EFFECTIVE READING PROGRAMS

EFFECTIVE READING PROGRAMS

THE ADMINISTRATOR'S ROLE

Floyd Boschee, Ed.D.

Associate Professor, Division of Educational Administration
School of Education, University of South Dakota
Vermillion, South Dakota

Bruce M. Whitehead, Ed.D.

Principal, Hellgate Elementary School
Visiting Assistant Professor
School of Education, University of Montana
Missoula, Montana

Marlys Ann Boschee, Ed.D.

Assistant Professor, Division of Curriculum and Instruction
School of Education, University of South Dakota
Vermillion, South Dakota

TECHNOMIC
PUBLISHING CO., INC.

LANCASTER · BASEL

Effective Reading Programs

a **TECHNOMIC**® publication

Published in the Western Hemisphere by
Technomic Publishing Company, Inc.
851 New Holland Avenue, Box 3535
Lancaster, Pennsylvania 17604 U.S.A.

Distributed in the Rest of the World by
Technomic Publishing AG
Missionsstrasse 44
CH-4055 Basel, Switzerland

Printed in the United States of America
10 9 8 7 6 5 4 3 2 1

Main entry under title:
   Effective Reading Programs: The Administrator's Role

A Technomic Publishing Company book
Bibliography: p.
Includes index p. 231

Library of Congress Catalog Card No. 92-83977
ISBN No. 0-87762-988-9

To our children and grandchildren

CONTENTS

FOREWORD

During my tenure as Superintendent of Public Instruction for the state of South Dakota, I had the opportunity to visit schools of all sizes in many different communities — both rural and urban. I was always somewhat amazed at how I could accurately determine the type of leadership present in a school simply by walking through its halls and briefly observing classroom activities. It has been my observation that the most effective education takes place in those schools where the administrator is an active participant in the day-to-day activities of the students and teachers.

Unfortunately, many administrators have found it difficult to break away from the stereotype of administrator as "head disciplinarian and evaluator" of both students and teachers, "public defender" of programs when they come under fire, and "liaison" between teachers and the upper echelons of school administration. As well, many schools of education have not emphasized the role of the administrator in the planning and implementation of curricular programs, even though recent research indicates that administrator involvement is critical to improving the effectiveness of our educational systems. New approaches to curriculum development, such as school-based management and shared decision-making programs, call for the integration of administrators into the proactive elements of curriculum, but many people who are already in administrative positions and many who are in training to fill those positions are having difficulty making the transition from the perceived "traditional" role of the administrator to the new role of "team leader" as presented in these innovative programs. *Effective Reading Programs: The Administrator's Role* is designed to guide administrators through this transitional phase of educational planning in a key area of learning.

Reading is a basic life skill, upon which all other learning is dependent. It is also an area of which educational analysts have become increasingly critical. Parents and others in local communities have begun expressing concerns over both the content and the instructional methodologies used. New technologies are having an impact on the mediums of instruction to which educators have access. A plethora of articles have been written describing various solutions to these educational dilemmas from various perspectives, and many administrators, teachers, and lay persons are finding it difficult to wade through the differing opinions and proposals. In many ways the situation has become confusing and chaotic. However, I see one clear message emerging from all the discussion—a successful reading program, regardless of the specific approach to teaching, needs to be a well-planned, well-led team effort. All members of the instructional team need to be adequately knowledgeable of approaches to teaching reading so they can make appropriate decisions concerning the day-to-day presentation of materials; all need to be aware of the importance of evaluation and accountability and be willing to take the time to use them effectively; all need to understand the importance of involving parents and others in the continuing process of teaching and assume such responsibilities are part of their job.

The authors of this volume clearly point to the administrator as the key to successfully implementing such a program. Individual chapters provide clear, practical methods for dealing with problems of assessment and accountability, public relations, creating an appropriate learning environment, adopting a specific reading approach, structuring groups, and developing inservice training. As well, the authors provide methods for using computers and other advanced technology to improve the efficiency of reading programs. Most importantly, this volume represents a shift in how the administrator should view his or her position in the development of a reading program that will meet the goals and objectives set forth in such reports as *America 2000*.

The need for change in our schools is great; the problems are many.

Some would say that the answer is better, more equitable financing, and certainly all schools could benefit from an infusion of funds. Some would say that other social institutions need to do a better job of helping young people develop moral and personal standards that contribute to their desire to learn, and to be sure schools would run more smoothly if teachers and administrators did not have to deal with the problems of broken homes, drug abuse, and violence. However, it is probably naive and unrealistic to expect that these solutions to educational problems will be forthcoming in the near future. What can be done in the short term is the adoption of more interactive programs and the development of focused leadership in our schools. *Effective Reading Programs: The Administrator's Role* can assist administrators in expediting change in their schools, thereby allowing the entire instructional team to more adequately prepare young people for the future.

Gordon A. Diedtrich, Ed.D.
School Administrator
Former State Superintendent of Public Instruction
Professor of Educational Administration

Increasingly, educational administrators, teachers, political leaders, employers, and the public are discovering that effective reading programs are essential for producing a basic life skill, reading. Reading is a prerequisite to the abilities to conceptualize, organize, and verbalize thoughts, as well as to problem solving, personal management, and interpersonal skills.

School administrators and reading supervisors, in particular, must understand that changes in society inevitably require changes in education and in reading programs. This understanding must go beyond conventional rhetorical statements about the importance of reading programs; it is necessary to incorporate specific purposeful actions such as those presented in this book.

Our intent in writing *Effective Reading Programs: The Administrator's Role* is to assist aspiring and practicing school administrators and reading supervisors to strengthen current reading programs. Reading should not be thought of as a subject that is taught by an individual teacher. It constitutes a program that needs direction, organization, evaluation, and nourishing.

ORGANIZATION AND CONTENT

Readers should view this book as an authoritative and practical source of information for school administrators, language arts directors, and reading supervisors. It is organized into eight chapters.

Chapter One lays the groundwork for this book. Discussion centers on "common sense" leadership skills needed by elementary school principals, the research findings on effective leadership skills, the positive contributions made by a Reading Curriculum Advisory Committee and a Steering Committee, and the accountability axioms for principals, teachers, parents, and students.

Chapter Two considers how *America 2000,* workplace requirements, school-based management and shared decision making, and Chapter 1 programs stimulate effective reading programs.

Chapter Three sets the main objective for reading, analyzes the three reading models, and appraises the four approaches used for reading instruction. It summarizes students' reflections on reading instruction, critiques the qualities of an effective reading teacher, categorizes students' strengths and weaknesses, and examines the importance of using an informal reading inventory and a reading interest inventory. It also presents the five principles that make a difference in reading achievement, considers the spectacular changes in society and children today, evaluates the Reading Recovery program, and summarizes the components of an effective reading program.

Chapter Four analyzes student assessment and the research on administrative involvement in reading and language arts programs, the elements that make up good management of reading and language arts programs, and the issues and controversies associated with the administrator's role in reading and language arts programs.

Chapter Five presents strategies for developing reading groups. Distinctive features of small cooperative groups, the uniqueness of the chronological anatomy of various age groups, the value of peer or same-age grouping, guidelines for structuring small cooperative groups, and sociometry are discussed. This model is the basis for the step-by-step process of how to implement small cooperative learning groups with technology.

Chapter Six explores the difference between heterogeneous and homogeneous grouping, how an elementary school principal can shape the composition of classrooms, how to identify the characteristics that should be considered when assigning students to classes, and what characteristics should be given priority when assigning students to classes. Software has been developed to enable the elementary school principal to work smarter rather than harder in shaping the composition of elementary school classrooms.

Chapter Seven focuses on change. It presents the National Assessment of Educational Progress reading assessment report, defines a paradigm, and describes paradigm paralysis. A comparison is made between traditional education and outcome-based education. It also summarizes the dramatic success of outcome-based education programs, analyzes the procedure for an outcome-based language arts curriculum, and describes and illustrates the components for an outcome-based model.

Chapter Eight discusses the impact a public relations program can have on a reading program, the role of an elementary school principal in developing a public relations plan to strengthen a reading program, the importance of internal and external groups for a sound public relations program in reading, and criteria that should be used to assess a public relations program for reading.

ACKNOWLEDGEMENTS

We would like to express a sincere appreciation to Karen Westergaard, English instructor at Black Hills State University, Spearfish, South Dakota; Marlene J. Lang, English instructor at the University of South Dakota, Vermillion, South Dakota; and Charlotte S. Whitehead, elementary school teacher, Missoula, Montana, for editing and for their promptness and patience. Gratitude is also extended to Brenda Rae Dronen, first grade teacher, Prairie View Elementary School, Eden Prairie, Minnesota, for originating the concept for *The Classmate;* to Barbara Ann Baird for accessing classroom resources; to Robert Bowker, elementary school principal; and to the third grade teachers, Jolley Elementary School, Vermillion, South Dakota, who so willingly cooperated and provided classroom data for the pilot test.

CHAPTER ONE

Principals and Quality Leadership

"Education makes a people easy to lead,
but difficult to drive;
easy to govern,
but impossible to enslave."

— LORD BROUGHAM

As you read and study:

. . . Consider the "common sense" leadership skills needed by
elementary school principals.

. . . Compare the research findings on effective leadership skills to the
"common sense" leadership skills.

. . . Analyze the skills needed to be a reading program manager.

. . . Summarize the positive contributions that can be made by a
Reading Curriculum Advisory Committee and a Steering
Committee.

. . . Appraise the accountability axioms for principals, teachers,
parents, and students.

Over the past decade, elementary school principals have placed a
greater focus on direct involvement in reading programs. They are now
beginning to realize that administrative priorities often are teacher
priorities as well. As a result, principals are beginning to separate myth
from reality.

Reasons for this newfound knowledge include the international emphasis on reading, an emphasis on school reform, and the advent of the
information age. The recent increase in the amount of theoretical and
instructional research is staggering. For example, Dowhower (1989)

and Dykstra (1984) found that prior to 1980 slightly more than 100 published research articles focused on reading. Today, over 1,000 articles are published annually, and more than fifty journals are devoted exclusively to elementary and secondary education.

The dearth of published research on reading programs in the past also reflects a limited knowledge of terminology and use of various practices by school administrators. Specifically, reading, grouping, levelization, and comprehension were the four common concepts principals were required to know to administer a reading program. Present and future elementary school principals must not only retain those four basic concepts, but must add and implement, among others, such precepts as bottom-up, top-down, interactive, schema theory, concept-based, ready-based, data-driven, text-based, metacognition, literal, interpretive, applied, objective-based, criterion-referenced, holistic, whole language, literature-based, language experience, story framing, and story mapping (Dowhower, 1989).

Some of the phraseologies are merely new names for old ideas. Even so, effective instructional leadership will require elementary school principals to be familiar with all of the concepts for developing and sustaining effective reading programs.

LEADERSHIP SKILLS IN READING

Elementary school principals must address a number of questions. Why do 23 million Americans lack the basic reading and writing skills needed to cope with everyday situations? Why is this number growing by 10 percent each year? Why are 30 million adults functionally illiterate? In response to the illiteracy dilemma worldwide, the United Nations passed a resolution declaring the first year of the last decade in the twentieth century as an International Literacy year, calling upon all educators to make literacy their top priority.

The last decade of the twentieth century will be an exciting era for principals and teachers. It can be a time for renewal and change as a result of the overwhelming support from the United States Congress and the International Reading Association (IRA). For example, House and Senate members on Capitol Hill are continuing to review teacher training proposals and federal grants for the National Board of Professional Teaching Standards, and the IRA is increasing its involvement in solving the literacy problem.

According to the president of the International Reading Association

(1989), more emphasis should be placed on new administrative roles in reading. These roles include principals as leaders, managers, and organizers of reading programs.

Common Sense Leadership

Members of the Administration and Reading Committee of the Indiana State Reading Council identified twenty-three common sense characteristics related to outstanding reading leadership (Rodgers, 1989). Effective reading administrators should:

(1) Ensure that reading becomes a top priority within their schools by identifying and communicating clearly defined goals to teachers, students, and parents.

(2) Be committed to reading as a goal and believe nearly all students can learn to read.

(3) Have high expectations and deeply felt visions of great futures for their students.

(4) Understand the principles of learning and recognize good teaching strategies.

(5) Know how to coordinate and help coordinate the reading curriculum.

(6) Provide books and instructional materials for classroom teachers as budgets permit.

(7) Encourage sharing and use of available resources in the school and community.

(8) Observe in classrooms regularly, know what is happening, and provide helpful feedback.

(9) Treat teachers with dignity and perceive them as able, dependable, and worthy.

(10) Coach, model, and show appreciation to teachers.

(11) Know the strengths and weaknesses of teachers and seek ways to help them.

(12) Arrange grade-level (team) meetings and planning sessions to encourage sharing of ideas (see ''Vowel Rap'' at the end of this chapter).

(13) Provide consultant help and staff development opportunities as needed.

(14) Have ongoing planning, implementation, and evaluation of the reading program.

(15) Encourage teachers to read quality literature to students.

(16) Ensure that students have *daily* opportunities to read.

(17) Plan incentives for students to read via *Book It!*, *Book Quest*, or the *100 Club*.

(18) Encourage parental involvement and communicate with parents via newsletters, notes, phone calls, and meetings.

(19) Solicit parent volunteers and view the education of children as a partnership between home and school.

(20) Be cognizant of people's ideas and demonstrate sensitivity toward the feelings of others.

(21) Enhance school spirit and work to create a positive, cooperative, stimulating, and orderly school climate.

(22) Help build a desire to achieve, encourage students to excel, and contribute to the common good.

(23) Maintain a sense of humor.

The aforementioned characteristics are essential in the development of leadership. Having leadership ability is paramount to having and implementing a sense of vision. When dealing with reading programs, good administrators must put a bold face upon their beliefs and standards, yet base their decisions on goals that juxtapose the school and community.

Focused Leadership

According to the National Institute of Business Management (1989), quality leadership means developing goals and objectives around simple themes such as (1) What do you want? (2) When do you need it? (3) Who is to do it? (4) Can it be done? (5) Is it for real? and (6) What are the recommendations? Bringing principals into the realm of quality leadership means ''setting goals with teeth.'' Today, the lack of focused goal setting is an inclusive leadership problem. In essence, effective leadership means that goals must be specific and forceful if others are to seriously support them. Below are six major questions with sub-questions that school principals must ask and answer in order to develop an effective reading program:

(1) What exactly do you want? Do you want administrative participation in the reading program? Do you want whole language, basals, a literature-based program, or a combination?

(2) When do you want it? What is the implementation date for the reading adoption? When will the recommendation be submitted to the superintendent and the school board?

(3) Who does what? Is there a reading committee, and who will be selected? Is there a steering committee? Will administrators, board members, parents, and students be included? Who will make the recommendations to the board?

(4) Do we have the resources? Is a literature-based program affordable? Will all teachers be able to teach a literature-based program? How much inservice will be needed?

(5) Are you really serious? Is there truly a commitment to a new reading adoption? Are all administrators, parents, and teachers positive about the change? Is everyone willing to put in the hours needed for the adoption?

(6) What are the recommendations? Are the recommendations specific and clear? Are evaluation time lines built into the recommendations?

The focused leadership goal-setting questions mentioned above must be addressed by school principals in order to achieve effective reading programs. The next step, reading management, is equally important for school principals to practice.

PRINCIPALS AS READING MANAGERS

As reading managers, elementary school principals must determine, develop, and implement policies and procedures. They must also coordinate physical and human resources to attain reading program goals and objectives. In essence, principals help teachers teach by aiding them in accomplishing tasks and goals. Under good reading management, teachers are not burdened by office duties or extraneous activities. Rather, they teach classes without interruption.

The seven major duties required of principals for managing and improving reading curricula are shown in Figure 1.1.

Following are sixteen lesser known and frequently forgotten techniques that are also important to principals for managing a reading program:

(1) Process and follow up on staff requests for custodial work such as replacing a burned-out light bulb in a supply closet or fixing a broken pencil sharpener.

(2) Make telephone calls for teachers to arrange for an important speaker.

1. Maintain adequate student and school records for easy access by staff members.

2. Prepare daily or weekly bulletins to communicate with staff members in the area of reading.

3. Utilize the budget to maximize the purchase of quality reading and language arts materials.

4. Recruit and select the best possible teachers and aides to work in reading and language arts programs.

5. Develop the best possible class schedules for effective reading time.

6. Provide staff members with easy access to supplies and equipment.

7. Monitor reading to ensure that school goals and objectives are emulated and that the scope and sequence of reading is followed.

Figure 1.1. Seven major duties for managing a reading curriculum.

(3) Find free material for the reading program.

(4) Make sure enough paper is easily accessible for the copying machine.

(5) Troubleshoot possible problems with broken-down audiovisual equipment immediately, or avoid problems by keeping equipment in good shape.

(6) Maintain an open door and expect to be interrupted by everyone.

(7) Help teachers with students who are ill.

(8) Clean up after a sick student if the custodian is not around.

(9) Make sure the temperature is comfortable in all the classrooms.

(10) Help teachers with the Christmas program when the backdrop disintegrates.

(11) Arrange occasional early outs for staff, and carry out the plan even when disappointed with several teachers.

(12) Support a teacher's request for equipment at a PTA meeting.

(13) Make a copy of and file all important information so that it can be retrieved in less than sixty seconds.

(14) Provide staff members with copies of important school documents and schedules.

(15) Worry less about the support of and more about supporting staff members.

(16) Smile.

As shown, principals should be managers as well as humane and technical assistants to teachers and consultants of reading. Assistance in reading includes (1) goal and objective formulation, (2) material selection, (3) audiovisual use, (4) acquisition of resource people, (5) facility use and improvement, (6) evaluation reviews, (7) field trips, and (8) special services. Effective school principals provide technical assistance to teachers to enhance the reading skills for all children.

In addition to assistance that principals give to teachers, they should initiate and facilitate an instructional assessment of needs and identification of problem points in reading. This is accomplished through the following activities:

(1) Clearly establish that unmet needs are the basis for selecting improvement areas.
(2) Set up a data base and data collection procedure.
(3) Establish criteria for selecting reading programs.
(4) Provide adequate time, resources, and personnel to handle the reading program.
(5) Set up an organizational network to ensure the broadest possible participation and widest dissemination of information.
(6) Ensure maximum, quality, and effective efforts.

As noted, successful principals must obtain and evaluate reading and make this information available. Too often, pupil performances, course data, and community characteristics are not included in analyzing school reading programs.

Although they may not appear essential, a myriad of other administrative behaviors in instructional development can ensure the success of elementary school principals. The nine distinct tips illustrated in Figure 1.2 can, if practiced over time, make a difference between successful and mediocre instructional leaders in reading.

Principals soon realize that effective reading programs depend on dedicated, effective professionals. Teachers are most effective in a humanistic environment in which the morale is high. The most common human relations skills that contribute to a positive school environment and high faculty and student morale are practiced when principals

- formulate a program of clinical supervision
- provide open channels for faculty input
- stimulate and motivate faculty members to maximum performance

---

1. Teach a class, any class.

2. Coordinate intergrade and intragrade meetings.

3. Visit classes as often as possible.

4. Make rounds in the morning to be available to teachers before the school day begins.

5. Arrange field trips and buses for teachers.

6. Take part in field trips.

7. Visit a teacher's classroom after pupils are dismissed and before staff release time to offer assistance in any way.

8. Listen to children read.

9. Read aloud to children.

Figure 1.2. "Tips" for success in the principalship.

- provide relevant faculty meetings, called only when necessary
- develop a biweekly bulletin for school staff and parents
- know as many of the students' names as possible
- allow faculty members to meet doctor and dental appointments
- encourage special service people to relieve teachers whenever possible
- encourage faculty members to occasionally observe and help in special services classrooms
- occasionally buy snacks for faculty members
- have lunch with students whenever possible
- send notes to students on their birthdays and on other special occasions
- read to classes whenever possible
- use a V.I.P. program to acknowledge students
- make home and hospital visits when possible

The administrative behaviors listed above assist elementary school principals in developing and maintaining quality reading programs. A principal's positive attitude results in high morale for faculty, and a jovial faculty generates happy and productive students. This may sound too simple, but it is a fundamental precept for any well-managed reading program.

The organizational structure used to implement a reading program is another important axiom. Organization can be based on an old, familiar concept in which administrators make all the decisions and delegate to their faculty, or administrators can encourage the "bubble up" concept by establishing a Reading Curriculum Advisory Committee.

Reading Curriculum Advisory Committee

Administrators can involve others by utilizing a Reading Curriculum Advisory Committee comprised of members who can formulate opinions and discover alternative approaches to solve problems. An advisory committee can continuously provide individual, budgetary, cost, community, and resource information. Additionally, the committee can work to eliminate the accruing and recording of superfluous data. It can also help decide what is to be researched, who should have access to the data, and how to construct the best reading program possible.

Principals should be *ex officio* members on the Reading Curriculum Advisory Committee. As *ex officio* members, they can stimulate ideas and guide discussion, moving through an agenda. Principals need not fear that such committees will make impulsive or erroneous decisions; the sole function of Reading Curriculum Advisory Committees is to make recommendations. Principals are encouraged to glean as much information as possible from committees. Failure to listen to and utilize information from Reading Curriculum Advisory Committees can force an elementary school principal into early retirement.

Assuming that most elementary school principals desire staff involvement coupled with strong leadership, the benefits of Reading Curriculum Advisory Committees are readily evident. Committees, according to Tankard (1974), are particularly effective for improving the reading curriculum when the following characteristics exist:

(1) Improvements are concerned with minor revisions in or modifications of the present reading curriculum.
(2) Information relative to the present reading program is sought from staff (boosts staff morale and gives ownership).
(3) Sufficient time is available to engage in extensive study.
(4) Staff development is recommended for improvement.
(5) Communication and coordination between departments and schools is deemed essential for improvement.

(6) Staff assistance in program interpretation and implementation is desired.

If a Reading Curriculum Advisory Committee is sanctioned by central administration, principals should take great care in selecting a process to determine committee membership, establishing a steering committee, setting the calendar, and defining the goals and objectives for the committee. In addition, well-balanced grade level representation is paramount to any successful approach in developing and implementing reading program changes.

Committee Membership

Membership selection should be based upon, but not limited to, the following criteria:

- grade levels affected
- subject area specialists
- staff leadership
- talents useful to committee composition
- staff cooperativeness
- special services
- optional: school board members and parents

Selection of committee members is somewhat political and should be approached with care and thought. Principals may ask some faculty to serve because of their specialization, but most of the Reading Curriculum Advisory Committee members should be volunteers. Other acceptable methods to use for committee membership selection are peer choices, evolvement, and administrative preferences. Administrative selection should only be used if the other methods are not feasible.

Committee Meetings

Reading Curriculum Advisory Committee meetings should be held in comfortable environments. The meeting room should have the following characteristics:

- comfortable work seats
- circular seating arrangements
- tables with room for participants to spread their papers out
- good acoustics (Bradley, 1985)

Appropriate refreshments should be available for the group, and desk name tags should be provided (people seem to resent name tags that they have to wear). The first meeting should be organized so that committee members get to know each other. To accomplish this task, administrators can have members share their grade level assignments, special interests, educational backgrounds and experiences, and hobbies. Becoming familiar with other committee members usually helps individuals feel more comfortable.

After committee members have been introduced and the principal has described the task to be accomplished, general discussion can commence. For instance, members may begin to brainstorm, an activity that permits an infusion of information and interchange among the members. The activity, a procedure for resolving problems, should also focus on the goals and objectives.

Reading Steering Committee

A Reading Steering Committee should be selected from the Advisory Committee, with members limited to the five most respected individuals. The primary tasks for this committee are developing goals, objectives, calendar dates, and deadlines for the Advisory Committee. The members must be flexible and willing to meet as often as possible. As the driving force of the larger group, the Steering Committee provides the energy and direction needed to plan and implement the reading adoption.

A primary function of the Steering Committee is to assess the existing reading program, which includes reviewing objectives, content, and effectiveness. Objectives can be ascertained in terms of learners' behavior, commonly called "behavioral objectives"; those stated in terms of teachers' behavior are called "instructional objectives." But since very exact statements are needed to describe performance of designated reading tasks, the term "performance objectives" seems preferable to "behavioral objectives." Content can be substantiated by reviewing course outlines, high school offerings, scope and sequence charts, curriculum guides, accreditation reports, and state reports. Effectiveness can be confirmed by reviewing standardized tests, reading inventories, school attendance, and school graduation records.

Delegated groups can provide information to the Steering Committee. This imbuement of information not only aids the committee, but supplies valuable feedback to school administrators who can use the data to set priorities and to select specific areas for curriculum improvement in reading. The Steering Committee should ask the following questions to access information about the reading program:

- Does the program meet the most critical needs of the school population?
- Does the program change pupil behavior?
- Is the program financially sound?
- Is the program manageable administratively?
- Are results commensurate to the cost and effort?

In the process of reviewing a reading program, elementary school principals should

- clarify any misunderstandings about the reading program and make provisions for changing or modifying the program
- analyze and compare the total instructional curriculum as it relates to the reading program, and identify areas where intervention is required by the principal
- examine the organizational structure of the reading program and determine possible rearrangements of staff members, materials, and resources
- research other reading programs at local, regional, state, and national levels
- institute a staff development program in the area of reading to include inservice and clinical supervision techniques
- develop learning alternatives for gifted children as well as for children having difficulty with reading
- conduct an inventory of facilities to determine architectural problems related to the reading program
- develop better utilization of interior and exterior space for reading

Subsequent Advisory Committee Actions

The Steering Committee reports its findings to the Reading Curriculum Advisory Committee, which has the responsibility to make a recommendation to the school superintendent or school board. Reading and language arts recommendations should be well researched, factual, and timely. After the recommendation is made, the committee should remain active to assist with implementation, inservice, and program evaluation.

The Reading Curriculum Advisory Committee can assist the principal with the reading program by

- identifying significant components
- determining the best utilization of material
- educating staff members and parents
- reporting progress (Moorman and Thomas, 1983)

Wilson (1981) believes that committees are essential to the development of a good reading diagnosis program. The advantages of a Reading Curriculum Advisory Committee are that

- Principals are kept well informed.
- Specialists working together have less conflict of interests.
- Overlapping responsibilities are diminished.
- Attention is concentrated on utilizing all the resources of schools (Wilson, 1981).

A Reading Curriculum Advisory Committee is most helpful to principals who think the reading process is inadequate. For principals unfamiliar with reading and language arts who feel locked in and unable to initiate or implement worthwhile changes, an advisory committee is especially useful.

RESEARCH, COMMON SENSE, AND ACCOUNTABILITY

The common sense nature of many of the research findings on effective school leadership is neither profound nor revolutionary. The research community, however, has validated many common sense concepts mentioned earlier about effective leadership and effective schools. Unfortunately, as Berliner (1981, p. 224) noted, ''Common sense is not common practice, as a visit to schools will reveal.''

Principal Accountability

A summary of research on effective schools by Culyer (1988) makes it clear that leadership by building principals is the single factor that determines whether schools are effective or ineffective. These six demonstrated attributes of principal accountability determine success:

- [supporting a] developmental curriculum
- providing appropriate materials to each teacher
- providing program development rather than relying on staff development
- ensuring that mastery teaching does occur on a consistent basis

- recognizing and rewarding teachers, pupils, and parents
- communicating with pupils, parents, and professionals on a regular and meaningful basis (pp. 366–367)

The accountability attributes mentioned above are essential for effective elementary school leadership. But, as Lessinger (cited by Culyer, 1988, pp. 367–368) emphasized, "It's insane to be held accountable for another person; no one is given that power. The only thing a professional can be held accountable for is using sound judgment."

Teacher Accountability

A review of a vast amount of research on effective teachers and schools suggests that seven areas of teacher accountability are especially important. Teachers demonstrate accountability by

- conducting [student] diagnosis at the beginning of the term and throughout the year
- providing appropriate materials and experiences based on the results of [student] diagnosis
- providing direct instruction [explanation, demonstration, guided practice, feedback, and correction]
- consistently using mastery teaching strategies
- providing appropriate reinforcement opportunities [relates to educationally significant outcomes; precludes the common use of copying board work students cannot read]
- creating a classroom environment that encourages pupils to do their best
- communicating with pupils and parents on a regular basis (Culyer, 1988, pp. 365–366)

These teacher accountability attributes are essential components of effective schools. What happens behind the classroom door is "all important." Accountability on the part of teachers, administrators, and ultimately schools, provides a basis for quality education.

Parent Accountability

Principals and teachers, according to Culyer (1988, p. 368), "represent one-third of the accountability partnership." The efforts of professionals can be enhanced if responsible parents

- send [their] children to school prepared to learn, ensuring that their children have sufficient rest and sleep, nourishing meals, and balanced time among television, recreational reading, homework, and leisure time
- support the school on a continual basis
- encourage and reward children for academic and social growth
- provide a wealth of reading material at home
- provide a quiet place for homework

Educating children cannot be left entirely to our schools. Because learning begins at home, parents must shoulder responsibilities. As Eckard (1991, p. 1) indicates, "Between birth and age eighteen, children spend just 9 percent of their time in school. That's why home environment is so important." Principals must strive to have a positive working relationship with parents within their school attendance areas. Students are given a better opportunity to learn when schools, families, and communities work together.

Pupil Accountability

Pupils are a major part of the "accountability partnership." "Education," Watson (1978, p. 209) notes, "is not something that is or can be done to children; it is something that children do for themselves with the assistance of their parents and educators." Pupils can demonstrate accountability by

- coming to school each day prepared both physically and academically
- consistently attending to the learning at hand, whether it is teacher-directed (e.g., working in small groups) or independent study
- learning from mistakes (correcting errors results in additional learning)
- applying learning to everyday situations (using information learned in health to care for the body)
- facilitating communication between the home and school (Culyer, 1988)

Students have to be held accountable for their learning, but if they fail, the influences of home or school should also be considered as contributing factors. Principals must put forth concerted efforts to make the "accountability triangle" work. Only when schools, parents, and students work cooperatively will the children acquire the skills they need to be successful in the twenty-first century.

SUMMARY

Principals' understanding of management skills is crucial to curriculum design and change in reading programs, since principals are perceived by community leaders, parents, teachers, and students as persons responsible for school leadership and for initiating and permitting instructional change. As educational administrators, principals are also perceived as allocators or withholders of resources and information needed for program modification. They do make a difference in the development of quality reading programs.

A positive attitude, enthusiasm, sound management skills, and organization are essential ingredients for the development and implementation of effective reading programs. As the field of reading becomes more complex, principals will have to become even more responsible for assisting reading teachers in the classrooms. Only when school administrators are actively involved in reading programs will schools function as coordinated units on the journey to excellence. In truth, elementary school principals may not only make a difference, they may make the actual difference.

"VOWEL RAP"[1]

I was sitting in my classroom paying no mind.
When all of a sudden, she came from behind.
The teacher caught me staring down the floor.
Said if I didn't do something, I'd be out the door.

So I sat up in my chair and paid attention,
and the whole wide world took on a new dimension.
I opened up my storybook, and what did I see?
Those special little letters from "A" to "Z."

[1]Special thanks are extended to Debbie McCoy for granting permission to use the "Vowel Rap." Debbie developed the vowel rap with her family, husband, Tom, and children, Brian and Kristen, while traveling from Texas to Colorado. Debbie teaches second grade in the Branch Elementary School, Muroc School District, Edwards Air Force Base, California.

Each one has a sound, a sound of its own,
blend those sounds together for an educated tone.
The twenty-six letters in the alphabet—
you'll be jiving and driving toward the right step.

a-b-c-d-e-f-g-h-i
See it's just as simple as eating pie.
j-k-l-m-n-o-p-q-r
You are getting closer; it's not very far.
s-t-u-v-w-x-y-z
Don't come in a straggling, just listen to me.
Twenty-six letters in the alphabet—
five of them are vowels, the rest are consonants.

The first vowel of them all is the letter "a."
ă like in apple, long ā as in cane.
Another "a" sound, the strangest of all,
is the sound of ä in the little word ball.

A mighty strong vowel is the letter "e."
ĕ like an elephant, long ē as in bee.
There's an amazing thing about the letter "e."
It's a powerful letter, just listen to me.
At the end of a word the "e" gains its fame.
Its silence makes the other vowel say its own name.

Now the next vowel in line is the letter "i."
ĭ like in igloo, long ī as in fine.
A mighty fine letter is the letter "i."
It refers to the best—me, myself, and I.

The roundest of the vowels is the letter "o."
ŏ as in octopus, long ō as in hoe.
Two sounds for this vowel are much too few.
It gathers up a third sound—ö as in too.

Now keep right on trying, we're almost through;
You'll find the things we're learning really are true.
Don't let your brain get lazy on me.
You soon will see that reading is Key.

The final main vowel is the letter "u."
ŭ as in umbrella, long ū as in mule.
Now you're probably thinking that your brain is full,
but try to remember the ü sound in pull.

Can you imagine all the times you will need to read?
I don't mean just in school, but for every need.
So let's end this rap on a positive thought.
Knowing how to read, you will learn a lot.

—by the McCoy family

REFERENCES

Berliner, D. C. 1981. "Academic Learning Time and Reading Achievement," in *Comprehension and Teaching: Research Reviews*, John T. Guthrie, ed. Newark, DE: International Reading Association, p. 224.

Bradley, L. H. 1985. *Curriculum Leadership and Development Handbook.* Englewood Cliffs, NJ: Prentice-Hall, Inc., p. 19.

Culyer, R. 1988. "Accountability as a Partnership," *The Clearing House*, 61:365−368.

Dowhower, S. L. 1989. "A Principal's Guide to Reading Terminology," *Principal*, 68(3):36−39.

Dykstra, R. 1984. *Handbook of Reading Research.* New York, NY: Longman, pp. 19−20.

Eckard, L., ed. 1991. "Home," *101 Ways Parents Can Help Students Achieve.* Alexandria, VA: American Association of School Administrators, p. 1.

Moorman, G. B. and K. J. Thomas. 1983. *Designing Reading Programs.* Dubuque, IA: Kendall/Hunt Publishing Company.

Rodgers, N. 1989. *What Can the Principal Do to Enhance the Reading Program.* Indianapolis, IN: Department of Education, Office of School Assistance.

Tankard, G. G., Jr. 1974. *Curriculum Improvement: An Administrator's Guide.* West Nyack, NY: Parker.

Watson, B. 1978. "Excellence: What It Is and How It Can Be Achieved," *Phi Delta Kappan*, 60:209.

Wilson, R. M. 1981. *Diagnostic and Remedial Reading for Classroom and Clinic.* Columbus, OH: Merrill Publishing Company.

CHAPTER TWO

Stimulators for Effective Reading Programs

"Between good sense and good taste there is the same difference as between cause and effect."

— DES JUGEMENTS

As you read and study:

. . . Summarize how *America 2000* can stimulate the development of an effective reading program.

. . . Relate the workplace requirements to an effective reading program.

. . . Analyze the merits of school-based management and shared decision making.

. . . Identify the successful attributes for a Chapter 1 reading program.

. . . Correlate Cetron's forecast with *America 2000,* workplace requirements, school-based management and shared decision making, and Chapter 1.

In an attempt to analyze and internalize who the stimulators might be for effective reading programs in our schools, confusion enters, reminiscent of the perplexity recorded in Culyer's (1988) description of education and accountability. A thought from an unknown author seems appropriate:

There was an important job to be done and Everybody was asked to do it. Everybody was sure Somebody would do it. Anybody could have done it, but Nobody did it. Somebody got angry about that because it was

Everybody's job. Everybody thought Anybody could do it, but Nobody realized that Everybody wouldn't. It ended up that Everybody blamed Somebody when actually Nobody asked Anybody. (p. 365)

To develop effective reading programs, the "who's" should be studied and analyzed. Who can influence? Who can help? Who is directly responsible? Failure to ponder the "who's" will cause Everybody to blame Somebody when actually Nobody asked Anybody.

AMERICA 2000

The education community and the general public experienced rays of hope when an Education Summit in 1989, which included the Governors' Association and the President of the United States, sanctioned six primary goals to secure America's educational well-being by the year 2000. These goals, worked out on a bipartisan basis, include "school readiness, school completion, student achievement and citizenship, mathematics and science, adult literacy and lifelong learning, and safe, disciplined, and drug free schools" (McCune, 1990, p. 4).

This plan, called *America 2000,* is a long-term national ideology, not a federal program that relies primarily on local control and local initiative because the United States Constitution limits the federal government's role. The concept, however, "can help by setting standards, highlighting examples, contributing some funds, providing some flexibility in exchange for accountability, and pushing and prodding — then pushing and prodding some more" (U.S. Department of Education, 1991, p. 2).

The blueprint for *America 2000* consists of four segments pursued simultaneously. The journey to excellence consists of the following:

(1) For today's students, we must radically improve today's schools, all 110,000 of them — make them better and more accountable.

(2) For tomorrow's students, we must invent new schools to meet the demands of a new century.

(3) For those of us already out of school and in the work force, we must keep learning if we are to live and work successfully in today's world. A "Nation at Risk" must become a "Nation of Students."

(4) For schools to succeed, we must look beyond their classrooms to our communities and families. Schools will never be much better

than the commitment of their communities. Each of our communities must become a place where learning can happen (U.S. Department of Education, 1991).

However, *America 2000* represents only an ideology and not a specific educational plan. Top-down management, especially in the form of governmentally-driven educational recommendation, does not address how schools are to implement a better educational program. Principals and teachers are left to increase learner outcomes. Thus, education reform can neither occur solely in the form of a federal philosophy driven by policy makers, nor can reform occur exclusively from an individual school site. Cooperation between policy makers and those directly educating (parents, teachers, and principals) is needed to guide a good idea into a workable strategy. As John I. Goodlad (1992) states, "There can be positive progress toward school improvement when the ideas perceived by thoughtful, inquiring educators are endorsed by policy makers" (p. 236).

Although an educational reform such as *America 2000* has it followers and detractors, for the first time ever an "all-inclusive" infrastructure has been developed. Now the plan must be implemented.

Who Are the Players?

The players for the four-part *America 2000* vision include all Americans. More specifically, the concept, which depends upon the long-term commitment of all Americans, delegates responsibilities to the president, Department of Education, cabinet, Congress, governors, business leaders, and community (U.S. Department of Education, 1991). *America 2000* begins a wave of reform. To actually reform our schools, President Bill Clinton suggests, "Strong leaders create strong schools. Research and common sense suggest that administrators can do a great deal to advance school reform. I believe that they must and will lead the second wave of reform" (Amundson, 1988, p. 17).

The school principal becomes integral to making an administrative goal become an actual learner outcome. The principal performs the role of "instructional leader [who is] responsible for directing and managing the teaching/learning process of the school and maintaining [the] learning climate" (Robinson, 1986, p. 22). Accountability as to whether or not the school is effective in student achievement of learning objectives, usually measured by test scores, is shouldered by the school principal.

For effective learner outcomes, the principal remains the key figure of leadership. To promote effective student learning, the principal must exercise leadership by:

- providing an assertive instructional role
- being goal and task oriented
- being well organized
- conveying high expectations for students and staff
- defining policies well and communicating them clearly
- visiting classrooms frequently
- maintaining high visibility and availability to students and staff
- supporting staff strongly
- having adept skills to maintain parent and community relations (Robinson, 1985)

There is nothing riveted in *America 2000* that "prevents creative teaching; the goals only preclude the kind of 'feel good' programs in which students end up illiterate and incompetent" (Seeley, 1991, p. 3). Compared to the report, "A Nation at Risk," which merely gave a summary of the shortcomings in American education, it is the responsibility of school administrators to balance educational reform to produce "A Nation of Scholars," a great influence and stimulator for an effective reading program.

WORKPLACE REQUIREMENTS

Are our schools preparing our young people for the workplace? What are the workplace requirements? Recently, the Secretary of the U.S. Department of Labor established a Commission on Achieving Necessary Skills (SCANS) to examine the demands of the workplace to determine whether American young people were meeting them. The results from the discussions and meetings with business owners, public employers, unions, and supervisors in plants, shops, and stores are widespread and disturbing. The explosive growth of technology and globalization of commerce and industry during the last quarter of the twentieth century are not reflected in how young people are prepared for the workplace. "More than half of the young people," according to the respondents, "left school without the knowledge or foundation required to find or hold a good job" (U.S. Department of Labor, 1991, p. 1).

Research by SCANS reveals that workplace know-how consists of competencies and a foundation. The five competencies for effective job performance consist of

- resources: (individual) identifies, organizes, plans, and allocates resources
- interpersonal: (individual) works with others
- information: (individual) acquires and uses information
- systems: (individual) understands complex interrelationships
- technology: (individual) works with a variety of technology (U.S. Department of Education, 1991)

The three-part foundation for young people in the workplace requires

- basic skills: (individual) *reads*, writes, performs arithmetic and mathematical operations, listens, and speaks [emphasis added]
- thinking skills: (individual) thinks creatively, makes decisions, solves problems, visualizes, knows how to learn, and reasons
- personal qualities: (individual) displays responsibility, self-esteem, sociability, self-management, and integrity and honesty (U.S. Department of Education, 1991)

The eight requirements mentioned above are essential preparation for all students, both those going directly to work and those planning post-secondary education. In the broadest sense, the competencies are applicable from the shop floor to the executive suite. They are "the attributes that today's high-performance employer seeks in tomorrow's employee" (U.S. Department of Education, 1991, p. 6).

Although the workplace involves complex interplay among the five competencies and the three elements of the foundation, employees will *first be required to read* adequately to understand and interpret charts, correspondence, diagrams, graphs, manuals, records, tables, and specifications. Members of the commission postulate that "without the ability to read a diverse set of materials, workers cannot locate the descriptive and quantitative information needed to make decisions or to recommend courses of action" (U.S. Department of Labor, 1991, p. 6).

The Real World

The message is universal. Today's job market for our young people requires command of the basic skills, the old 3 Rs. They are (1) reading to ferret out detailed and quantitative information and to understand what it means, (2) writing to prepare charts, correspondence, graphs, instructions, or proposals, and (3) mathematics and computational skills to maintain records, use spreadsheets, estimate results, or to apply statistical process controls. According to the SCANS report by the U.S.

Department of Labor (1991, p. 8), "Less than half of all young adults have achieved these reading and writing minimums [and] even fewer can handle the mathematics" required in the workplace today. This is exemplified by the situation described.

A first year English teacher called his former college professor to speak with him about a situation that was jeopardizing his job. The teacher had informed the school administrator that two ninth grade and two tenth grade classes he was teaching did not read at their grade levels. The administrator responded by saying, "The problem is not the reading level of students but a lack of classroom discipline." The teacher was then directed to observe "good teaching" in a United States history class conducted by a veteran teacher.

During observation, the first year teacher noted that this veteran teacher read to students using an opaque projector; no class misbehavior was noticeable. That, in the administrator's mind, was good teaching, namely because students did not misbehave.

The college professor, who, incidentally, taught a tests and measurements course in which the teacher was a student a year previous to his first teaching assignment, advised this first year teacher to administer a test that would measure the reading level of students. Taking this advice, the first year teacher administered the "Zip Scale for Determining Reading Level" test to the students. The results from this highly reliable and useable test, shown in Figures 2.1 and 2.2, indicate that only eight (17 percent) out of forty-eight ninth grade students in this school were at or above the ninth grade level in reading and forty students (83 percent) were below. At the tenth grade level, seventeen (32 percent) out of fifty-three students were at or above the tenth grade level in reading and thirty-six students (68 percent) were below.

This situation—in which reading levels were greatly varied, a number of students were reading below grade level, and the school administrator inaccurately analyzed the problem—could be happening in schools across America. Carnevale, Gainer, and Meltzer (1990, p. 19) cite an educational assessment that "indicates that there is a large nationwide population of 'intermediate literates' who only have fourth to eighth grade literacy equivalency . . . and who have not obtained functional or employable literacy level." Unfortunately, the intermediate literates will make up nearly 65 percent of the entry-level work force over the next fifteen years.

How will the fourth to eighth grade literacy group fare in the workplace? This question is not rhetorical; it is as real as the baby boom that has gone bust, creating fewer young workers. This smaller cluster

Reading Level (Ninth Grade)	Number of Students (Forty-Eight) at Reading Level	Percent at Reading Level
12	1	2
11	0	0
10	4	8
9	3	6
8	2	4
7	7	15
6	9	19
5	11	23
4	1	2
3	5	10
2	3	6
1	2	4

Note: Percents do not total 100 due to rounding.
The names of teachers, school, and administrator have been omitted for confidentiality.

Figure 2.1. Ninth grade students' reading level.

Reading Level (Tenth Grade)	Number of Students (Fifty-Three) at Reading Level	Percent at Reading Level
12	6	11
11	2	4
10	9	17
9	8	15
8	1	2
7	2	4
6	12	23
5	7	13
4	3	6
3	1	2
2	0	0
1	2	4

Note: Percents do not total 100 due to rounding.
The names of teachers, school, and administrator have been omitted for confidentiality.

Figure 2.2. Tenth grade students' reading level.

of young people entering the workplace will be challenged by tomorrow's jobs. For example, MDC, Inc. (1988) predicts that in the year 2000:

> New jobs will require a work force whose median level of education is 13.5 years. That means, on average, that the workers who fill tomorrow's jobs will have to have some college-level training. Not to be the boss, mind you, but just to hold a job. (p. 36)

Jobs in the twenty-first century will be substantially different from those that were created in the past. Least-skilled jobs will disappear and high-skilled positions will increase, requiring workers to have computer, interpersonal, problem-solving, and better basic academic skills.

Reading has historically been considered the fundamental skill needed by all human beings. How can the fundamental skills of reading be improved? How can schools prepare a better work force? Who is responsible? Who should be responsible? These and many more questions can and should be asked. You, the readers, aspiring or practicing school administrators, should be able to provide some answers for the questions posed. As Doyle (1992, p. 513) states, "Being 'as good as we have been' will not be good enough—not in business and not in education." Research findings on workplace requirements should stimulate administrators to develop and implement reading programs that will help young people prepare for useful, productive, and satisfying lives.

SCHOOL-BASED MANAGEMENT AND SHARED DECISION MAKING

School-based management and *shared decision making* are popular terms that describe school reorganization today. The President of the United States and the National Governors' Association have indicated that school reorganization is essential if America is to accomplish the six major goals set forth at the Educational Summit meeting in 1989. Clearly, education is on the public agenda; the charge is to stop "creating a soup-kitchen labor force in a post-industrial economy" (MDC, Inc., 1988, p. 2).

Who are the major players for reorganizing schools? What should they try to change, and why must change occur? The immediate task is to identify the traits that leaders need to assert a sense of direction, to promote creativity, and to foster participation in an enthusiasm for the restructuring process. School-based management can be an essential feature for restructuring schools because according to Elmore (1991),

> Top-down change will not work. All too often in the past, educational change efforts proceeded without consultation with the implementers. We have made the classroom, the teacher, and school almost genetically resistant to any attempt to fundamentally alter what goes on, and for very good reasons. People have learned in classrooms to protect themselves against bad ideas. They have learned it so well that they are now resistant to good ideas. One of the things we must do to this system is to soften it up. By letting people at the work site, the school, make more of the decisions that matter, we can soften the resistance to change. (p. 18)

The three "broad pressures" on public elementary and secondary schools can be classified as economic, political, and social. They not only create expectations for change, but "they also create the necessity for thinking about the relationship between school organization, teaching, and learning" (Elmore, 1991, p. 17).

Although the pressure to restructure American public schools has economic, political, and social implications, boards of education, school superintendents, central administrative staff, principals, teachers, and parents are considered the key players. In fact, state level statutes

> place the responsibilities for operation of local school systems in the hands of the School Board, and by its designatee, the Superintendent as Chief Executive Officer. The Board may delegate, but not abdicate, its powers or duties under [most state statutes]. The Board delegates decentralized decision-making authority to the Faculty Council in matters of curriculum, staffing, budgeting, and building level organizational/management subject to all current conditions and restrictions contained in Board policy and regulations, Master Agreements (as may be modified from time to time), establish district and curriculum requirements. (Site-Based Management, 1991)

Thus school boards, superintendents, central administrative staff, principals, teachers, and parents become the "who's" that must be involved in restructuring the public schools. However, before a change can be initiated and implemented, the participants must understand the benefits of school-based management in order to overcome the barriers that exist.

Advantages of School-Based Management

School-based management, which has become an increasingly important strategy for guiding school improvement, is a response to the need for an adaptive organizational model in education that forges the critical link

between school-site authority and improved student learning. The underlying assumption is that greater decision-making authority at the school
level will enable individual schools to respond more efficiently, effectively, and flexibly to the needs of its unique student population by harnessing two forces: the expertise of school professionals and the involvement of parents and the community. (Mutchler and Duttweiler, 1989, p. 1)

As the Winona, Minnesota Independent School District recognizes,

Education will be most effective when carried out by people who feel a
sense of ownership and responsibility for the process. Those most closely
affected by decisions ought to play a significant role in making those
decisions. This means that teachers, along with principals, should be
involved in solving building-wide problems while the Superintendent and
the Board of Education make district-wide decisions. (Site-Based Management, 1991)

Schools could expand a site-based management council by including
support staff (clerical, maintenance, food service, etc.), parents, students (middle school and senior high only), and a business/industry
person. No single group of stakeholders should comprise more than 50
percent of the site team. Each site within a district would have a site
team, such as the Winona Independent School District has established,
representing all stakeholders, which would meet monthly throughout the
school session to assure that their site meets district staff development
requirements, and to develop building goals for each year. Each site
could design their own system of operation, preferably one by consensus, and determine length and member replacement policies. Teams need
to select a facilitator, preferably a volunteer, but not necessarily a site
team member or a principal. The facilitator needs to be neutral in
opinion, keep the team on task, and work toward bringing the team to a
consensus decision. The site team should record meeting minutes and
distribute copies to all stakeholders and present a summary of activities
to the school board at least yearly.

School-based management means a significant change in the way most
school districts are managed today.

The school board and superintendent both encourage and permit site
teams to take risks and try new ways of education improvement. Principals, also, share many of the building-level decisions. Central office
administrators work with site teams in providing service, information,
and assistance to teams. All stakeholders in the district are represented
as decisions are made. As trust builds and site teams become more

comfortable in their work, they will solicit task forces comprised of other site stakeholders to assist them with their work. (McIntire, 1992)

The concept suggests that most decisions about how individual schools operate should not be made by school superintendents or school boards, but by the schools themselves. As Henderson (1991, p. 1) reveals, "Our experience has led us to believe that a bottom-up, school-by-school approach is by far the most promising strategy for rescuing our troubled schools."

Why should school districts adopt school-based management? What are the advantages? In an attempt to answer these questions, the American Association of School Administrators, the National Association of Elementary School Principals, and the National Association of Secondary School Principals convened a task force to identify the advantages of school-based management. Focusing on school districts that had adopted school-based management, the task force found that:

- It formally recognizes the expertise and competence of those who work in individual schools to make decisions to improve learning.
- It gives teachers, other staff members, and the community increased input into decisions.
- It shifts the emphasis in staff development; teachers are more directly involved in determining what they need.
- It focuses accountability for decisions; one individual — typically the superintendent or a building principal — has ultimate responsibility for any decision.
- It brings both financial and instructional resources in line with the instructional goals developed in each school.
- It helps to provide better services and programs to students.
- It nurtures and stimulates new leaders at all levels; as one task force member said, "Superstars emerge from the process. There is a rebirth."
- It increases both the quantity and the quality of communication, which is more likely to be informal — in face-to-face meetings, for example. (Fullbright, 1988)

School-based management can enrich the climate for educators and students. As illustrated in Figure 2.3, it gives building principals and teachers the flexibility to make school-level decisions to meet the needs of students.

Decisions	Decision Makers' Role			
	School Board	District	Principal	Faculty
Budget Allocations				
Building Level Capital Outlay/General Fund	finalize	finalize	decide	advise
Personnel				
Building Level Addition/Reduction				
—certified staff	finalize	finalize	decide	advise
—administration (principal)	finalize	decide	no input	advise
—administration (district)	finalize	decide	advise	inform
Instructional Assignments				
—certified/noncertified staff	finalize	finalize	decide	advise
—department chairpersons	finalize	finalize	advise	decide
Staff Development				
—district	finalize	finalize	decide	advise
—building	finalize	finalize	advise	decide
Curricular/Cocurricular				
District Policy/Process	finalize	decide	advise	advise
Building Policy/Process	finalize	finalize	decide	advise
Classroom/Grade Policy/ Process	finalize	finalize	advise	decide

Figure 2.3. Site-based management decision making schema. Source: Site-Based Management. 1991. Winona, MN: Winona Public Schools, Independent School District No. 861.

Site teams cannot, independently, change an area of district operation which is a district-wide function. District-wide functions are those areas that either impact all sites in the district, or are areas which require school board approval. Examples of those types of district-wide functions include: budget allocations, transportation, food service, etc. Every effort will be made to work with site teams who wish to study, change, or try something new which involves district-wide responsibilities. The site teams will need to work with the superintendent to determine if these types of changes can be attempted. (McIntire, 1992)

John Goodlad (1983), a noted educator, researcher, and author of *A Place Called School,* strongly endorses local school decision making. His strategy for school reorganization calls for "school by school" because the greatest impediment to educational reform is the failure to recognize individual schools as social systems and as the focal points for improvement. Accordingly, school-based management may not be a panacea, but "it is a process, based on democratic principles, which has worked where it has been given a chance" (Marburger, 1989, p. 74).

CHAPTER 1 PROGRAM

Chapter 1, a stimulator for reading programs, is a federally sponsored and funded program designated for educationally deprived students in public and nonpublic schools. In framing the Hawkins-Stafford Elementary and Secondary School Improvement Amendments of 1988, P.L. 100-297, Congress specifically acknowledged that "enhancing educational opportunities is an investment in the future of the Nation" (South Dakota State Department of Education and Cultural Affairs, 1991).

Congress reauthorized Chapter 1 in 1988 to emphasize accountability and program effectiveness. This requires local school districts to identify unsuccessful projects and modify those that need improvement.

Successful Program Attributes

A study of Chapter 1 projects that have been highly successful in meeting the needs of disadvantaged students provides a model for program attributes selected by the U.S. Department of Education. The program attributes and achievement indicators found to be consistently successful are as follows:

(1) Clear project goals and objectives that emphasize high expectations for student learning and behavior
(2) Appropriate instructional materials, methods, and approaches that result in maximum use of academic learning time
(3) Coordination with the regular program
(4) Student progress monitoring to provide for regular feedback and reinforcement
(5) Strong leadership
(6) Professional development and training of school and Chapter 1 staff and parents
(7) Parent/community involvement
(8) Positive school/classroom climate
(9) Excellence recognized and rewarded
(10) Evaluation results used for program project improvement (South Dakota State Department of Education and Cultural Affairs, 1991, PA-1-2)

These ten program attributes serve as guidelines for Chapter 1 schools to help disadvantaged students improve their reading skills and comprehension. Elementary school principals should utilize the established guidelines, implement what research says about the teaching and learning process (illustrated in Chapters Five and Six), and consider Chapter 1 as a major source for improving reading programs.

As society continuously changes, "U.S. children are entering school less prepared now than five years ago . . . with a third of them starting school not ready to learn" (Haspel, 1992, p. 5). The message is simple but universal. If our young people leave school without a good foundation in reading, they and society will pay a very high price.

Elementary school principals responsible for Chapter 1 programs usually have questions. To establish an awareness of what can and cannot be done, the twenty-one most frequently asked questions and answers are presented.

CHAPTER 1 PROGRAM:
QUESTIONS AND ANSWERS[2]

(1) How are Chapter 1 program allocations determined?

Each year each state receives its allocation from the U.S. Department of Education. Each state then has the responsibility to suballocate these funds to local school districts. The allocation for each school district is based on a formula dependent on the number of children aged five to seventeen residing in the district who are
- from low income families
- from families receiving aid to dependent children (ADC)
- in local institutions for neglected or delinquent children
- in foster homes supported by public funds

The latest decennial census provides information about children aged five to seventeen in a school district from low income families. This is the primary data source used to determine local education agency (LEA) allocations.

(2) Why do some schools with smaller enrollments have larger allocations than those schools with larger enrollments?

It is entirely possible that a smaller school district will reflect more low income as determined by the U.S. Census Bureau. Allocations are based upon the 1990 census, and school districts are

[2]Chapter 1 questions and answers were prepared by the South Dakota State Department of Education and Cultural Affairs. Used with permission.

always guaranteed 85 percent of the previous year's allocation.

(3) What is the responsibility of Chapter 1 to students attending private schools?

LEAs that have students attending private schools, after consultation with appropriate private school administrators, must make arrangements for Chapter 1 services. The services must be provided at a neutral location and be *equal* to that provided in the public schools.

(4) Can limited English proficiency (LEP) students be enrolled in Chapter 1?

LEP children should be selected for Chapter 1 services on the same basis as non-LEP children. Language problems do not qualify LEP students for Chapter 1 services.

(5) Must diagnostic tests be given every year?

The decision to give diagnostic tests is a local program determination. Formal and informal assessments of student progress or areas of weaknesses are encouraged. Some students who are having learning difficulties need more frequent assessment than other participants.

(6) A school's evaluation results this year were not very good. Has the school failed in meeting the students' needs?

Possibly not. There are numerous reasons why a decline in test scores occurs. They range from technical problems in test administration, to student motivation, to the program itself. Generally, if appropriate services are provided, gains occur. Also, a need might exist to do further diagnosis, change strategies, or improve concentration of services. LEAs may qualify for program improvement processes.

(7) Parents in many communities are very difficult to involve in Chapter 1. What is suggested?

Research shows a high correlation between Chapter 1 student academic success and parental participation. Publications on parental involvement are available from the Chapter 1 office.

(8) Is parental permission required to enroll a student in Chapter 1 and to administer diagnostic tests?

No. Chapter 1 instructional services and diagnostic testing are part of, or an extension of, the regular program of instruction. Diagnostic tests are not considered a psychological or other type of test for which parental consent is required. However, communicating with parents about their child's participation and learning needs is important and strongly encouraged.

(9) If parents request that their child not participate in Chapter 1, what should be done?

Although this is a local decision, it is suggested that the request be honored. It is unlikely that appropriate educational gains can be made if parents, and likely the student, are negative about the services.

When this occurs, the LEA should evaluate if parents have been properly informed about the program and the potential progress their child could make in the Chapter 1 program. It may be a communication problem rather than a program problem.

(10) May special education students participate in Chapter 1 programs?

Yes. Some students who qualify for special education services may also qualify and receive Chapter 1 services. Special education students may participate if

- The project is designed to meet educational deprivation needs rather than a child's handicapping condition.
- They are selected on the same basis as other participants.
- They participate jointly with services at intensities that take into account participant needs and abilities without preference to a handicapped condition.
- They can be reasonably expected to accomplish the project's objectives and make gains.

LEAs may *not* use Chapter 1 funds for services they are required to provide under Public Law 94-142 or other funds.

(11) Can the regular program's basal reading or literature series and mathematics series be used in Chapter 1?

Chapter 1 requires supplemental program services designated to meet special educational needs of each student. Using the same materials in the same way that they are used in the regular reading and mathematics programs will result in supplanting.

The fine line between supplemental services and supplanting is simply too difficult to distinguish if assistance with classroom basal series is provided. Many publishers have numerous *supplemental* materials that accompany their basal series. These and other materials that are coordinated with the regular classroom approach are appropriate to meeting Chapter 1 student needs.

(12) Can Chapter 1 students be helped with their daily assignments or homework?

This answer relates to the previous question. Again, the responsibility to provide a supplementary program designed to meet specific student needs must be met. Daily assignments and homework are generally not considered appropriate supplemental services designed to meet long-term needs of identified participants.

(13) Can students be served who are absent for long periods of time?

Absenteeism is *not* a criterion for student selection in Chapter 1. It is normal for average and above average students to be absent as well as low achievers. However, if a Chapter 1 student has an extended absence, the responsibility to assist with classroom work missed is not the program's. There is a likely need for reteaching.

(14) Must personalized education plans (PEP) be written for each Chapter 1 student?

PEPs are not required by law, but, if used, they can be valuable when there is teacher turnover and for communicating to other teachers and parents.

(15) What should be done about the school work that students miss when they participate in Chapter 1?

Coordination of instruction between Chapter 1 and the regular classroom is extremely important. It is expected that classroom teachers will make curricular adjustments to compensate for the participant's time in the program. It is demoralizing to participants to have extensive makeup work to complete after receiving Chapter 1 assistance.

(16) Must students be pulled out of class to provide Chapter 1 services?

Chapter 1 regulations state that the supplement, not supplant, does *not* require that services be provided outside of the regular classroom or program.

(17) What certification must teachers have to teach or tutor in Chapter 1?

Staff members who teach in the program must possess the same (state) certification as a regular teacher who teaches an identical subject or grade level in a regular class. There are no special additional state or federal requirements.

(18) May students from private schools participate in Chapter 1 programs?

LEAs must give students from private schools the opportunity to participate if they reside in the project area. Chapter 1 services cannot be provided on the premises of private schools but must be provided on an equitable basis at a location that is neither physically nor educationally identified with a private school.

(19) Why is coordination between Chapter 1 and regular classroom teachers important?

Coordination of the Chapter 1 program with other school programs increases opportunities to learn by reinforcing basic skills in different instructional settings. Also, because Chapter 1 is a diagnostic and prescriptive program, it is important that Chapter 1 teachers and regular classroom teachers communicate and coordinate their programs.

(20) What is meant by size, scope, and quality?

The law does not define how to meet these requirements, but Chapter 1 services should generally involve small classes (size), more hours of instruction in reading and math (scope), and special teachers and aides and more appropriate instructional approaches and materials (quality).

(21) Can Chapter 1 personnel be assigned non-Chapter 1 duties?

Full-time Chapter 1 personnel may be assigned non-Chapter 1 duties if similarly situated personnel are assigned these duties and the time spent does not exceed one period or sixty minutes per day.

THE FUTURE: WHAT'S IN STORE

"We'd better fire up our engines, because we have an enormous challenge ahead of us," warned Secretary of Education Lamar Alexander (Zakariya, 1991, p. A6). American students, according to the National Assessment of Educational Progress (NAEP) twenty-year summary, are no farther ahead academically than they were in the 1970s.

In forecasting what the future holds for American education, Cetron (1990, p. 30) believes that "education will be respected as a valuable and prestigious profession by the twenty-first century." Some selected excerpts from Cetron's predictions are as follows.

- Education will be the major public agenda into the twenty-first century.
- The growing mismatch between the literacy of the labor force and the competency required by available jobs will be greatest among the "best" jobs where educational demands are greatest.
- The emphasis on school reform and restructuring will continue throughout the 1990s.
- The "back-to-basics" movement will become the "forward-to-future" basics (movement).
- Accountability at all levels will be the buzzword for the 1990s.
- All community stakeholders (parents, students, teachers,

business leaders, and others) will continue to demand more involvement in the decisions governing education.

Forecasts and results from testing programs give credence to the importance and value of the four stimulators—*America 2000*, workplace requirements, school-based management and shared decision making, and Chapter 1—addressed in this chapter. Elementary school principals have an opportunity to provide the leadership for new, improved, redesigned, exciting, and more effective schools. The public is demanding it.

REFERENCES

Amundson, K. 1988. *Challenges for School Leaders*. Arlington, VA: American Association of School Administrators, p. 17.

Carnevale, A. P., L. J. Gainer, and A. S. Meltzer. 1990. *Workplace Basics*. San Francisco, CA: Jossey-Bass Publishers, pp. 19, 36.

Cetron, M. 1990. "Cetron's Latest Forecast of Education's Critical Trends," *The School Administrator*, 47:29−31.

Culyer, R. 1988. "Accountability as a Partnership," *The Clearing House*, 61:365.

Doyle, D. P. 1992. "The Challenge, the Opportunity," *Phi Delta Kappan*, 73:513.

Elmore, R. 1991. "Leadership for Change: Superintendents and Restructuring," *The Superintendents' Leadership Role in School-Based Improvement*. Documentation of Colloquia of the 1990−1991 School-Based Improvement Project. Boston, MA: Office of Community Education, Massachusetts Department of Education, pp. 17, 18.

Fullbright, L., ed. 1988. *School-Based Management: A Strategy for Better Learning*. Arlington, VA: American Association of School Administrators, p. 7.

Goodlad, J. I. 1983. *A Place Called School: Prospects for the Future*. New York, NY: McGraw Hill Book Company.

———. 1992. "On Taking School Reform Seriously," *Phi Delta Kappan*, 74(3):236.

Haspel, D. E. 1992. "Report Urges School to Reach Out for 'Readiness,' " *Leadership News*, 94:5.

Henderson, A. T. 1991. *Access*. An Access printout on school based improvement and effective schools: A perfect match for bottom-up reform. Columbia, MD: The National Committee for Citizens in Education (February):1.

Marburger, C. L. 1989. *One School at a Time*. Columbia, MD: The National Committee for Citizens in Education, p. 74.

McCune, S. D. 1990. "Implementing the Governors' Goals: What Will It Take?" *Noteworthy*. Aurora, CO: Mid-Continent Regional Educational Laboratory, p. 4.

McIntire, R. 1992. *Winona Public Schools: Shared Decision-Making for Building Site Teams*. A district document. Winona, MN: Winona Public Schools, Independent School District No. 861.

MDC, Inc. 1988. "Executive Summary," *America's Shame, America's Hope*. Technical report prepared for the Charles Stewart Mott Foundation by MDC, Inc. Flint, MI: Charles Stewart Mott Foundation, p. 2.

———. 1988. "The Future: Can We Get There from Here?" *America's Shame, America's Hope*. Technical report prepared for the Charles Stewart Mott Foundation by MDC, Inc. Flint, MI: Charles Stewart Mott Foundation, p. 36.

Mutchler, S. E. and P. C. Duttweiler. 1989. *Implementing Shared Decision Making in School-Based Management: Barriers to Changing Traditional Behavior*. Technical report sponsored by the Office of Educational Research and Improvement, U.S. Department of Education. Austin, TX: Southwest Educational Development Laboratory, p. 1.

Robinson, G. E. 1985. "Effective Schools Research: A Guide to School Improvement," *Concerns in Education* (February).

———. 1986. "Learning Expectancy: A Force Changing Education," *Concerns in Education* (February):22.

Seeley, D. S. 1991. "The 'Sleeper' in America 2000," *Network for Public Schools*, 17(3):3.

Site-Based Management. 1991. "Site-Based Management Decision Making Schema," Winona, MN: Winona Public Schools, Independent School District No. 861.

South Dakota State Department of Education and Cultural Affairs. 1991. *Chapter 1 State Plan for Program Improvement*. Prepared by the South Dakota State Department of Education and Cultural Affairs, Pierre, SD, p. 1.

———. 1991. *South Dakota Technical Assistance Handbook*. Prepared by the South Dakota State Department of Education and Cultural Affairs, Pierre, SD, PA-2-3.

U.S. Department of Education. 1991. *AMERICA 2000: An Education Strategy*. Prepared by the U.S. Department of Education, Washington, D.C., pp. 2, 23−24.

U.S. Department of Labor. 1991. *What Work Requires of Schools: A Scans Report for AMERICA 2000*. An executive summary prepared by the Secretary's Commission on Achieving Necessary Skills (SCANS), Washington, D.C., pp. 1−6, 8.

Zakariya, S. B., ed. 1991. "Common Measures," *Education Vital Signs*. A supplement to *The American School Board Journal* and *The Executive Educator* (December): A6.

Reading: What Works

*"Reason and calm judgement, the qualities
specifically belonging to a leader."*

TACITUS

As you read and study:

. . . Determine the main objective of reading.

. . . Analyze the three reading models.

. . . Appraise the four approaches used for reading instruction.

. . . Summarize students' reflections on reading instruction.

. . . Critique the qualities of an effective reading teacher.

. . . Categorize students' strengths and weaknesses in reading.

. . . Discover the importance of using an informal reading inventory.

. . . Compile a reading interest inventory.

. . . Analyze the five principles that make a difference in reading
    achievement.

. . . Consider the spectacular changes in society and children today.

. . . Evaluate the Reading Recovery program.

. . . Summarize the components of an effective reading program.

Optimism about reading and reading programs is currently under a
cloud. We are familiar with denunciation and criticism, which reveal
their emotional sources in their peevish and undiscriminating tone. The
condemnations testify to the heat of feelings rather than the light of
thought. As Vacca, Vacca, and Gove (1991) state,

In the pressured world of teaching it's easy to lose sight of what you

believe about children, reading, and how children learn to read. . . .
Inquiry into what you do and why you do it is one of the best tools you
have for understanding teaching and improving instruction. (p. 3)

Reading is essential in the school curriculum. The primary objective
is to provide all children not only with the ability to read but also the
desire to choose to read and to enjoy reading. Teachers should have the
expertise to diagnose and prescribe proper instruction for the individual
child. There is neither a model nor a certain approach, as some tend to
assert, which guarantees that all children will learn how to read. As the
research indicates, "No one approach to teaching reading yields consistently superior results. A combination is probably best" (Gunning,
1992, p. 391). It is the responsibility of administrators and teachers to
be knowledgeable about "what works" for students, to diagnose and to
prescribe the proper method for reading instruction.

READING AND REALITY

Children are unique and learn to read just as they have learned to talk
and walk. Not all of this happens at the same age. Subsequently, "We
won't produce a nation of readers by trying to cram all our young readers
into a single mold. The varied nature of student learning should be
informing both our classroom practice and our research agenda" (Harris, 1989, p. 259). Administrators and teachers must focus on the reasons
for reading and on the end result, not the means. Only when we begin
to look at and respond to the strengths that students possess, will the
debates on whether students should be taught to read using a skills or a
whole language approach to reading instruction become insignificant.
The students and how they learn will be significant if "we make the
connection between the ways in which children learn language and the
ways in which they use language" (Taylor, 1989, pp. 192−193).

Administrators and teachers should know that reading is a process of
organizing knowledge and resources in ways that allow each student the
opportunity to predict and understand print. Also, reading is an activity
that allows one to comprehend, understand, and enjoy printed texts. It
is a communication between the author and the reader.

How can administrators comprehend and explain this process and
focus on what works in reading instruction? First, they must become
familiar with the models and approaches used in teaching reading. This

step is important to understand what is happening in the classroom. The model and approach that a teacher chooses to use in reading instruction represents the teacher's implicit theory becoming an explicit theory. Our task as administrators is to understand the complexity of the literacy behavior of young children because educators need to "use these understandings to support and enhance children's learning opportunities" (Taylor, 1989, p. 193).

Reading theories can be characterized by three models and four major instructional approaches. The models of reading differ in terms of their semantic, syntactic, and graphophonemic information. None of the reading models is a complete picture because they do not encompass the social nature of reading.

THE THREE READING MODELS

The authors do not recommend one of the following models over another because each model has positive instructional purposes that are necessary and beneficial in teaching reading. The following descriptions of the three models of reading instruction are used only to review inherent characteristics of each model. Administrators should encourage teachers to use a combination of strategies and techniques in reading instruction that gives students "the best of all worlds." Only then will reading instruction be focused on "reading, writing, listening, and speaking — all the elements of language — as an integrated whole, not a jumble of individual skills. This reading approach gains strength from literature, basals, and whole language strategies" (Cochran, 1989, p. 39). It is critical to use a comprehensive plan in teaching reading and to select techniques from all three models and to "combine them with good, creative teaching practices" (Cochran, 1989, p. 39).

Bottom-Up Model

The Bottom-Up Model conjectures that the process of translating meaning begins with print and is initiated by the decoding of print. The emphasis is on phonics instruction so that students will acquire independence in word identification (Trachtenburg, 1990). Sounds are associated with graphic symbols and the process has students learning letters, sounds, and words in isolation before reading sentences, paragraphs, stories, and books. Bottom-up models of reading are described as "data driven" and can be analogous to a person who is learning how to drive a car as

> The beginner finds the mechanics of operating the automobile so demanding that he or she must focus exclusively on driving. However, with practice the skilled driver pays little conscious attention to the mechanics of driving and is able to converse with a passenger or listen to the radio. Likewise, the beginning reader must practice decoding print to speech so rapidly that decoding becomes "automatic." (Vacca, Vacca, and Gove, 1987, p. 15)

Individual subskills are regarded as hierarchical and are taught in sequence. Some teachers begin with the vowels and their sounds, and then the consonants. Others progress through the letters of the alphabet from A to Z. Instruction is based on "sequential, letter-by-letter, word-by-word process, as indicated by the isolated phonics and vocabulary instruction and the focus on perfection in oral reading" (Jones, 1982, p. 773).

To facilitate phonics instruction in the bottom-up model and to enable teachers whose implicit theory places an emphasis on phonics instruction, it is recommended that teachers use a blend of a whole-part-whole sequence. Using this sequence of reading instruction and combining it with excellent literature would be beneficial to students. The authors recommend the whole-part-whole concept. It can be facilitated by following Trachtenburg's (1990) three stages:

(1) Whole: Read, comprehend, and enjoy a whole, quality literature selection.
(2) Part: Provide instruction in a high-utility phonic element by drawing from or extending the preceding literature selection.
(3) Whole: Apply the new phonic skill when reading (and enjoying) another whole, high-quality literature selection.

This method of teaching phonics is a good option for students to learn the letters, sounds, and rules while providing for a natural, meaningful, and intrinsic use of language. The whole-part-whole method combines students' knowledge and reinforces their ability to recognize and pronounce letters and words by using sentences, paragraphs, and stories.

Top-Down Model

The Top-Down Model assumes that the process of translating print begins with the prior knowledge of the reader. It stresses "that information processing during reading is triggered by the reader's prior knowledge and experience in relation to the writer's message'' (Vacca, Vacca, and Gove, 1991, p. 20). The process is initiated by making predictions or educated guesses about the meaning of the units of print and involves speaking, writing, reading, and listening.

The reader decodes graphic sounds to ''check out'' his or her hypotheses about the meaning of the printed words. The process is conceptually driven. The following story provides an example of how reading is conceptually driven.

Flan and Glock

Flan was a flim.
Glock was a plopper.
It was unusual for a flim and a plopper to be crods, but
Flan and Glock were crods. They medged together.
Flan was keaded to moak at a mox. Glock wanted to kead
there too. But the lear said he could not kead there.
Glock anged that the lear said he could not kead there
because he was a plopper. (Vacca, Vacca, and Gove, 1991, p. 21)

By reading the short story above, one could perceive that Flan and Glock are names of two persons and proper nouns. The verbs are medged and keaded. By using ''educated guesses'' it is understood that Glock was being discriminated against. ''Both prior knowledge and graphophonic information were required to make these guesses'' (Vacca, Vacca, and Gove, 1991, p. 21). The process is a combination of the bottom-up and top-down models. It is difficult to separate the two entirely.

Interactive Model

The Interactive Model uses prior knowledge and print to combine both the top-down and bottom-up models of reading. ''Neither prior knowledge nor graphophonic information is used exclusively . . . [and] the process of reading is initiated by formulating hypotheses about meaning and by decoding letters and words'' (Vacca, Vacca, and Gove, 1991, p. 21). It assumes that the readers can begin by using either the decoding of graphic symbols, letters, syntactic and semantic context of a word, or their prior knowledge to make hypotheses about the text. Consequently, ''The crucial difference between bottom-up models and the interactive model is that in the latter, information processing occurs from the top-down, as well as from the bottom-up'' (Jones, 1982, p. 774).

From years of teaching reading in the elementary school we would prefer to identify with the interactive approach. Some students needed to be taught using the bottom-up approach and some needed the top-down. It was our responsibility to diagnose and prescribe the right model for the individual child.

THE FOUR APPROACHES

The four major approaches are individualized prescriptive, basal reading, language experience, and literature based. These approaches (illustrated in Figure 3.1) can be placed on an instructional continuum with the skills perspective on the extreme left and the whole language perspective at the far right.

Individualized Prescriptive Approach

The Individualized Prescriptive Approach is a skills approach that is located at the far left of the continuum (Figure 3.1) because phonics instruction is emphasized. If you visit or listen to reading instruction as it takes place in elementary schools, you will likely hear the teacher give prescribed commands such as:

"Read the first paragraph on page twenty-two and tell me what Jane did at the circus."

S					H
U					O
B	Individualized	Basal	Language	Individualized	L
S	Prescriptive	Reading	Experience	Personalized	I
K					S
I					T
L					I
L					C

Figure 3.1. Range of four approaches and position on a Subskill-Holistic Instructional Continuum. Adapted from Vacca, J. L., R. T. Vacca, and M. K. Gove. 1987. *Reading and Learning to Read.* Glenview, IL: Scott, Foresman and Company, p. 39.

"Take time to sound out the words you don't know."

"The five vocabulary words on the chart need to be memorized for today's lesson."

"All of you read the following paragraph about 'The Clown' out loud."

"Remember the rule for changing the *y* to *i* and adding the ending" or "*i* before *e* except after *c*, or when sounding like /*a*/ as in *neighbor* and *weigh*."

This form of instruction views reading as a part-to-whole process.

The two main methods used to teach phonics are known as the analytic and synthetic phonics methods. The analytic method is preferred because it places an emphasis on the sound-symbol relationships by using an analysis of words that are familiar to students. An example of the individualized prescriptive approach is as follows:

- Observe a list of known words with a common phonic element, for example, the initial consonant *t*.
- Begin questioning as to how the words look/sound the same and how they are different.
- Elicit the common phonic element and discuss.
- Have the learners phrase a generalization about the element, for example, all the words start with the sound of the letter *t*. The sound of the letter *t* is /*t*/ as in top. (Vacca, Vacca, and Gove, 1987, p. 220)

The synthetic method uses a definite sequence to teach sound-symbol relationships. The sequence is as follows:

- Teach the letter names.
- Teach the sound(s) each letter represents.
- Drill on the sound-symbol relationships until rapidly recognized. Discuss rules and form generalizations about relationships that usually apply to words, that is, when vowels are short or long.
- Teach the blending together of separate sounds to make a word. Provide opportunity to apply blending to unknown words. (Vacca, Vacca, and Gove, 1987, p. 220)

It is recommended by the authors that phonics instruction be used if and when necessary. Teachers should form small groups and provide instruction on skills students need to learn. Do not assign page upon page of phonics lessons from a workbook. Always remember, the reason for phonics instruction is to help each student master the ability to read by joining letters, words, sentences, and texts independently. The reason for this recommendation is because

> The strongest functional connection between these two skills may run in the reverse direction. It is only the nature of reading that can make the content of a phonic lesson seem sensible; it is only the prospect of reading that can make them seem worthwhile. (Adams, 1990, p. 272)

Because phonics instruction is a means to an end, it should fulfill some distinctive condition, and it should be correlated with students' reading lessons. Since the ultimate goal is to enable students to become independent readers, phonics instruction "must be functional, useful, and contextual to be of value. It also should be planned and be systematic" (Gunning, 1992, p. 79).

From past experience in teaching and in helping students gain knowledge about letter sounds, it was beneficial to use bulletin boards that were "learning boards" to explain and illustrate specific skills. One favorite that was used for students of different grade levels is the one on the two sounds made by the letter *C, c*. The letter can be confusing for students when beginning to read because the two sounds are either the hard /k/ or soft /s/ sound. In teaching third grade students, the "*C, c* learning board" (see Figure 3.2) was on the classroom entry door. One day a fifth grade student on her way to music class stopped and asked, "What does this bulletin board mean?" After the rule was explained by using the cats (each family was a different color to separate visually the different sound classes) she looked at the teacher and said, "Oh! That is what that is all about." How many times had this fifth grade girl been told the rules for the sounds of the letter *C, c?* How many times had she been told that it depended on the vowel that followed? How many phonics work sheets had been completed using the vowels *a, o,* and *u* with the letter *C, c* to make the hard /k/ sound (cat, cot, cut) and *i, y, e,* with the letter *C, c* to make the soft /s/ sound in *city, cyclone,* and *cent.* This gives credibility to the old sayings that "seeing is believing" and "pictures are better than a thousand words." Learning bulletin boards are helpful because students can see and immediately use the information when speaking, reading, writing, and listening. They also provide an exceptional technique to integrate art and reading.

Basal Reading Approach

The use of basal reading material occupies the largest part of the instructional continuum and can be described as a comprehensive read-

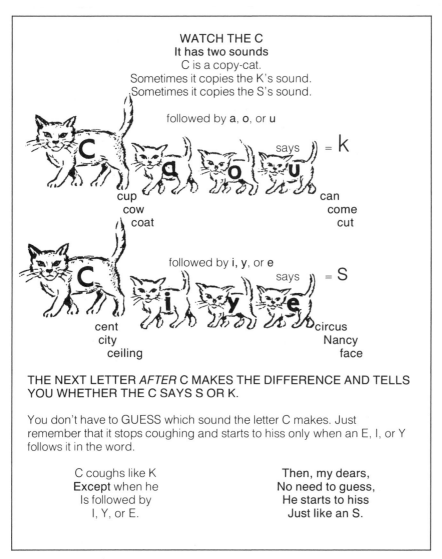

WATCH THE C
It has two sounds
C is a copy-cat.
Sometimes it copies the K's sound.
Sometimes it copies the S's sound.

followed by a, o, or u

says = k

cup
cow
coat

can
come
cut

followed by i, y, or e

says = S

cent
city
ceiling

circus
Nancy
face

THE NEXT LETTER *AFTER* C MAKES THE DIFFERENCE AND TELLS YOU WHETHER THE C SAYS S OR K.

You don't have to GUESS which sound the letter C makes. Just remember that it stops coughing and starts to hiss only when an E, I, or Y follows it in the word.

C coughs like K
Except when he
Is followed by
I, Y, or E.

Then, my dears,
No need to guess,
He starts to hiss
Just like an S.

Figure 3.2. The sound of the letter C (learning board). McEathron, M. 1952. *Your Child Can Read*. Buffalo, NY: Kenworthy Educational Service, Inc., p. 18. Reproduced by permission.

ing program. The directed reading lesson or directed reading activity is a familiar method used for organizing instruction with basal reading materials. ''Even with the rise in popularity of whole language and literature-based reading programs, teachers in more than 90 percent of U.S. classrooms use basal reading programs'' (Samuels and Farstrup, 1992, p. 146).

Basal readers do furnish a structure and most students do learn to read with them. However, basal readers fail to provide adequate practice in reading. As Au and Mason (1989, p. 64) indicate, "Basal activities and materials can be the basis for a good developmental reading program, but they should be seen only as a starting point and should be heavily supplemented with other activities and materials."

The major components of basal reading programs are:

(1) The readiness program
(2) Pre-primer and primer levels
(3) Word identification strand
(4) Comprehension strand
(5) Literature
(6) Language arts
(7) Management

Administrators and teachers must analyze the available materials used in reading instruction and differentiate between the "pros" and "cons" when using this approach in reading instruction. Gunning (1992) maintains that

> Basals are neither a method nor an approach to teaching reading. They are simply a carefully crafted set of materials. The core of the reading program is the teacher. It is the teacher who should decide how and when to use basals and whether to choose alternative materials. (p. 365)

Those who have a rigid reliance on the old paradigm of basals and ignore the teacher as core of the reading program mortify an effective reading program.

Language Experience Approach

The Language Experience Approach (LEA) is characteristic of the interactive and top-down models and is very personal. In the LEA, "the student — either individually or as a part of a small group — dictates a story about an actual, personal experience" (Samuels and Farstrup, 1992, p. 296). It integrates the processes of thinking, speaking, listening, writing, and reading. A child's story is typed or written by the teacher or another person, read aloud, and can be made into a book. This approach gives students with ability the opportunity to use their prior knowledge and personal experiences. Stories use words that are familiar and utilized in the everyday language of students. A description of the LEA approach is as follows:

What I can think about, I can talk about,
What I can say, I can write (or someone can write for me),
What I can write, I can read (and others can read too),
I can read what I have written, and I can also read what other people have
written for me to read. (Baghban, 1981, p. 13)

Literature-Based Approach

The Literature-Based Approach is located at the far right of the
continuum. It can be described as the approach that utilizes characteristics from the interactive and/or top-down model of reading instruction. "Literature-based reading programs are used by teachers who want
to provide for individual student differences in reading abilities and at
the same time focus on meaning, interest, and enjoyment" (Vacca,
Vacca, and Gove, 1987, p. 42).

How can a teacher get ready and plan for using this approach? The
most important components are to designate a time each day for reading
and to have many, many books available that students will enjoy and
choose to read. These books can be of varied reading levels, topics,
types, and interest. Interest is the key motivator in getting students to
read. The number of books must be adequate for the number of students
in the classroom.

The following questions and answers will assist in use of the literature-based approach in reading instruction.

(1) How do I set up a classroom library?

Stock the library with all types of books—trade books, library
books, Caldecott Medal books, Newbery Medal books, new
books, old books, fat books, picture books, little books, big books,
poetry books, plays, historical fiction, nonfiction, autobiog-
raphies, biographies, journals, magazines, fairy tales, nursery
rhymes, newspapers, books on dinosaurs, birds, animals, famous
people, and outer space. Include modern, realistic, and traditional
literature. Also, choose books that represent ethnic and minority
groups, mainstream Americans, and traditional and nontraditional
families. Acquire science, music, social studies books, . . . and
any books that interest students.

(2) Where can I find these books?

Buy, borrow, collect, find, and order them from book clubs. Use
resources—school, city, university, and state libraries. Check out
the rummage and garage sales in your area. Ask school ad-

ministrators, colleagues, parents, grandmothers, grandfathers, students, uncles, aunts, and friends. Explore and look in the boxes in the attic, the basement, and the garage. Shop at book stores.

(3) Where should this reading area be located?

Choose a corner or a special place in the classroom for reading. Organize the reading area and make it comfortable by having carpeting, rugs, pillows, or bean bags on the floor for students to sit or stretch out on. Any furniture can be used, even an old bathtub—just create an environment that enhances students' reading.

(4) What does the teacher do when the children are reading?

The change from product- to process-oriented instruction changes the teacher's role. The teacher is the facilitator, assisting the students when help is requested, making competent instructional decisions, helping students select books at proper reading levels, and modeling reading.

In more and more of today's classrooms the teacher often assumes a role of facilitator of learning, rather than dispenser of information. "He [she] is likely to be seen modeling reading and writing processes, conferring with individuals or groups of children about their reading and writing, and encouraging them to share their work" (O'Donnell and Wood, 1992, p. 4).

The teacher conferences with a student on a regular basis in a special place—away from other students—no distractions are allowed! These conferences are about five to ten minutes. The teacher uses a class list to make certain all students have a scheduled time. Conferencing is on a one-on-one basis. The teacher and the student have selected a procedure for recording individual student's reading selections, e.g., title, author, main idea, favorite character, and type of literature. The teacher could even have students retell a portion of the story that has been read. Retelling is excellent for measuring comprehension.

(5) What do students do when the teacher is having a conference?

Students will be cognizant of the rules established for the reading area and select a book to read. When choosing books to read, students should use the "rule of thumb" that involves the following:

(a) Choose a middle page of the book.

(b) Read the page silently.

(c) Every time the student encounters a word that is unknown or confusing, put down a thumb. When a second word is unknown, put down a finger. If all fingers are used for the one page, the book is too difficult and the student should choose another book.

Students may choose a story, poem, or play and read it with someone from their peer group. *The Small Grouper* (described in Chapter Five) can be of assistance if the teacher desires to pair students to be "buddy" readers. The teacher may have the students read portions of these books, stories, . . . orally before reading to the teacher. Most important, students will spend this time *reading,* either silently or orally. Also, students may be doing journal writing, writing letters, writing poetry, writing books, publishing stories—the list is endless. The teacher and the students will have ways to share these activities using the Author's Chair, class books, individual books, newspapers, and plays.

(6) How will the teacher assess student learning?

Assessment will be observational and ongoing. The teacher uses "kid watching," informal reading inventories, anecdotal records, checklists, observation, and portfolios of stories written and read orally. The strengths and needs of each child will be recorded in a notebook, on a card, or any method used by the individual teacher.

(7) How will group or individual assignments be made?

Assignments will be based on the needs of the student. The assignments can be individual or small group work. The teacher will become cognizant of the needs of individual students by reviewing the records of individual conferences to determine which students have the same reading problems, such as vowels, suffixes, prefixes, compound words, etc. These students can be brought together as a group and taught the skill. Grouping is a fast way to teach the same skill to several students at the same time, e.g., a few students need instruction on vowel sounds.

There are hundreds of other cooperative or independent activities such as creative writing, research, crafts, science experiments, and social studies projects that can be included with this approach. The objective is reading, reading, and more reading for the literature-based approach. After years of observation and study, Jewell and Zintz (1990, p. 243) conclude that the best way to teach children to read and write is by using a literacy program that is literature-based. "Research in literacy development over the past two decades strongly supports a literature-based program." Literature gives students an excellent opportunity to learn about themselves and their world. Literature-based reading instruction creates a community of readers.

To capture and to explore what works in reading instruction, administrators and teachers must be aware of what turns students on to want to read. It is important to find out what students perceive and how students can be motivated. Motivation and developing self-esteem are key ingredients to what will get students reading, which promotes literacy.

STUDENTS' REFLECTIONS ON
READING INSTRUCTION

Let us stop and reflect on what college seniors remembered about "what worked" in their reading instruction and about their teachers in elementary school. The students were elementary education majors enrolled in a required reading methods course prior to their student teaching semester. They were asked to answer two questions.

What do I believe about how children learn to read?

I believe children learn how to read

- when they have a positive and patient person teaching them
- when they receive positive feedback
- when they learn to identify the letters of the alphabet
- by learning the alphabet first and then sounding out words, sentences, paragraphs, and stories
- when they are read to
- by having good and positive role models — at home and at school
- through experience with different media
- through positive learning experiences
- by example and from experience
- when reading is an important and a continuous part of their lives
- being actively involved in reading activities
- by letting them read
- by knowing sight words and by practicing reading
- in many ways using small groups, large groups, one-on-one with teachers, or just by themselves
- through careful instruction and practice

- when it is enjoyable and interesting to them
- differently and at a different pace — some children need less instruction while others may need help all through school — it is important to remember each child's ability and differences
- by being exposed to written materials
- by memorizing what is said — nursery rhymes, poems, and echo reading
- by using spoken language — talking to and with children
- by receiving clear instruction and motivation from a teacher
- by receiving support from their teacher
- by being allowed to use their imaginations to create their own stories — this helps them know that letters and words are meaningful
- from effective teachers who can make reading interesting and fun for children — they become interested and are willing to learn
- by using the whole language approach and letting children use invented spellings

In describing your favorite reading teacher, what characteristics, teaching styles, and/or personality did the teacher possess?

My favorite reading teacher was

- My first grade teacher because she was kind and very understanding of all students and had control of the class. She had a very positive personality and was usually happy. She related well to her students and was helpful.
- My first grade teacher — I don't remember a lot about her teaching styles but she was fun and enthusiastic. She never became discouraged by students who could not read the words we were learning. In first grade, I don't recall the stories as being difficult but she always encouraged everyone, even on words that may be considered easy by some people.
- My second grade teacher because she was patient, kind, and had a sense of humor.
- My third grade teacher because she presented the material enthusiastically and seemed very knowledgeable. We played challenging and enjoyable word games. She gave us certificates for reading library books and used SRA material in the classroom. Every day, after lunch, she would read a chapter out of a novel (of our choosing). She used vocal variations and

dramatized the story so it was as if we were actually "seeing the story taking place."

- My third grade teacher because she was the most outgoing person I have ever met. Everyday we would start our class with a story. Sometimes we could bring a book, magazine, or newspaper article from home but most of the time she read to us about why reading is so important. She placed an emphasis on reading and had us believe in ourselves and that we were capable of learning to read. By the middle of the school year, we (as a class) were so excited about reading that every day a different student was given the chance to read one of the teacher's articles or books to the class. We loved it because we thought she was the greatest reader in the world and for us to be able to read something that she chose was a great feeling. I learned from her.

- My third grade teacher because she was great at motivating children. She brought a large bathtub into the classroom which students painted, decorated, and placed pillows in. When our work was finished, students could get a book and read it in the bathtub. Everyone had a chance and would choose to be in the bathtub reading when it was their turn. Consequently, students were reading.

- My third grade teacher because she was excited about teaching reading, which created excitement and enthusiasm in students. She would have all students involved in reading but never put pressure on the students if they made a mistake. I think the most important characteristic of this teacher was that she truly cared about each individual in her classroom.

- My fourth grade teacher because she was a very intriguing woman who always seemed to read about things that were important to us at that particular time in our lives. Also, we could sit on the floor in a semi-circle.

- My fourth grade teacher because she made her students feel like we were already great at reading. This gave us confidence. She encouraged us to read what we were interested in. The best thing that she did for all students and what we all really loved about our teacher was the time she spent reading to us each day.

- My sixth grade teacher because she was fun and we could do projects about books we read on our own. I remember reading a book about Abraham Lincoln, carving Lincoln's face on a bar of soap, and how impressed this teacher was with my project.

- My seventh grade teacher is the one who I will never forget. He made reading fun for us and was very willing to help us learn. He encouraged us for the smallest accomplishments and praised us for our efforts. We would play games such as homonym basketball.

- Mr. R. because he is the only reading teacher I remember. Reading time seemed to be a fun time for my group and me. Mr. R. did not always act serious and authoritative. He laughed with us when he or someone made a humorous mistake. Reading time was nonthreatening.

- She was very energetic and fun. She believed reading increased knowledge. She created a playhouse which was decorated with various books and reading animals and was raised above floor level. This is where students earned their free time to go and read in this special reading area.

- She was able to make any story exciting and consequently students wanted to learn more about the author and read more. She took the time to read and discuss the story with students.

- She was super-sweet! She was kind to everyone. Somehow she got through to us by making reading enjoyable. Sometimes we would act out stories or do activities that the characters in the story would do. She was a very warm-hearted person.

- She was energetic, kind, and cheerful. She read to us every day and we read out loud to each other from the same book. We started with short, easy stories and then went on to longer more interesting stories. Reading became fun for us and we looked forward to getting new books.

- She believed that reading anything and everything was the best way to be a good reader. She was excited about reading, read to us daily, and helped us discover the joy that reading can give to students.

- She was friendly, caring, and made the story come alive by using different voice intonations and speech. She was full of energy.

- The teacher who let us choose the books we wanted to read but helped us to make choices that were challenging. She was indirect, focused, and had a warm and open personality. She recognized and developed each student's individuality and uniqueness. It was important to her that we were reading.

- She made reading exciting. Her personality was very outgoing, she involved the entire class in reading and stressed how important reading was to us in and out of the classroom.
- She was a very warm, friendly woman. She made me feel very secure and I wasn't afraid to make a mistake. She made reading fun and to this day I love to read.
- She was patient and would allow me to sound out words in class before interrupting me. She would also encourage the slower readers in class to read out loud and would not allow other students to make any upsetting remarks about the slow readers.
- When I first learned how to read—my teacher knew how to teach, made reading fun, exciting, and had us read out loud in class with her assistance and provided positive feedback. We also took our books home and read to our parents. I found that to be the most rewarding of all—I think my parents did, too.
- The one who always gave us free time to read every day and allowed us to use the library.
- The teacher with a positive attitude.
- The one who had many books available for me to read and let me start a class newspaper.
- The person who took time to spend with each student and made sure everyone understood the material. She created a positive attitude about reading and integrated reading into fun time and work time. She also used learning centers and let students read along with taped stories. She took time to read to us every day.

One student could not recall a teacher in elementary school who influenced her in reading, but she had a favorite English teacher in high school who did. This makes one wonder why or ask what happened in reading class during the preceding eight years of this student's formal education.

We direct the solicited comments from future teachers specifically at the classroom teacher. They characterize humanistic values about teachers who (1) encourage students to read in a positive way, (2) let students choose reading material, (3) value and model reading, and (4) let students know that they are important.

Qualities of an Effective Teacher

The qualities that are considered important for an effective teacher are

- Warmth: The teacher should have a caring attitude for all students and a concern for their social, emotional, and intellectual needs.
- Enthusiasm: Arousing interest in the teaching and learning processes is essential for being an effective teacher.
- Cognitive organization: The teacher must know how to organize learning material for students (e.g., the teacher needs to diagnose and prescribe the correct reading materials and use the proper instructional approach for the students).
- Indirectness: The teacher uses varied instructional methods that will best connect students with the subject (students of all ages remember 90 percent of what they say as they do a task) (Boschee, 1989, p. 22).

The above qualities are analogous to what effective teachers do. For example, "The mediocre teacher tells. The good teacher explains. The superior teacher demonstrates. The great teacher inspires" (Alcorn, Kinder, and Schunert, 1964, p. 6).

The school administrator should also consider the qualities of McGregor's X and Y theories and Ouchi's Z theory in selecting teachers for reading instruction. Flexibility is one of greatest assets of teachers. They must have the knowledge and expertise to modify reading instruction to fit the needs of students. McGregor's X and Y theories and Ouchi's Z theory, illustrated in Figure 3.3, can be utilized as a beginning point in deciding the type of teacher who should be facilitating reading instruction for students in our schools.

Effective teachers understand the nature of reading, serve as role models, and enjoy reading. They truly believe that reading is a part of language and important in communication, more than completing skill exercises or a complex skill. Reading "instruction demands much more than merely drilling children, asking them for correct answers, and following the suggestions offered in the teacher's manual" (Hayes, 1991, p. 11). Effective reading teachers do not look for a panacea; they understand the complex nature of reading and reading instruction. They monitor students' comprehension, not by placing an emphasis on correct answers and rote memory, but by utilizing open-ended questions that use

Consider your approach to the teaching and learning processes and
determine whether you are an X, Y, or Z type teacher.

Theory X	Theory Y	Theory Z
1. Students dislike work and will avoid it.	1. Learning is as natural as play.	1. Students and teachers work as a team.
2. Students must be forced to work.	2. Students are self-motivated and will strive to accomplish objectives.	2. Teachers clarify objectives to gain students' support for learning.
3. Students want to be directed and will avoid responsibility.	3. Students will learn to accept and seek responsibility.	3. Teachers and students view learning as a journey.

Note: Teachers should be flexible and adapt to students' needs. Some students must be directed
until they can become self-directed.

Figure 3.3. Theories X, Y, and Z teacher characteristics. Source: Boschee, F. 1989.
Grouping = Growth. Dubuque, IA: Kendall/Hunt Publishing Company, p. 21.
Reproduced by permission.

"why" and "how" to facilitate and place an emphasis on comprehension, analysis, synthesis, and evaluation which causes students to think.

Effective reading teachers also value the importance of having students who "like to read and that . . . read willingly in order to acquire
information and enrich their lives" (Hayes, 1991, p. 9). Reading instruction should give students the tools necessary to read different forms
of printed material. This will fulfill students' reading needs with other
reading materials to meet the desired goals of the school district's
reading program. Basal readers are normally used as a beginning point,
a guide, a resource, or a tool. However, effective reading teachers will
help students "learn to be strategic in making sense of what they read
and use reading in their world outside of school" (Hayes, 1991, p. 11).

Determining What Works

Students' strengths and weaknesses can be assessed by asking some
general questions about a school district's literacy program, which is

dependent on the adopted reading philosophy, goals, and objectives. Relevant questions are as follows:

- Where are students in their literacy development?
- At what level are they reading?
- Are they reading up to their ability?
- How well do they comprehend what they read?
- How adequate are students' reading vocabularies?
- What word attack skills do they use effectively?
- Do they know how to study?
- What comprehension and word attack strategies do students use?
- What are their attitudes toward reading?
- What kind of books do they like to read?
- Do they read on their own?
- Do they enjoy reading?
- How well do they write?
- What kinds of writing tasks have they attempted?
- Are students' reading and writing improving?
- Which students seem to have special needs in reading and writing? (Gunning, 1992, p. 460)

The information from the aforementioned questions will provide administrators and teachers with insights on what type of reading instruction is needed for students in that school or district.

Informal Reading Inventories

An informal reading inventory (IRI) provides information about the independent, instructional, frustration, and listening capacity levels for each student. The independent level is considered to be the level where students can read and comprehend with little or no assistance. The instructional level is the position where students can comprehend and learn with the teacher's guidance. The frustration level occurs when students become frustrated while reading required materials that are too difficult. The teacher should avoid this level at all times. The listening capacity level indicates how well the students can read if the teacher eliminates word recognition problems.

Teachers who have completed a course in remedial reading instruction should have exposure to varied reading inventories. Teachers can construct their own IRI using selections from a basal reading series or commercial inventories. It is recommended by the authors that teachers with no prior knowledge of an IRI seek assistance from the school's reading specialist or a teacher who has had specific training in the selection, construction, administration, and interpretation of an informal reading inventory. As illustrated in Figure 3.4, commercial informal reading inventories are available.

The informal reading inventory, a diagnostic instrument, determines how students interact with print when reading orally or silently, ascertains appropriate reading levels, and finds out how students interact with printed material. It will assist teachers in selecting and matching reading materials of appropriate difficulty for students, and in assessing the reading skills and abilities of students. The IRI can be administered to individual students or adapted and used as a silent group reading test.

Reading Interest Inventories

Another reading inventory that provides teachers with reading material that can help in turning students on to reading is the interest inventory. These inventories are comprised of teachers' questions or they can be purchased. The reading interest inventory listed here was developed by students in a reading methods course at the University of South Dakota for their "Bag of Tricks" to teach reading. It consists of thirty questions from which teachers can pick and choose to use with students in their classrooms and/or schools.

Inventory Title	Publisher	Grade
Analytic Reading	Merrill	1–8
Basic Reading	Kendall/Hunt	1–8
Burns/Roe Informal Reading	Houghton Mifflin	1–12
Classroom Reading	Brown	1–8
Qualitative Reading	Scott, Foresman/Little, Brown	1–8

Figure 3.4. Commercial informal reading inventories. Gunning, T. G. 1992. *Creating Reading Instruction for All Children*. Needham Heights, MA: Allyn and Bacon, p. 469. Reproduced by permission.

Reading Interest Inventory

(1) Who are you?
(2) How old are you?
(3) When is your birthday?
(4) How would you describe yourself?
(5) Do you live in a city or in the country?
(6) What sports do you enjoy?
(7) Who is your hero? Why?
(8) What is the name of your favorite book?
(9) Why did the author write the book?
(10) Who is your favorite character from a book you read?
(11) What do you like to read?
(12) Would you like to have more time during class to read on your own?
(13) Do you read at home?
(14) Do you like to have someone read to you?
(15) Do you like to read out loud?
(16) Do you have a library card?
(17) What is your favorite subject?
(18) What animals do you like?
(19) If you could go to the movies, what would you choose to see?
(20) What section of the newspaper do you like the most?
(21) What magazines would you like to read?
(22) I wish I had more time in school to _____.
(23) What is something special that you can do that you would enjoy teaching or showing the class?
(24) How many people are in your family?
(25) If you could visit any country, what country would you choose? Why?
(26) What is your hobby or what would be your hobby if you had one?
(27) What is your favorite thing to do after school? What do you like to do when not in school? If you're not in school I would find you doing _____.
(28) What do you want to be when you grow up?
(29) I enjoy _____.
(30) Reading is _____.

An interest inventory gives teachers information about students' interests and attitudes towards reading. It provides teachers with needed insights for accruing books that students in the classroom will be eager to read. Using some or all of the inventory questions will assist teachers to find "what works" for each child. Always remember, each child is an unique individual and possesses different likes and dislikes. The ultimate goal in reading instruction should be to motivate each student to read a myriad of print media, to comprehend what is read, and to enjoy reading.

HOW TO AND WHAT TO DO

It is a well-known fact that to become good and proficient at any skill one needs to practice. Why is it that more students have not been given the opportunity to practice reading? What type of reading program will help meet the literacy needs of students today and equip them for their future? It is time to endorse reading programs that allow children to read. Utilizing children's books can help achieve greater levels of success in learning reading skills and also reading for enjoyment. The five principles that can make a significant difference in a reading program, if followed faithfully, are:

(1) Children learn to read by reading.
(2) Reading should be easy — but not too easy.
(3) Instruction should be functional and contextual.
(4) Make connections. Build a bridge between children's experiences and what they are about to read.
(5) Build self-esteem. (Gunning, 1992, pp. 14 – 17)

The above five principles can even be a part of the self-fulfilling prophecy. School administrators, from their first course in school administration, learned about the beneficial results of expressing to students that "we have confidence in them." Now apply those principles and this prophecy, and believe in your students. Help the teachers in your school to gain the knowledge and expertise to diagnose, to prescribe, and to make learning to read important and relevant.

Reading instruction must become focused on reading as a language and a thinking process. In order to promote reading instruction that will be language-conscious, and alleviate the differences between language learning in school and the language students use at home or in their life space, the following will be beneficial:

(1) Instead of learning words to read, read to learn words.

(2) Instead of learning phonics to read, read to learn phonics.

(3) Instead of beginning readers reading to their teacher, the teacher should read to them.

(4) Instead of teachers or materials asking questions, children should ask them.

(5) Instead of thinking of children as deriving meaning from print, think of children bringing meaning to print. Meaning is not in the ink found on a page of print, but in the minds of students. (Tovey, Johnson, and Szporer, 1986, pp. 12 – 14)

Learning to read must be perceived as language learning. Administrators and teachers should work collaboratively to bring about the needed changes in reading instruction. It is essential that students be given the opportunity to ''link their linguistic competence and cognitive abilities'' (Tovey, Johnson, and Szporer, 1986, p. 15). When this happens, the school administrator and anyone who enters the classroom during reading instruction, according to Tovey et al. (1986, p. 15), will hear:

''What do you like about the book you're reading?''

''What do you think it is?''

''If you have trouble with a word while reading, don't be afraid to ask for help.''

''Who had the science section of *The New York Times?*''

''Did you ever notice that 'float' is also like 'goat' and 'boat'?''

''What do you think the author is trying to say?''

Reading is a meaningful and enjoyable process. Use what each student has in his or her cognitive map to facilitate learning how to read.

CHANGES IN CHILDREN AND SOCIETY

The roof is leaking! Quick, get the buckets! In this metaphor, a reading program was a once-beautiful home that deteriorated over time. The owners, realizing this, try to repair the obvious damage, but somehow they overlook the leaky roof. So they redo the plaster, repair the windows, replace the doors – giving attention to everything but the roof. The house continues to deteriorate and nobody seems to notice the roof. But until the roof is repaired, the house will never be beautiful or fully functional (Hodgkinson, 1991).

Where is the leaky roof in our reading programs? Is it the spectacular changes in children who now attend school? Is it the continuous use of traditional reading programs? Or, is it both?

Spectacular Changes in Children

Education demographer Harold Hodgkinson believes that the spectacular changes in children who now attend school constitute the leaky
roof in our reading programs. Fully one-third of our nation's children
are at risk of failure before they enter kindergarten. The assertion is
supported by the statistics issued by the U.S. House of Representatives
Select Committee on Children, Youth, and Families, which show the
following:

- One-fourth of all preschool children in the U.S. live in poverty.
- Seven out of ten women with children are active members of the
  work force.
- The work force has quadrupled in the past twenty years, pushing
  the number of single-parent families towards 25 percent; 16.2
  million children are being raised in single-parent families, and
  that number is expected to increase 30 percent by the year 2000.
- Fifteen million children are being raised by single mothers
  whose annual income averages about $11,400 in 1988 dollars,
  while the average couple makes $34,000. The number of babies
  born addicted to cocaine reached 350,000 a year by 1989; those
  who survive birth are poorly coordinated and have strikingly
  short attention spans. (Anderson and Jeffrey, 1992, p. 26)

For better or worse, the family image has changed significantly. The
traditional household of one mother, one father, and two children has
decreased from 60 percent in the 1950s to 4 percent today. Also,
communities across America are experiencing more violent and higher
crime rates, more poverty among the populace, a neglect of disadvantaged youth by public institutions, and the dissipation of good
teachers. In general, at-risk youth are not confined to the ghetto, the
poor, or newly arrived immigrants. Rather, they are symptomatic of
disturbing conditions in all American communities.

At-risk children "require a very high level of psychological and
academic development . . . to be successful both in school and later in
adult life" (Comer, 1987, p. 13). Subsequently, school administrators
will have to learn new strategies and behaviors on how to organize
effective reading programs. The ability to work smarter, not harder, will
become the measure of achievement. In reality, reading is a social and
educational intervention that is analogous to Albert Einstein's statement:
"Perfection of means and confusion of ends seem to characterize our
age" (Amundson, 1988, p. 51).

A Proven Solution

A local strategy for school administrators is to underwrite and support an intervention reading program to supplement the school district's current reading program. Because there are spectacular changes in children who now attend school, the Reading Recovery program is one viable vehicle to positively affect those children who need help to overcome the barriers to becoming successful readers. Imagine what a school could be like if all children could experience prosperity in reading. Could the school dropout rate decline? Could society be more literate? Positive reading results could influence most or all of America's education goals. The goals are as follows:

(1) All children will start school ready to learn.

(2) The high school graduation will increase to at least 90 percent.

(3) American students will leave grades four, eight, and twelve having demonstrated competency in challenging subject matter including English, mathematics, science, history, and geography; and every school in America will ensure that all students learn to use their minds well, so they may be prepared for responsible citizenship, further learning, and productive employment in our modern economy.

(4) United States students will be first in the world in science and mathematics achievement.

(5) Every adult will be literate and will possess the knowledge and skills necessary to compete in a global economy and exercise the rights and responsibilities of citizenship.

(6) Every school in America will be free of drugs and violence and will offer a disciplined environment conducive to learning (U.S. Department of Education, 1991, p. 9).

School administrators, teachers, and the American public must ask the hard question: ''Can any of the goals be achieved without effective reading programs?'' An answer to the question can be found in John Dewey's *Democracy and Education* (1916), where he so eloquently wrote that

A society which is mobile, which is full of channels for the distribution of change occurring anywhere must see to it that its members are educated to personal initiative and adaptability. Otherwise, they will be overwhelmed by the changes in which they are caught and whose significance or connections they do not perceive. (Glatthorn, 1987, p. 41)

With that thought in mind, administrators especially, should consider an alternative to help students become proficient readers.

READING RECOVERY

An example of a reading program that has been developed by educator and psychologist Marie Clay of New Zealand and used in that country since 1970 is the Reading Recovery program. Clay defines Reading Recovery as "a strategic process that takes place in the reader's mind; that reading and writing are interconnected, reciprocal processes; that it is most productive to intervene early, before children become trapped in a cycle of reading failure" (Dyer, 1992, p. 10). The state of Ohio has experienced success with the program since 1984.

Reading Recovery is getting more recognition today because it seeks to help students who are at risk due to the consequences caused by failure in reading. Past experience has shown that for some children, whatever the reason, regular classroom instruction

> is not enough to assure that they become readers and writers. They need extra help to make that critical breakthrough that suggests that they understand the underlying processes. Traditional remedial programs do help but do not make it possible for at-risk readers to "catch up"; these programs do not usually create independent readers who can keep on learning. (Pinnell, 1989, p. 180)

Reading failure is costly in dollars and to the individual student. "Viewed from the short-term perspective of annual costs, Reading Recovery is less expensive than first grade retention, but more expensive than typical Chapter 1 services or special education services. However, [as illustrated in Figures 3.5 and 3.6], the short-term investment in Reading Recovery has significant long-term payoffs" (Dyer, 1992, p. 15). Reading Recovery offers an effective way for schools to use financial resources for the good of students. It is a cost-benefit program.

Students who cannot read suffer from low self-esteem and have academic difficulties. Reading Recovery is a one-time intervention that occurs when students are enrolled in first grade. Its aim is to assist those children who are in the lowest 20 percent in reading and writing achievement. Dyer (1992, p. 10) believes that its purpose is to help children "without regard to intelligence, ethnic group, language achievements, school history, physical handicaps, or learning dis-

Intervention	Annual Cost	Average Years in Program	Total Program Time	Total Cost per Student
Retention (first grade)[1]	$5,208 (all costs)	1 year	1,080 hours	$5,208 (all costs)
Chapter 1[2]	$943	5 years	525 hours	$4,715*
Special Education[3] ("learning disabled")	$1,651	6 years	1,512 hours	$9,906*
Reading Recovery[4]	$2,063	½ year	40 hours	$2,063

*Cost in 1990–91 dollars; inflation and salary increases are not included.

[1]Cost for one child retained in first grade who received *all school services* (food, transportation, etc.) for one additional year, assumed to be the annual per pupil expenditure nationwide fo r current operations of $5,028, in 1990–91, as reported in *Estimates of School Statistics: 1990–91*, National Education Association (1991). The time for this intervention was estimated assuming a 6-hour school day × a 180-day school year.

[2]Annual *teacher salary cost* of instruction for one student in Chapter 1 pull-out program. Calculated by dividing the national average of teacher salaries for 1990–91 ($33,015) reported in NEA *Estimates of School Statistics: 1990–91,* by the average number of Chapter 1 students taught by each Chapter 1 teacher per year. The average number of students taught per teacher was calculated from data in the U.S. Department of Education report *The Current Operation of the Chapter 1 Program* (1987), and assuming a 6-hour teacher day with 7 classes of 5 students each, equaling a teaching load of 35 students. The study also was the source of data used to calculate the time for this intervention: an average Chapter 1 pull-out resource session of 35 minutes per day × 180 days per year, × 5 years, which is the average length of time students receive Chapter 1 services in elementary school.

[3]Annual *teacher salary cost* of instruction for one student classified as "learning disabled" taught in pull-out resource room program for one year. Calculated by dividing the national average of teacher salaries for 1990–91 ($33,015) by the average total number of students classified "learning disabled" taught by each teacher in a resource room pull-out program (a teaching load of 20 students per day), as reported in the U.S. Department of Education study *Patterns in Special Education Service Delivery and Cost* (Moore et al., 1988). The time for this intervention was also calculated from data in the study, which reports the typical student classified as "learning disabled" spends 7 hours per week in resource pull-out programs. Given a 36-week school year, this is 252 hours per year, or 1,512 hours over the course of 6 years of elementary school.

NOTE: These costs only include teacher salaries. Costs do *not* include items such as the *annual* cost of *assessment* of students, which was reported in the study *Patterns of Special Education Services Delivery and Cost* to be $1,273 per Special Education student in 1985 –86. Estimates also do not include time and salary costs for Special Education students beyond sixth grade.

[4]Annual *teacher salary cost* of Reading Recovery instruction for one student calculated by taking half the national average of salaries for teachers for 1990–91 ($33,015 divided by 2 = $16,508) and dividing this number by the average number of students (8) taught by one Reading Recovery teacher teaching Reading Recovery half of each day for one year. The time for this intervention was calculated using a tutoring session of 30 minutes each day, for a 16-week period.

Figure 3.5. Reading Recovery savings: comparison of teacher time and salary costs per pupil, with grade retention, Chapter 1, and Special Education in the elementary grades (in 1990–91 dollars). Source: Dyer, P. C. 1992. "Reading Recovery: A Cost Effectiveness and Educational-Outcomes Analysis," *ERS Spectrum*, 10:1. Reproduced by permission.

• Expected benefits from one Reading Recovery teacher working one year:	
Avoid 2 grade one retentions, @ $5,208 each	$10,416
Avoid need to serve two students in Chapter 1 programs (each child served for five years), @ $4,715 each	$9,430
Avoid misclassification of one Special Education student in "learning disabled" resource program (child served for six years during elementary school)	$9,906
Total cost savings	$29,752
• Less cost of one Reading Recovery teacher (half year's full-time salary)	(16,508)
• Net savings per Reading Recovery teacher	$13,244

Figure 3.6. Potential long-term Reading Recovery cost-benefit for one Reading Recovery teacher working with eight students during one year (in 1990–91). Source: Dyer, P. C. 1992. "Reading Recovery: A Cost Effectiveness and Educational-Outcomes Analysis," *ERS Spectrum*, 10:1. Reproduced by permission.

abilities." The goal of the program is to provide assistance and one-to-one individualized instruction for students so they have the opportunity to develop into independent readers. The duration of Reading Recovery instruction is twelve to sixteen weeks. Students will be in a pull-out program but Reading Recovery is not intended to be a substitute for the school district's selected reading and writing instruction; it is a supplementary program.

The Reading Recovery teacher must receive special training through inservice education because Reading Recovery is not a teacher-proof, commercially prepared package. The training continues for a year and teachers learn how to design intervention strategies to meet individual learning needs. Students will receive instruction on a one-to-one basis and each lesson will be for one-half hour daily. The teacher directs

the rereading of familiar "little" books, takes a "running record" of independent reading, works with the student on reading strategies as needed, supports the child in writing a message or a story, and reads a new "little" book with the child. (Dyer, 1992, p. 11)

Each teacher works individually with four children per day and undertakes other educational duties during the rest of the day.

The primary principle of the Reading Recovery program correlates with what most administrators and teachers have believed about children and their ability to learn to read. The effects of implementing a Reading Recovery program in a school can be assessed as having immediate effects as well as long-range effects on students. These effects are as follows.

Immediate Effects of Reading Recovery

- Reduce retention in first grade.
- Reduce referrals to special programs.
- Build self-esteem in students.
- Develop independent readers, writers, and problem solvers.
- Achieve higher test scores.
- Turn good teachers into better teachers.
- Provide a vehicle for parental involvement.

Long-Range Effects of Reading Recovery

- Reduce the dropout rate.
- Produce a more literate community.

The Reading Recovery program reduces reading failure and is designed to assist those students who are at risk before they become labeled and categorized as remedial. Reading Recovery can also be an asset to the model, strategy, or method used by the teacher in individual classrooms for reading instruction. Some fundamental theoretical assumptions of Reading Recovery that correlate with other reading models are as follows:

- Reading is a strategic, in-the-head process.
- Reading and writing are reciprocal processes.
- Children learn to read by reading.
- School literacy instruction influences children's conceptions of reading.
- It is productive to intervene early.
- Knowledgeable and sensitive teachers are the key. (Pinnell, 1989, pp. 169–170)

Reading Recovery saves money and reduces a school district's dependence on the current practices of retaining students, labeling, tracking, and categorizing students. These are not even educational practices. They are educational stumbling blocks for some students.

If a company offered a better product that would cost less and take less time to develop, business and industry would not hesitate one minute to have that product become a reality.

> American students, teachers, parents, and taxpayers deserve no less. With the research evidence that Reading Recovery is not only education- ally effective, but also cost-effective, this early intervention deserves careful consideration by all those responsible for the education of children. (Dyer, 1991, p. 18)

It is important that administrators remember well John Dewey and his conviction that school is not a preparation for life, but it is life. Let's work to make students literate and to become lifelong readers.

COMPONENTS OF A GOOD READING PROGRAM

The changes in society, research about reading instruction, and methods students use to master the complex activity of learning how to read have brought focus on various components and conditions that are instrumental in a good reading program. Schools can no longer be satisfied with just teaching students how to identify and how to pro- nounce words. Reading experts state that

> Before students can truly be said to be readers, they must have the ability to read the words they see, understand the ideas those words convey, integrate information from a variety of sources, and use all the informa- tion to understand complex ideas. (Kline, Brodinsky, and Amundson, 1990, p. 1)

According to recent research, a good reading program should include the following components and characteristics:

- phonics instruction
- the opportunity for children to do "meaningful" reading
- an emphasis on comprehension, not just word attack skills
- opportunities for listening, speaking, reading, and writing
- inclusion and applicability in all curricular subjects (Kline, Brodinsky, and Amundson, 1990, pp. 2−3)

Administrators need to evaluate reading instruction that is practiced in the classrooms to ensure that the above components and charac- teristics are included in the reading program.

In conclusion, the fifteen goals for reading endorsed by the American Association of School Administrators (1990) can serve as a guide in choosing ''what works'' in reading instruction. These goals are as follows:

- Incorporate both whole language and skill-based instruction into the reading curriculum.
- Extend and deepen formal reading instruction in content areas and in middle and secondary schools.
- Enrich materials and motivate students to read for pleasure and as a habit.
- Vary and extend teaching capabilities.
- Establish or extend school district reading priorities, goals, and standards.
- Reach problem students.
- Teach higher-level skills.
- Offer more effective inservice training.
- Encourage greater comprehension.
- Individualize instruction to a greater degree.
- Make greater, more effective use of computers.
- Seek new materials, more time, and higher scores for reading instruction.
- Involve parents more deeply.
- Establish stronger leadership structures in the reading program.
- Increase the use of children's literature in reading instruction. (Kline, Brodinsky, and Amundson, 1990, p. 8)

Finally, the teaching of reading and deciding ''what works'' will be dependent on the school district's philosophy, administrator and teacher philosophy, interpretation of research, the students' prior experience with print, prior knowledge, and level of instruction. Educators should always be cognizant that reading is a part of the language process and you, the administrator, must provide the environment for students to master the task of reading. Barbara Bush states that

Every American child deserves a school that takes to heart its most challenging and important mission; to teach all students to read. The child who attends such a school is much more likely to become a productive and contributing adult—and a happier one, too. (Kline, Brodinsky, and Amundson, 1990, p. 1)

Administrators do have a moral obligation to do whatever is necessary to guarantee that all students receive reading instruction that will provide them success in learning how to read, learning how to comprehend, and learning to read for enjoyment. The reading success of individual students and productivity of educational systems should be preeminent to the school administrator. Research has provided the basis for promising techniques and approaches that can be used in different school districts to provide all students with the ability to become literate during their first years of school and to put students on the road to success in life.

REFERENCES

Adams, M. J. 1990. *Beginning to Read: Thinking and Learning about Print.* Cambridge, MA: MIT Press.

Alcorn, M. D., J. S. Kinder, and J. R. Schunert. 1964. *Better Teaching in Secondary Schools (Rev. Ed.).* Chicago, IL: Holt, Rinehart and Winston, Inc.

Amundson, K. 1988. *Challenges for School Leaders.* Arlington, VA: American Association of School Administrators.

Anderson, T. R. and J. Jeffrey. 1992. "Restructuring Schools with the Forgotten Solution: Community Education," in *Educational Restructuring and the Community Education Process*, Larry E. Decker and Valerie A. Rommney, eds., Alexandria, VA: National Community Education Association, p. 26.

Au, K. H. and J. M. Mason. 1989. "Elementary Reading Programs," in *The Administration and Supervision of Reading Programs*, S. B. Wepner, J. T. Feeley, and D. S. Stricland, eds., New York, NY: Teachers College Press, pp. 60–75.

Baghban, M. 1981. "Practicality and Literacy," a paper presented at the *26th Annual Meeting of the International Reading Association, New Orleans, LA, April 17–May 1, 1981.* ERIC Reproduction Service No. ED 206 411.

Boschee, F. 1989. *Grouping = Growth.* Dubuque, IA: Kendall/Hunt Publishing Company.

Clay, M. M. 1985. *The Early Detection of Reading Difficulties, Third Edition.* Auckland, New Zealand: Heineman Educational Books.

Cochran, J. M. 1989. "The Best of All Worlds," *Instructor*, 98(9):38–41.

Comer, J. P. 1987. "New Haven's School–Community Connection," *Educational Leadership*, 44(6):13.

Dyer, P. C. 1992. "Reading Recovery: A Cost-Effectiveness and Educational-Outcomes Analysis," *ERS Spectrum* (10):1, 10–18.

Glatthorn, A. A. 1987. *Curriculum Leadership*. Glenview, IL: Scott, Foresman and Company, p. 41.

Gunning, T. G. 1992. *Creating Reading Instruction for All Children*. Boston, MA: Allyn and Bacon.

Harris, P. 1989. "New Findings in the Great Debate," *Phi Delta Kappan*, 71:259.

Hayes, B. L. 1991. *Effective Strategies for Teaching Reading*. Boston, MA: Allyn and Bacon.

Hodgkinson, H. 1991. "School Reform vs. Reality," *Phi Delta Kappan*, 73:9 – 16.

Jewell, M. G. and M. V. Zintz. 1990. *Learning to Read and Write Naturally, Second Edition*. Dubuque, IA: Kendall/Hunt Publishing Company.

Jones, L. L. 1982. "An Interactive View of Reading: Implications for the Classroom," *The Reading Teacher*, 35:772 – 777.

Kline, L., B. Brodinsky, and K. Amundson. 1990. *Teaching Reading*. Arlington, VA: American Association of School Administrators (Critical Issues Report).

McEathron, M. 1952. *Your Child Can Read*. Buffalo, NY: Educational Service, Inc., p. 18.

O'Donnell, M. P. and M. Wood. 1992. *Becoming a Reader*. Boston, MA: Allyn and Bacon.

Pinnell, G. S. 1989. "Reading Recovery: Helping At-Risk Children Learn to Read," *The Elementary School Journal*, 90(2):161 – 183.

Samuels, S. J. and A. E. Farstrup, eds. 1992. *What Research Has to Say about Reading Instruction*. Newark, DE: International Reading Association.

Taylor, D. 1989. "Toward a Unified Theory of Literacy Learning and Instructional Practices," *Phi Delta Kappan*, 71:184 – 193.

Tovey, D. R., L. G. Johnson, and M. Szporer. 1986. "Remedying 'The 180° Syndrome' in Reading," *Childhood Education*, 63(1):11 – 15.

Trachtenburg, P. 1990. "Using Children's Literature to Enhance Phonics Instruction," *The Reading Teacher*, 43:648 – 652.

U.S. Department of Education. 1991. *America 2000: An Education Strategy*. Prepared by the U.S. Department of Education, Washington, D.C., p. 9.

Vacca, J. L., R. T. Vacca, and M. K. Gove. 1987. *Reading and Learning to Read*. Glenview, IL: Scott, Foresman and Company.

———. 1991. *Reading and Learning to Read, Second Edition*. New York: Harper Collins Publishers.

CHAPTER FOUR

Supervising Student Assessment

*"Where there is an open mind,
there will always be a frontier."*

CHARLES F. KETTERING

As you read and study:

. . . Analyze the research on administrator involvement in reading and
language arts programs.

. . . Consider what elements make up good management of reading
and language arts programs.

. . . Summarize issues and controversies associated with the
administrator's role in reading and language arts.

Accountability is having a major effect on education. Current standardized tests are being questioned by educational researchers, teachers,
and administrators. Many educators claim that we are asking standardized testing to do too much, that we need to broaden the scope of
assessment and to find alternative ways to assess students. Individual
teachers no longer want to focus just on raising test scores in reading and
other subject areas; instead, they want credible student assessments that
reflect and support sound instructional practices. Moreover, they want
assessments that address conceptual understanding and problem-solving
abilities. In their search for assistance with reading assessments,
teachers are turning more to administrators and reading supervisors for
guidance. Many small school districts, however, have only one administrator, who becomes the reading supervisor by default. Larger
school systems may have several reading specialists. For the purposes

75

of this chapter, any or all reading specialists or supervisors will be referred to as administrators because of their role in implementing and assessing reading programs. As a result, administrators are becoming a focal point in this quest for better student assessments.

Proactive administrators are making changes in student assessment. The purpose of this chapter is to review how successful administrators are making a difference in reading through the use of alternative assessment techniques. One of the first steps in reviewing this process is to ask ourselves some very important questions:

- What is the role of the administrator in student assessment, and how has it been increasing?
- What current supervisory practices in student assessment are being used?
- What is the concern among administrators regarding standardized testing?
- Why are more administrators searching for alternatives?
- What specific assessment alternatives are available?
- Where will new developments lead us?

ADMINISTRATIVE ROLE

A major national debate exists regarding how to handle reading and language arts assessment and what the role of the administrator is in assessment. The area of reading and language arts is a concern due to the number of remedial students who have a limited proficiency of reading and writing. As shown in Figure 4.1, Thomas Snyder (1990) states that about 12 percent of all children in public schools participated in remedial reading during the 1987 – 88 school year, as opposed to 7 percent who participated in remedial math programs.

The number of remedial reading students has alarmed many educators, parents, and community members, and has resulted in administrators turning their focus to the area of reading and reading assessment. Many administrators have now made reading and language arts their number one goal, along with mathematics. With the increased attention on reading and reading assessments, some administrators have become confused as to why some assessments are used and others are not. For example, in the area of language arts and reading, some principals do not know a portfolio from a file folder, or a cloze procedure from a miscue analysis.

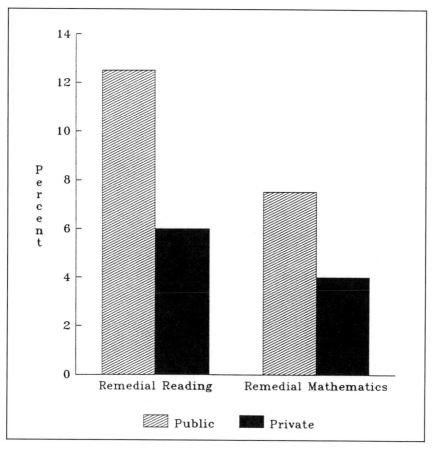

Figure 4.1. Percent of elementary school children participating in selected school programs, by control of school: 1987–88. Source: Adapted from Snyder, T. D. 1990. "Trends in Education," *Principal*, 70(1):6.

With this in mind, many administrators are asking questions about assessment and assessment problems, many of which relate directly to concerns about student assessment at local school levels. As a result, the purpose of this chapter is not to debate nor to address the monstrous issue of national assessment and curriculum, but to address the problem of supervision and assessment at the building level. In other words, what role can the local principal play in reviewing assessment procedures? As an example, let's say you as the administrator decide to investigate your reading and language arts program from an assessment standpoint and you utilize the survey provided in Figure 4.2.

Describe the status of your reading program by scoring each statement on the scale of "1" (not at all like our program) to "5" (very much like our program). If you have no knowledge of an item, put an X through the item number at the left. After completing the rating, circle the number in front of the five items you feel should receive special attention in improving the program for students.

PROGRAM GOALS/DESIRED OUTCOMES

1. Carefully stated goals/desired outcomes have been developed for the reading program.   1 2 3 4 5

CURRICULUM

2. Program uses the district/classroom curriculum as a guide to providing reading instruction.   1 2 3 4 5

3. Regular classroom staff have worked together to design a reading curriculum that is based on current research.   1 2 3 4 5

4. The main goal of the reading curriculum is to teach reading comprehension and to teach word recognition skills within that context.   1 2 3 4 5

5. A variety of reading materials and real-life purposes for reading are included in the reading curriculum.   1 2 3 4 5

6. Interpretive and critical reading strategies are a regular part of the curriculum.   1 2 3 4 5

INSTRUCTION

7. Teachers teach that the goals of reading are to think and understand.   1 2 3 4 5

8. Teachers teach students how to adjust their reading strategies when reading different types of materials.   1 2 3 4 5

9. Teachers guide students to read for meaning rather than word-by-word accuracy.   1 2 3 4 5

10. Teachers guide students to establish their own purposes for reading so they know why they are reading and what information they seek.   1 2 3 4 5

Figure 4.2. Reading program assessment instrument.

Following the implementation of the survey, you check the results and find that:

- Most of the teachers do not know how to give an Individual Reading Inventory (IRI).
- A portfolio assessment program is only being used by a limited number of staff members.
- A lesson involving a literature novel given to sixth graders is the same as one observed recently in a fourth grade class.
- A report card sent home does not reflect children's reading comprehension levels and/or word recognition skills.

If you have ever experienced even one of the above situations as an administrator, you are already aware that quality assessment can be very important.

There is hope for improvement in assessment procedures as teachers and administrators become more knowledgeable about assessment, reading levels, and strategies. Administrators are finding out more about teaching and learning and becoming more efficient in assessing reading (Cohen, 1988). As administrators of reading teachers, our new role is to make sure that curriculum and assessment follow current reading research, based on the notion that reading is the process of making meaning, rather than focusing on narrow subskills. In this role, administrators need to assist teachers by providing up-to-date staff development and inservice in the area of whole language and literature-based reading.

In addition, administrators need to inform their school board members, parents, and community members about new research developments happening in their school. Successful administrators maintain strong community support for programs in language arts and assessment. Once any new program has been selected for a school, the school board and community should be informed about its rationale and procedures. Good public relations techniques can strengthen any program.

CURRENT SUPERVISORY PRACTICES IN ASSESSMENT

Over the past decade, administrators have found reading materials limited in scope or lacking in literary substance. Reliance on single text programs is not preparing our children for the future. Our knowledge of how to help teachers integrate subject areas across the curriculum with reading, as well as how to evaluate the success of that integration, has also been limited.

Trade books, basal readers, literature anthologies, microcomputers, and videotapes are all important but are dependent upon efficient assessment, organization, and instruction on behalf of the teacher. Research findings are clear—learning is enhanced if subject areas are integrated and if oral and written activities are included.

Reading assessment will be enhanced when integrated learning is prevalent and students begin to meld all the bits and pieces into a whole. When teachers begin to integrate listening, speaking, and writing with life experiences, reading instruction will become clearer and more effective.

In the past, assessment techniques have relied overly much on published test forms constrained by narrow psychometric constructs of reliability and validity. Assessment has been done primarily on a mandatory and rigid basis. Previous models have been overly represented by mastery learning of discrete skills and multiple choice measures of word identification, word meaning, and comprehension of small units. Teachers stop every other month or at the end of each quarter, to test and then mechanistically regroup for the next week's instruction. As a result, assessments have been test-centered rather than teacher- and pupil-centered (Pikulski, 1989).

With problems in reading assessments becoming more pronounced, administrators have had to become more knowledgeable about assessment strategies. Figure 4.3 reveals data from a recent study completed by Crane (1990). The study indicates that a majority of elementary principals in the northwest have taken at least one course in each of the following areas: supervision of language arts, reading in the content area, supervision of reading, children's literature, teaching language arts, and elementary reading. Crane also noted in her study, as shown in Figure 4.4., that 85 percent of the elementary principals indicated they had taught reading in the classroom. As illustrated by Crane's study, more principals are realizing the need to have taught reading in the classroom as well as to have taken graduate level courses in reading and language arts. Only through a better knowledge of reading can they become better at assessing the assessors. Armed with more knowledge, administrators have begun to ask themselves several important questions:

Courses	F	% N*
Supervision Language Arts	22	55.0
Reading in Content Areas	22	55.0
Supervision of Reading	23	57.5
Diagnosis of Reading Problems	15	37.5
Elementary Reading	30	75.0
Children's Literature	21	52.5
Linguistics	8	20.0
Teaching Language Arts	29	72.5

*$N = 40$.

Figure 4.3. Principals: courses taken in reading. Source: Crane, G. M. 1989. "Leadership Characteristics of Elementary School Principals Related to Reading Achievement," Ed.D. dissertation, University of Montana, p. 150.

- Who knows the total curriculum best?
- Who is in the best position to make accurate observations and interpretations of what is happening in the classroom?
- Who is best able to interpret growth and provide documentation?

It has been established that administrators are the key to any successful language arts program. They have a total view of curriculum, assessment, and students from kindergarten through high school. Top building-level administrators know most of the children and are able to follow their progress from grade to grade. Information garnered in previous

Response	F	% N*
No	6	15.0
Yes	34	85.0

*$N = 40$.

Figure 4.4. Principals: teaching of reading. Source: Crane, G. M. 1989. "Leadership Characteristics of Elementary School Principals Related to Reading Achievement," Ed.D. dissertation, University of Montana, p. 152.

grades is often helpful to teachers trying to find out "why Johnny can't read."

Administrators are also becoming more aware of learning styles and their effect on student behavior and reading. Who could possibly be better at matching learning styles of teachers and students than the principal? According to Dunn (1990), learning styles have an impact on how teachers will teach children and how they will assess students. Research completed by Dunn indicates students using learning style strengths demonstrate statistically significant increases in academic achievement and improved attitudes.

Top administrators not only know how to utilize learning styles, they also know how to improve language arts programs. They know such programs are anchored in authentic literary experiences (Valencia and Pearson, 1990) and can be easily assessed. This means that tasks and texts should relate as much as possible to language experiences of the children. In addition, assessment of student work should be a continuous, ongoing process that reflects the developmental growth of students. Skills and strategies should be assessed only when needed, and assessments should reflect student literary knowledge (Farstrup, 1990). For example, a teacher could check reading and writing progress by having students read (grade-level appropriate) full-length selections that are experientially based. After reading the selection, students would then write a short summary of the story. Selected writing samples could then be scored holistically (Lytle and Botel, 1990) by making a general comparison score (ranking) with other anchor papers or quality descriptors. An analytic score could also be made from a profile of subscores based upon a number of specific features of a composition (such as organization, coherence, spelling, etc.). Teachers, naturally, could generate their own system rather than adopt a ready-made system of holistic or analytic scoring. Some children might even assume part of the responsibility for assessing their own growth.

Administrators must understand that assessment practices of effective teachers are linked and loosely interwoven with these essentials of reading:

- Student reading levels should be continuously monitored and assessed.
- Students learn to read by reading.
- Language experiences are the foundation of the reading process.

- Reading is an interactive process utilizing writing, speaking, and listening skills.
- Students read at their own individual rate.
- Students read a wide variety of material.
- Family and school are essential partners in reading instruction.

Administrators need to become more aware of the essentials of reading and assessment and they need to become more confident and effective observers of curriculum. Supervision techniques in reading assessment improve as administrators discover and make use of better whole language approaches. They know our children and our teachers better and are able to meet their needs more effectively. Unfortunately, this creates a dilemma: our new knowledge of reading instruction is at odds with old assessment instruments due to an overreliance on standardized testing.

STANDARDIZED TESTING

Standardized tests are the most visible and widely used vehicles for assessing student achievement in the United States (Dreher and Singer, 1984). Since the mid-1970s, statewide assessment has grown exponentially. According to Pearson et al. (1989), at least forty-six states had state-regulated tests in 1989, and half of these states used standardized testing. Haney and Madaus (1989) report an increase of testing by citing the average number of published column inches devoted to articles on testing and curriculum in the *Education Index*.

As shown in Figure 4.5, the average number of column inches in the *Education Index* devoted to articles on curriculum has increased only moderately over the past fifty years. In contrast, the average number of column inches devoted to testing has increased dramatically from 30 inches in the 1930s to over 300 inches in the 1980s. Because of the prevalence of standardized testing, administrators cannot overlook the use and the practical application of standardized test data. Some educators have preferred criteria-referenced tests, whereas others have noted that norm-referenced tests have provided important data in this age of high teacher and student mobility. Arguing for a national standardized curriculum for basic skills, Porter (1983, p. 26) suggests that standardized tests are the ''mechanism available for making clear and forceful the goals of education.'' Furthermore, standardized testing is

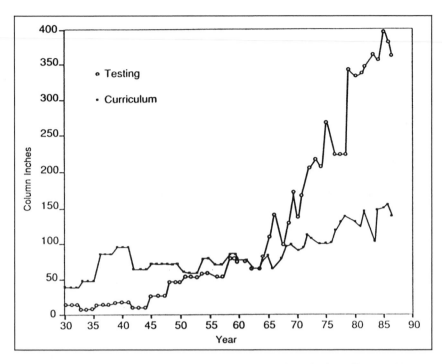

Figure 4.5. Education index listings under testing and curriculum. Source: Haney, W. and G. Madaus. 1989. "Searching for Alternatives to Standardized Tests: Whys, Whats, and Whithers," *Phi Delta Kappan*, 70:685. Reproduced by permission.

recognized as a major component by the U.S. Department of Education in defining effective schools.

Standardized testing has served many schools over the years and has become a part of our national educational system. Unfortunately, many educators have forgotten that standardized testing provides only a partial picture of student achievement, and teachers and administrators are beginning to ask questions (Whitehead and Santee, 1987).

A national debate over standardized testing and a national standardized curriculum is raging, and it appears that standardized testing might be running amok (Shepard, 1989). Longstanding complaints about this type of testing are increasing. Many administrators are finding logical inconsistencies among mandated standardized tests, approved textbooks, and mandated curriculum (Anderson et al., 1985). The growing dissatisfaction has led to questions about standardized testing and a review of some of the negative assessment aspects of standardized tests, which include:

- test-driven curriculum
- cost-effectiveness
- test schizophrenia
- deprofessionalization

Test-driven curricula may stem from the fact that many school boards are demanding higher test scores. This charge places tremendous pressure on supervisors to deliver. Thus, a test-driven environment is created in which textbooks and materials are geared to the test objectives, whether or not these objectives are appropriate for the long-term needs of students and society. The faculty, then, struggles on a day-to-day basis trying to "teach to a test," but is continually told not to "teach to the test." Finally, supervisors hope that teachers teach objectives that will correlate with the test so that higher scores can be achieved.

Cost-effectiveness of standardized testing is also under discussion. The high cost of test materials has raised the eyebrows of teachers and administrators. These individuals are wondering if some of this cost might be diverted to other types of tests. Dreher and Singer (1984) note that the cost of administering standardized tests is estimated to be $40 million annually. Clearly, significant school resources (time and money) are invested in standardized testing.

Testing schizophrenia is a real concern. This phenomenon is encountered by students, teachers, and administrators. Many students are petrified when taking such tests. According to Livingston, Castle, and Nations (1989), testing students for skills that they lack causes failure. Students' failures on standardized tests affect not only them but also parents, teachers, and schools. Some students shut down for a week, others go home crying. Teachers are admonished and monitored in many schools for poor test scores. After reading test scores in the local paper, parents become alarmed, often thinking test scores are absolute. This type of test hysteria and pressure leads to cheating and taking shortcuts. Morale problems surface and deprofessionalism becomes evident. Parents, teachers, and board members become frustrated, confused, and angry.

SEARCHING FOR ALTERNATIVES

There is very little material that is new when it comes to assessing educational progress on the basis of standardized test scores. Administrators differ widely in their perceptions on this problem and in the significance that they apply to the issue. Previous assessment instruments have been narrowly focused and measurement-driven, causing an "academic trickle-down effect." Decisions on what to teach and when to teach it have become obscured by politics.

Many aspects of measurement-driven curriculum can be positive if kept in balance. Teachers need to be spontaneous in their approach and must be encouraged by administrators to be creative as well as accountable. Curriculum should be related to real life experiences as often as possible. In addition, unique approaches need to be utilized in reading and language arts such as media technology involving computer word processing. For example, first graders in a Montana school are using the IBM Children's Publishing software program to generate pages of children's writing with computerized illustrations. Such written work can be used to assess how a child is progressing through the simple use of a portfolio system.

Not all assessments have to be creative. Some teachers are utilizing standardized tests effectively. Standardized tests can be used to note possible areas of strength, as well as to denote areas to be expanded. Teachers can use standardized tests in a more practical manner by targeting students who may need assistance in a specific area rather than subjecting the entire class to a barrage of subskills and workbook pages (Whitehead and Santee, 1987).

Many individuals do not even realize standardized tests are a problem. Some administrators feel that standardized tests quickly solve their documentation problems at a cost and "if [they] can buy [their] way out of a problem, [they] don't have a problem" (Mackay, 1988, p. 194).

Unfortunately, this conventional wisdom has led many administrators to fashion their student assessments around individual critical skills. Curriculum is broken into fixed sequences of reading and writing, with an emphasis on mastery of specific skills. From an administrative standpoint, some of this sounds logical. According to proponents, basic skills diagnosed as critical deficiencies can be isolated and learned (U.S. Department of Education, 1990). The process involved provides assessment of a clear structure for learning, and facilitates assessment of students' progress. In addition, a common vocabulary can be used throughout supplemental instructional programs to assist children having difficulty.

However, this approach also creates a problem. According to the U.S. Department of Education (1990) this process

- underestimates the capability of students
- postpones more challenging and interesting work for too long and, in some cases, forever
- fails to provide a context for learning or for meaningfully employing the skills that are taught
- reinforces academic failure over the long term

Students should be able to obtain the "whole picture" from this approach, but generally they are not able to integrate pieces into a useful knowledge base and thus do not challenge themselves. For instance, children with spelling problems are not encouraged to write stories because they lack spelling skills. As a result, these children do not have the opportunity to improve their vocabulary or to expand upon their language experience through writing. They become easily frustrated and soon become failure prone.

This approach also poses problems for teachers and administrators. Specifically, the greatest concern for administrators is teachers locking themselves into ditto and workbook cycles for assessment purposes. Specific skill assessment data is easy to chart and use on a percentage basis, and, as a result, teachers often prefer this approach. Additional assessment alternatives should provide teachers with some new avenues (Hiebert and Calfee, 1989). Teaching should be a balanced program and should reduce tendencies to overemphasize discrete skills. With more information about student ability and student achievement, teachers can stress underlying thinking processes along with skills.

A curriculum based on mastery of specific skills not only poses problems for students in transferring their skills to larger contexts, but it is also conducive to the formation of homogeneous group settings, i.e., tracking. Administrators are rightfully concerned with the long-term effects of tracking.

Tracking, which allows teachers to break up academic tasks into small manageable steps and allows "easier assessment," has some positive aspects. Direct instruction seems to be facilitated and pacing appears to be improved. Moreover, excessive time for practice and feedback is provided.

So, what is the problem? The problem with tracking lies in the lack of time and resources with which to aid students on an individual basis. In a language arts homogeneous tracking situation, a person could walk into any room having disadvantaged students and find 80 percent of the students with their hand in the air, waiting for help. Generally, no teacher aides are available, little peer tutoring is possible, and the teacher alone cannot help each student on a one-to-one basis. Feedback and assessment are difficult because the teacher often is too overwhelmed with work to meet these demands. Moreover, differentiated arrangements exacerbate further problems. Students in the low group feel bad about being "Blackbirds" who rarely listen to good readers. They become frustrated with having to wait for help and with the endless sea of dittoes and workbook pages they must complete. These frustrations often surface in disciplinary problems, which, in turn, create problems for the administrator who must work to resolve conflicts.

Many times students remain in their tracking groups regardless of success. If students in low groups develop comprehension and fluency skills, they generally remain with the group because teachers desperately need at least one student to read and model for the other children. Having at least one higher functioning student in the entire class also helps maintain a teacher's sanity. Occasionally, however, an observant parent, supervisor, or other teacher realizes what is happening and asks for assessment information. Following a quick screening check, the teacher of the low group agrees that the student has been doing better recently, and the child is quietly slipped into the next reading level group.

Hopefully, through better assessment procedures and techniques, administrators can encourage staff to move these children into more appropriate groups. With more accurate assessment data, teachers will be able to utilize cooperative teaching strategies and develop more flexible and temporary ability-grouped arrangements. Teachers will be able to maximize individual help to low-achieving students on an *ad hoc* basis rather than on a long-term group-based arrangement. With these changes, administrators can view assessment from a new perspective. Ineffective language arts programs, oral language, reading, and writing can be assessed as a whole process.

We have learned to ascertain what students can discuss, what they understand as they read, and what they are capable of saying when they write. The following are some general recommendations in improving assessment programs:

- Be aware that most assessment instruments provide only a partial measure of a student's ability and achievement.
- Utilize assessment instruments designed to measure student abilities in speaking, reading, and writing as they apply to real life experiences.

- Assess subskills of speaking, reading, and writing, used only with meaningful content.
- Assess language arts directly in an integrated multimedia environment. For example, teachers can use computer word processing as a tool to evaluate student creativity, writing, and spelling skills in social studies and science as well as in reading and language arts.
- Use nationally normed standardized testing information for comparison purposes as long as other varied additional assessments are utilized.

Integrating Chapter 1 into a regular classroom can also help. Chapter 1 staff have a wealth of knowledge about more effective ways to assess students, and can assist teachers in this regard. In addition, staff can contribute suggestions on how to help ''marginal students'' who are sometimes called ''lifers'' (U.S. Department of Education, 1990).

A major role of an administrator in searching for alternative assessments is to make sure that curriculum goals are in place. Basic goals for a language arts program are suggested below:

- The student reads for a variety of purposes.
- The student constructs meaning from text.
- The student expands and refines understanding by integrating reading with writing, speaking, and listening.
- The student has a lifelong desire to read, and reads to understand the diverse perspectives in a multicultural society.

These goals can be transformed into more specific objectives or focus areas. All assessments should relate back to specific objectives and eventually to the original goal. The above goals should be used as examples; school districts should formulate their own individual set of goals. Instructional goals should relate to district goals when writing curriculum, as illustrated in Figure 4.6.

As shown in Figure 4.6, daily lesson plans should either directly or indirectly reflect a district's reading philosophy and goals. The process is analogous to a staircase because the district's philosophy and goals are the first step in the planning process, followed by program philosophy, learner outcomes, outlines, and lesson plans. The final step is student instruction in the classroom. Administrators need to assess their reading and language arts programs to determine if district philosophy and goals are underpinning instruction. To illustrate this

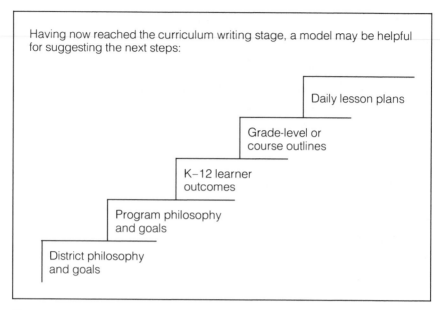

Having now reached the curriculum writing stage, a model may be helpful for suggesting the next steps:

Daily lesson plans

Grade-level or
course outlines

K–12 learner
outcomes

Program philosophy
and goals

District philosophy
and goals

Figure 4.6. Four-step model for curriculum writing. Source: Montana Office of Public Instruction. 1990. *The Curriculum Process Guide: Developing Curriculum for the 1990s.*

process, the authors have provided the Montana Whole Language Planning and Assessment Model (Montana Office of Public Instruction, 1991) which includes philosophy, a primary literature goal, an objective, focus areas, a specific focus area, materials, strategies, and assessments (see Figure 4.7.). When implementing the model, administrators should have staff meet and determine specific focus resources, strategies, and assessments for each focus area. Figure 4.8 illustrates such a format used by Hellgate Elementary, Missoula, Montana.

As depicted in Figure 4.8, the first learner outcome or focus area relates to grapho/phonic relationships. The primary resource is the text, with the strategy being the use of charts and/or a cloze activity. The assessment could be cloze in nature or observation. Teachers use this document as a guide and are not limited to any specific items. For example, if a teacher did not want to use the text as a resource, he or she could use other written material such as works of literature.

The purpose of this example is to provide a model or framework from which district and teacher level curricula can be developed and assessed. The principal's role is to assist staff in developing specific focus areas or learner goals as well as developing a specific plan for the formation of instructional strategies, the acquisition of resources, and the types of assessments utilized. The model curriculum can be viewed as a menu offering a focus for each of the model goals, objectives, student focus areas, materials, strategies, and methods for assessment. The key is to assist teachers with developing effective practices or strategies and assessments used to reach the goal.

This type of model can actively involve administrators, teachers, students, trustees, specialists, parents, community, and, when appropriate, state resource people. These individuals should be involved

PHILOSOPHY:	Communication and language arts are the study of language and language use. Language arts develops from a need to create a process of social interaction, to comprehend experience, to express oneself, to assess, and to communicate. Language begins through interactive, cognitive, and affective processes such as speaking, expressing nonverbally, writing, listening, observing, and reading. Thinking, media, and literature are inherent in these processes.
MODEL PRIMARY GOAL:	Students read for a variety of purposes.
OBJECTIVE:	Students read a balanced variety of real books to become real readers. Emphasis is on literature experiences that provide a vehicle for integrating instruction.
FOCUS AREAS:	These include folktales, poetry, rhymes, animal stories, newspapers, magazines, picture books, informational books, and plays. *Folktales as a specific area:* • material—story books, filmstrips, movies, and videos • strategy—mapping, story framing, and different endings • assessment—writing samples, retelling, portfolio, and vocabulary check

Figure 4.7. The Montana plan.

SUBJECT AREA: Reading

LEVEL: Primary

GOAL: The student will associate the written form with the spoken word.

FOCUS STATEMENT: Students will learn that letters represent sounds which combine to make words and develop skills in language cuing systems.

FOCUS AREAS	RESOURCES	STRATEGY	ASSESSMENT
Grapho/Phonic (symbol-sound relationships, phonics)	text	charts, cloze, games	cloze test, observation
Syntactic (structure-grammar)	text, student writing, modeling	student writing, storytelling, modeling	writing samples, tests, conferencing
Semantic (meaning)	text, library books	mapping, language, webbing, experience, stories brainstorm, predicting	tests, teacher made materials, conferencing
Visual Configuration	word banks	direct teaching	student writing, student sample

Figure 4.8. Communication arts format for resources, strategies, and assessment.

in curriculum planning as well as in assessment planning. Principals who implement curriculum guides developed outside the local district sometimes have a tendency to circumvent important individuals who could make a significant contribution to the process.

The following principles were designed to make this model approach "user friendly" for administrators.

- Each strand of the language arts program should be tied to the district's philosophy.
- Each objective clarifies each goal, emphasizing skills, products, content, or processes that are listed under focus areas.
- Learner goals can be divided into grade-level clusters.
- Suggested effective practices or strategies provide administrators and teachers with recommended lessons or approaches to the goals. Although grade levels are specified, the developmental nature of the learner goals may require adapting strategies from one level to another.

SPECIFIC ASSESSMENT ALTERNATIVES

Administrators need to develop curriculum models as shown above and assist teachers in finding new alternatives in assessing student achievement. In addition, they need to provide ways to inservice staff on new strategies and techniques incorporated into models (Costa, 1989). Quality ideas always provide the best alternative approaches.

Inservice can be incorporated in a number of ways. For instance, some innovative supervisors have set aside one day per month on which students are dismissed early and staff are brought together to share or review new strategies and techniques in their field. Other administrators schedule specific days for staff development during the academic year. These inservice days can be used to share many ideas, including the specific assessment alternatives listed below. Some of the items are more innovative than others. Many of the examples provided are now back in vogue due to changes in principals' attitudes and classroom operations such as cooperative teaching. All of the assessment alternatives discussed in this chapter have been successfully utilized in classrooms and observed by the authors. They do work.

Portfolios

Student portfolios provide a way to collect a large body of finished and unfinished work. Basically, the teacher keeps a file of individual students' work or the work of an entire class. Dated entries allow a chronological view of student progress. Portfolios can include, but are not limited to, notes, papers, diagrams, drafts, sample writings, audiotapes or videotapes, letters, journal entries, logs, checklists, formal and informal tests, and anecdotal records. Teachers can select materials that best exemplify what the student has accomplished, or students select their papers for grading. The portfolio can be shared with parents or students and can be passed along as a continuous document from year to year. The value of a portfolio depends upon the accuracy and validity of the information collected.

Anecdotal Records

Anecdotal records are an old concept regaining popularity. Hopefully, with the advent of the portfolio system, anecdotal records will become more common in the classroom. Surprisingly enough, many newly trained teachers are not familiar with anecdotal records and their usefulness as a student assessment tool. Anecdotal records are notes that record the interactions observed in the classroom. Teachers need to accentuate the positive as much as possible when utilizing anecdotal records. Notes can be collected on individual children as well as on the class as a whole.

Daily/Weekly Writing Samples

Writing samples provide teachers with current assessments of students' progress. Children are asked to write for fifteen minutes in a comfortable, nonthreatening environment in order to obtain an appropriate and reliable sample. Material collected is reviewed and dated for documentation. Individual conferences can be used to review written samples before they are placed in a portfolio or sent home.

Audio and Video Records

Individual cassettes provide an excellent record of reading, behavior, use of picture cues, and eye-ear-voice matching. Cassettes provide documentation when conferencing with parents. The tapes are particularly helpful in recording progress made by the student. Thorough familiarization of students with the recording equipment will help get ''natural'' assessment recordings.

Miscue Analysis

Miscue analysis is a tool used to determine reading strategies used by a student. Teachers record the number of miscues a child makes during oral reading and/or retelling a story after the first reading. The teachers determine the quality or type of errors and/or the frequency of errors made by students.

Learning Profiles

Learning profiles provide an insight into the strategies used by children. The profiles also provide information on attitudes and learning styles. Information is collected via surveys and issue questionnaires on an individual basis. Many teachers develop learning profiles early in the year in order to address specific student needs and determine appropriate materials.

Journals and Logs

Students can accentuate language experience and writing skills through the development of journals and log records, which provide an up-to-the-minute view of how students are progressing and a current running record of what is happening within the classroom. For example, dialogue journals between students and teachers help provide very useful documentation of student work. Entries in journals and logs are usually made on a daily or weekly basis.

Checklists

Checklists can be teacher-made or obtained from curriculum guides. Developmental lists are useful as reference or quick assessment tools. Checklists serve as a method to document students' observable behavior, thoughts, and reflections made in the classroom.

Students' Work

A variety of students' work, in addition to writing samples, can be collected to assess academic growth in language arts. Puzzles, maps, pictures, and other projects provide important information relating to how a student is thinking and learning. Materials can be stored in folders, noting the contents on the cover (see *Portfolios*).

Self-Evaluation

Self-evaluation records help reveal the frustrations, difficulties, and positive aspects of being a student in a particular classroom. By expressing their feelings in a written form (journals), students can better understand their relationship with peers, teachers, and others. Students need to become aware of their own growth and achievements.

Conference Record

Information gathered during a student conference is useful in reassessing learner goals. Teachers can become aware of students' reasons for using a certain strategy to complete a lesson. Minisessions allow students to talk freely and express their feelings about what they are learning. A loose-leaf binder can be used to record statements made during the conferences in order to plan instructional practices at a later date.

Retelling

Students listen to or read stories, listen to or watch tapes, videos, and similar sources of information, and then restate the story or parts of the story in their own words.

Narrative

Students write statements reacting to or expressing feelings about a particular issue or subject.

Tests and Exams

Teachers, students, and publishers produce many different types of tests and exams. Examples of objective tests include true-false, multiple choice, fill-in-the-blank, short answer, and matching.

Primary Trait Scoring

In assessing student work, one or two traits are identified as the focus of the assessment for that assignment, and the writer is evaluated only on those traits.

Holistic Scoring

Holistic scoring is a method of assessment in which an essay is read for a general impression of quality and then assigned a score (often on a 5 to 1 scale). The standards for each score are determined by reading all student papers first and then grouping them into sets of similar quality.

Analytic Scoring

Analytic scoring is a method of assessment in which an essay is read and scored for specific criteria such as idea and content, organization, sentence fluency, use of standard writing conventions, voice, and word choice. The essay is scored on its success in meeting each of the criteria.

Cloze Test

The cloze test offers test items in sentence or phrase form that leaves a blank or blanks to be filled in, thereby completing a thought or idea.

Score Sheet/Rating Scale

A scoring sheet outlines each of the criteria that were established as achievement targets for students on a particular assignment. The scorer (teacher, self, or peer) evaluates the success of the speaker/writer in meeting each criterion on a continuum.

Teacher's Conference Record

Teachers should keep a record in chart form for each student when conducting writing. In the columns, the teacher records the title of each piece written and its date of submission, skills used correctly, and one or two skills taught for that piece.

Status of the Class Sheets

When conducting a writing workshop, teachers should use a status of the class grid as a lesson plan (Atwell, 1987). One grid per week is used for each class. Student names are written down the left side and the week days are written across the top. Each day before students begin work, students report what they will be doing that day (first draft, second draft, revision, or self-editing) and the teacher writes in an abbreviation for the activity.

In sum, there are a number of exciting alternative ways to assess students. Learning experiences and events in the area of language arts that can be used to accompany the assessment alternatives are illustrated in Figure 4.9.

WHERE WILL NEW DEVELOPMENTS LEAD US?

Appropriate assessment provides teachers with information useful in promoting students' growth in literacy. According to Wixson, Peters, and Weber (1987), new theories point to the close connection between assessment and learning. Future assessments will continue to be in a portfolio framework, which will allow teachers to document students as readers and writers. Some administrators will try to anchor portfolio assessments to grade-level benchmarks, reflecting set achievement standards.

This has been accomplished in some Hawaiian schools (Au et al., 1990). In the Kamehameha Elementary Education Program, for example, teachers elevated writing to the same level of importance as reading and used a portfolio outline for documentation. The plan is based on six aspects of literacy:

- ownership
- reading comprehension
- writing process
- word identification
- language and vocabulary knowledge
- voluntary reading

This plan will be used more often by teachers in the future. Utilizing comparable outlines will allow teachers to improve assessment in whole language environments.

K – 2	3 – 5	6 – 8	9 – 12
• Discussions	• Discussions	• In-depth book discussions	• In-depth book discussions
• Imaginary stories and poems	• Imaginary stories and poems	• Imaginary stories and poems	• Imaginary stories and poems
• Observations	• Observations	• Observations	• Observations
• Letters, thank you notes	• Letters, thank you notes	• Letters, thank you notes	• Letters, thank you notes
• Presentations	• Presentations	• Presentations	• Presentations
• Graphs, lists, charts	• Graphs, lists, charts	• Reader response journals	• Reader response journals
• Author's circle	• Author's circle	• Brainstorming	• Brainstorming
• Content area logs	• Content area logs	• Checklist for writing folders	• Informational reading/writing
• Informational reading/writing	• Informational reading/writing	• Essays	• Essays
• Reading/writing workshop	• Reading/writing workshop	• Information articles	• Information articles
		• Poetry journals	• Poetry journals

Figure 4.9. Suggested learning experiences/events. Montana Office of Public Instruction. 1991. *Communication Arts Curriculum Model*. Helena, Montana.

Increases in the cognitive sciences and the move to interdisciplinary curriculum has led to numerous language-based assessments. Direct observations, long-term projects, logs and journals, student interviews, and videotapes are just a few of the many language-based assessments being used in various disciplines. In order to ensure the success of these methods, administrators need to support staff development in the area of assessment.

For instance, teachers need to learn to give students more opportunities to evaluate themselves. When students take on the responsibility of monitoring themselves, they

- keep anecdotal record books or profiles on a daily basis
- retell stories with detail and consistency
- keep writing samples that are complete and inventive in nature
- develop reading logs
- check and evaluate their own papers
- ask open-ended questions
- share writing activities orally with other students

Not only will students be evaluating themselves, but they will also be able to monitor their own progress with the help of computer-related technology (Martinez and Lipson, 1989). Assessment supported by advanced technology will better serve the interests of learners and teachers. Technology will provide educators with an opportunity to have students address more complex problems encountered in real life experiences. For example, video terminals will provide simulations of social, political, economical, and environmental problems that will challenge and assess student knowledge at all levels. Computer-assisted simulations can be utilized in all subject areas, but will be particularly helpful in language arts-based curriculum.

Media technology and computers, however, are only a part of the answer to advances in reading and assessment. Major factors in any successful reading program are the administrators and teachers. As we have seen, more administrators are becoming knowledgeable about assessment, reading levels, and strategies. Furthermore, they are making sure that curriculum and assessment trends follow sound current research, and they are learning the importance of staff development.

The road to success is long and arduous. Administrators will have to play a major role in reeducating legislators, parents, school board members, and community members about assessment and how it relates to whole language and literature-based reading. To accomplish this, principals have to become public relations specialists as well as curriculum specialists. They also need to develop schoolwide plans for the collection and use of assessment information and work with staff to develop reading curriculum philosophies, operational goals, objectives, focus areas, strategies, and materials. And, most importantly, principals have to assist teachers in assessing students' abilities to read, speak, listen, and write in ways that allow students to communicate an understanding of real life and be ready for the workplace.

REFERENCES

Anderson, R. C., E. H. Hiebert, J. A. Scott, and I. A. Wilkenson. 1985. *Becoming a Nation of Readers*. Urbana, IL: University of Illinois Center for the Study of Reading.

Atwell, N. 1987. *In the Middle: Writing, Reading, and Learning with Adolescents*. Upper Montclair, NJ: Boynton/Cook.

Au, K. H., J. A. Scheu, A. J. Kawakami, and P. Herman. 1990. "Assessment and Accountability in a Whole Literacy Curriculum," *The Reading Teacher*, 43:574−577.

Cohen, M. 1988. "Designing State Assessment Systems," *Educational Leadership*, 69:583−588.

Costa, A. L. 1989. "Re-Assessing Assessment," *Educational Leadership*, 46(7):3.

Crane, G. M. 1989. "Leadership Characteristics of Elementary School Principals Related to Reading Achievement," Ed.D. dissertation, University of Montana, pp. 150−160.

Dreher, M. J. and H. Singer. 1984. "Making Standardized Tests Work for You," *Principal*, 63:20−24.

Dunn, R. 1990. "Rita Dunn Answers Questions on Learning Styles," *Educational Leadership*, 48(15):15−19.

Farstrup, A. E. 1990. "Overview: IRA and Assessment," *Reading Today*, 7(3):1.

Haney, W. and G. Madaus. 1989. "Searching for Alternatives to Standardized Tests: Whys, Whats, and Whithers," *Phi Delta Kappan*, 70:685.

Hiebert, E. H. and R. Calfee. 1989. "Advancing Academic Literacy through Teachers' Assessments," *Educational Leadership*, 46(7):50−54.

Livingston, C., S. Castle, and J. Nations. 1989. "Testing and Curriculum Reform: One School's Experience," *Educational Leadership*, 46(7):23−25.

Lytle, S. L. and M. Botel. 1990. "The Pennsylvania Framework for Reading, Writing and Talking across the Curriculum," The Pennsylvania Department of Education, pp. 138–139.

Mackay, H. 1988. *How to Swim with the Sharks*. New York, NY: William Morrow and Co., pp. 194–195.

Martinez, M. and J. Lipson. 1989. "Assessment for Learning," *Educational Leadership*, 46(7):73.

Montana Office of Public Instruction. 1991. *Communication Arts Curriculum Model*. Helena, Montana.

Pearson, D., C. W. Peters, and K. K. Wixson. 1989. "Theory and Practice in Statewide Reading Assessment: Closing the Gap," *Educational Leadership*, 46(7):59–60.

Pikulski, J. 1989. "The Assessment of Reading: A Time for Change," *The Reading Teacher*, 43(1):80–81.

Porter, A. C. 1983. "The Role of Testing in Effective Schools," *American Education*, 19(1):26.

Shepard, L. A. 1989. "Why We Need Better Assessments," *Educational Leadership*, 46(7):4–9.

Snyder, T. D. 1990. "Trends in Education," *Principal*, 70(1):6–10.

U.S. Department of Education. Office of Planning, Budget and Evaluation. 1990. *Better Schooling for Children of Poverty: Alternatives to Conventional Wisdom*. Washington, D.C.: Government Printing Office.

Valencia, S. and P. D. Pearson. 1987. "Reading Assessment: Time for a Change," *The Reading Teacher*, 40:726–732.

Whitehead, B. M. and P. Santee. 1987. "Using Standardized Test Results as an Instructional Guide," *The Clearing House*, 61:57–59.

Wixson, K. K., C. W. Peters, E. M. Weber, and E. D. Roeber. 1987. "New Directions in Statewide Reading Assessment," *The Reading Teacher*, 40:749–754.

Strategies for Reading Groups

"Let such teach others who themselves excel,
And censure freely who have written well."

ALEXANDER POPE

As you read and study:

. . . Identify the axiom for small group cooperative learning.
. . . Analyze the distinctive features of small group cooperative
learning.
. . . Imagine what can be learned about mutual goals,
interdependence, accountability, and responsibility.
. . . Formulate a uniqueness about the chronological anatomy of the
various age groups.
. . . Assess the value of peer or same-age tutoring.
. . . Construct the guidelines to follow for structuring small
cooperative learning groups.
. . . Define the term *sociometry*.
. . . Organize the process to construct a sociogram.
. . . Compare and contrast the student choice vs. teacher choice
sociograms.

In searching for an axiom about "small group cooperative learning,"
we must identify what is true and universal and can appropriately serve
as the base for understanding and explication that extend as far as our
analytical powers allow. We need to search for the most fundamental

possible descriptive statements that will embrace administrative, teaching, and learning behaviors in reading programs.

If such an axiom can be identified, the foundation is laid for establishing a theoretical construct that will not only include an alternative model for teaching reading but will also show the organic relationships that grouping has for the administrative, teaching, and learning processes in reading. It will also prevent individual idiosyncrasies from becoming major educational tenants, rigid sets of principals, or even guiding philosophies that inhibit the growth of students. This universal truth should help guide administrators and teachers in achieving an active learning model for students and alleviate the problem of rigidity in teaching reading.

THE AXIOM

In this chapter, small group cooperative learning will be considered as the axiom. Students need more than knowledge. They need to understand how to organize and connect knowledge that can be learned through class conversations. Thus, every child needs to be an active participant within the class culture. This concept is reinforced by Jerome Brunner (1986) in the textbook, *Actual Minds, Possible Worlds:*

> It is not just that the child must make knowledge his own, but that he must make it his own in a community of those who share his sense of belonging to a culture. It is this that leads me to emphasize not only discovery and invention but the importance of negotiating and sharing—in a word, of joint culture creating as an object of schooling and as an appropriate step en route to becoming a member of the adult society in which one lives out one's life. (p. 127)

Because learning is a social endeavor, reading must be viewed as social. Children can learn to read more easily if the classroom environment permits them to participate in the creation of a learning community. Yet, as Schaps and Solomon (1990, p. 40) indicate, "All too often, meeting children's needs for belonging and contributing is the missing variable in the school improvement equation." Therefore, the school and the school classroom should be places where children "learn to control knowledge rather than be controlled by it" (Berghoff and Egawa, 1991, p. 537).

Small Group Distinctiveness

Small group cooperative learning is an organizational structure in which a small group of students (consisting of two, three, four, five, or six students) work together to pursue goals through collaborative ventures. By working together, students can draw on each other's strengths and support each other in completing a task(s). This togetherness stimulates good communication skills, supportive relationships, and higher-level thinking abilities that contribute to higher student achievement.

A review of sixty research studies on small group cooperative learning by Slavin (1990) reveals two conditions that affect cooperative learning and student achievement positively. One of these conditions is group goals, or positive interdependence, in which students undertake a group task with a feeling of mutuality, each doing his or her own part for the benefit of the group. For example, the low achievers in the small group strive to do their best for the welfare of the entire group, and the high achievers, wanting to sustain their own high quality of work, will assist others in achieving the group task(s). As Johnson et al. (1984) submit, positive interdependence by small cooperative groups is achieved

through mutual goals (goal interdependence); divisions of labor (task interdependence); dividing materials, resources, or information among group members (resource interdependence); assigning students differing roles (role interdependence); and by giving joint rewards (reward interdependence). (p. 8)

In order for a learning situation to be cooperative, students must understand that they are positively interdependent with other members of the group. Merely asking students to work together is not enough.

The second condition for higher student achievement is individual accountability, or personal responsibility for learning material. Here, the small cooperative group's success is dependent upon the sum of group members' quiz scores or on evaluation of a report in which each small group member contributes his or her part or unit. Individual accountability is intended to maximize the achievement of each student in the small cooperative learning groups. Moreover, it is helpful if the level of mastery is determined so that students can render appropriate assistance and support to one another. Just assigning a task(s) to students and letting one student do all the work while others get equal credit for work completed is not a part of small group cooperative learning.

	Median Effect Size	No. of Studies
Group Goals and Individual Accountability	+ .30	32
Group Goals Only	+ .04	8
Individual Accountability	+ .12	9
No Group Goals or Individual Accountability	+ .05	2

Note: Effect sizes are different between small group cooperative learning and small group control classes on achievement measures divided by the post-test standard deviation. Only methodologically adequate studies of at least four weeks' duration are included.

Figure 5.1. Achievement effects of alternative forms of cooperative learning. Source: Slavin, R. E. 1988. "Cooperative Learning and Student Achievement," *Educational Leadership*, 46:32. Reproduced by permission.

The recent findings on small cooperative groups are supported by a previous study completed by Slavin. As shown in Figure 5.1, the success of small cooperative learning groups on achievement "depends substantially on the provision of group goals and individual accountability."

Contrasting with the positive effects method, group goals, and individual accountability, are those methods that use group goals only, those that use individual accountability only, and those that use no group goals or individual accountability. Here too, the research findings are conclusive. The key to higher achievement in small cooperative learning groups is inclusion of group goals and individual accountability.

An added positive dimension for small group cooperative learning is that it also addresses gender equity. Holmes (1991, p. 11) suggests that school administrators should make sure that "teachers are using instructional techniques that engage students, including cooperative learning, opportunities to work independently, and hands-on activities." The small cooperative process, if students are appropriately assigned, will enhance learning opportunities for girls as well as boys.

INTERDEPENDENCE AND
ACCOUNTABILITY = ACHIEVEMENT

Lessons can be learned about mutual goals, interdependence, accountability, responsibility, and achievement by reading the Caldecott Medal

Award winning children's book, *Drummer Hoff*, by watching a flock of geese make its way to a certain destination, and by analyzing the collaborative efforts between the two largest computer companies, Apple and IBM. In the children's book, Drummer Hoff was triumphant in firing off the cannon only after Private Parriage brought the carriage; Corporal Farrell brought the barrel; Sergeant Chowder brought the powder; Captain Brammer brought the rammer; Major Scott brought the shot; and General Border gave the order: FIRE, CLICK, and KAHBAHBLOOM (Emberley and Emberley, 1967).

Geese, as well, know the need for grouping and working together. As Hoyle, English, and Steffy (1985) point out:

> A flock of geese flying in formation knows the meaning of believing in group work. The lead goose creates a draft or vacuum for the geese following to the left and right. When the lead goose tires, another takes the lead role and the journey continues. By this wonder of nature a flock of geese can fly 78 percent farther than a single goose can fly. (p. 27)

The collaborative efforts between Apple and IBM, although limited to certain areas, have put aside some of the traditional rivalries because these two corporations cannot be competent in every area and because neither can afford to solo the venture. Even though pressure of the marketplace is a factor, the major goal of the two computer companies is to produce, by the year 2000, "a new generation of powerful, portable 'information appliances' that will make today's PCs seem as primitive as yesterday's typewriter" (Gifford, 1991, p. A22). Why the collaboration between two major computer companies? The major reasons, according to Gifford, are (1) to share resources, (2) to share costs and benefits, (3) to revise policies and practices that limit access to knowledge to school systems that enjoy the greatest wealth, and (4) to bring together interdisciplinary teams of scholars working on significant problems outside of institutional lines.

The aforementioned illustrations of cooperation focus on mutual group goals, or positive interdependence and individual accountability, or personal responsibility. Educators, likewise, should believe and trust in students' abilities to function in small cooperative groups. Small group reading activities containing appropriate conditions for students can make the journey to become better readers a meaningful and enjoyable experience. The challenge for administrators and teachers is to have a reading program that endorses inclusion with structure and eradicates exclusion. "After all," as Gifford (1991, p. A22) said, "if the blue-jeaned whiz kids of Apple can join forces with the buttoned-down brains of Big Blue, anything is possible."

CHRONOLOGICAL ANATOMY OF GROUPS[3]

The groups that permeate every child's learning environment should be understood, assessed, and worked with in ways that facilitate each child's full use of growth-producing learning opportunities within the educational environment and enterprise. The chronological anatomy of group effects for children will be of practical assistance to administrators, supervisors, and teachers who have the responsibility to understand and work with groups that comprise the "way of life" in schools and classrooms.

Kindergarten through Third Grade

Groups of primary age children are very different from groups of older children. Following are some significant characteristics of primary age children:

- Kindergarten through second grade children usually do not develop strong groups within specific peer norms.
- Third grade children are often just beginning to have group alliances, and peer pressure is usually not as powerful as in later years.
- Third graders are more likely to react to, adjust to, or act out against the expectations of significant adults in their lives than against fellow classmates.
- Children in the primary school age group tend to be more interested in parallel play (play side by side) than they are in groups.
- Kindergarten through third grade children, even when they are in groups, tend to follow a leader, either constructively or destructively, rather than making a group decision, overtly or covertly, about what action will take place.

[3]Much of the information that follows is excerpted from Joy Johnson, *Use of Groups in Schools: A Practical Manual for Everyone Who Works in Elementary and Secondary Schools.* Her consent is greatly appreciated.

- Praise and criticism have a great deal more meaning when they come from adults than when given by other children in the primary school age group.

A number of reasons explain why the above characteristics are true. Children in this age group are still very much in need of, and are controlled by, adults. This dependence is not only for physical need fulfillment but for emotional security as well. For example, the satisfaction that comes from having lunch with Mom combines the needs of hunger and caring.

During the early grades in school, children frequently develop a second part of their identity. The first is established at home where the basic issues of trust and mistrust are resolved. Throughout their first developmental stages, children have initial feelings about whether or not they are good people and whether or not the world is a good place in which to live. The way parents respond to children at home has a significant impact on youngsters at this time, which carries over to life outside the family. More specifically, children who are abused at home come to school expecting the world at school to be punitive as well. Likewise, youngsters who "rule the roost" during their early years also want to control the classroom as well.

The Formative Stage

The first three years in school are extremely important, not only to students' learning but also to their basic attitude toward life in general and toward themselves in particular. An important educational task in working with children in these formative years is to help them find their places within the classroom and among their peers, as well as to teach them beginning cognitive skills such as reading, writing, listening, and understanding concepts such as the importance of following directions.

Children in the primary grades have an opportunity not only to master new skills but to learn something about themselves and about groups. Those with self-doubts can find new ways to assure that they are worthwhile human beings. On the other hand, the children who begin school thinking they can do no wrong can be helped to discover and accept some of their vulnerabilities. As one first grade teacher said,

There are two children in my class this year with whom I work intensely. One is a girl who stays by herself and is trying to keep isolated both from her peers and from her learning. She gives up before she begins. I want her to learn to try. The other girl is a fast learner who works quickly and does her work well, but breaks into tears every time she makes one small error. Both of these children need to learn to accept themselves and not give up or dissolve.

Helping children in this age group learn how to evaluate themselves realistically and still feel adequate as people is one of the hardest, and most important, tasks that a teacher has to accomplish.

One of the best ways to do this, of course, is through the content taught: it is likely that the two students above will respond most directly when the teacher's comments are about work just completed. The teacher might ask the girl who has dissolved in tears to go to her desk and find five things she has achieved. The other girl might be asked to finish one small part of the assignment so that she can have a sense of accomplishment rather than an ongoing feeling of failure.

Cooperative Learning

There is yet another dimension to the learning that must take place for children in the primary grades, setting the stage for later cooperative learning. Most primary grades have moved to individualized learning programs because children do need to learn at their own speed and to feel unique and special. Furthermore, they need to learn how to respond to each other in constructive ways by learning how to nurture, to care, to listen, and to communicate honestly without hitting one another. When these skills are learned in the primary grades, they can be transmitted to positive group processes in the future. If these important skills are not mastered during these early school years, future positive group participation becomes increasingly difficult.

Teachers of children in the primary grades have found success in teaching cooperative skills through small group exercises, beginning with "pairing." Pairing two children together to complete any small task begins the process of learning to work in groups. The task might entail looking at a book together and then telling the story to another pair of students. Students might also read to each other in pairs. These cognitive concepts can be mastered in pairs, and, at the same time, the children gain beginning relationship skills.

Pairing has also been used effectively by special education teachers in classrooms of young children with behavior problems. Experts claim that pairing someone who is withdrawn with someone who is more active can offer each child additional alternatives for behavior, which are significant when the pairing is accompanied by activities that help the children try out their newly learned options. Oftentimes teachers of very young children who have difficulty controlling their behavior have helped children learn to express their feelings verbally rather than acting them out. One teacher, for example, created personalities for some of the most prevalent feelings that she saw acted out in her class. She gave each feeling a name (being sure to avoid use of names of any children in her class) such as Sad Sally, Mad Mark, Silly Susan, Blue Bob, Happy Harry, and many others. Each of these ''personalities'' became real to the children as she told stories about them, articulating the mood that the name represented. She also drew faces on the board to show what they looked like when they felt that way. As the children became excited about meeting these new characters, they learned how to translate their own feelings to the names on the board.

This ''verbal acting out program'' was successful, not only in controlling behavior, but also in helping children learn to identify some of the feelings that they were experiencing and some of the ways these feelings became actions. The use of ''pairing'' for this program gave each child more individualized time and made the effort to share feelings rather than act them out a two-person project. Each child learned to help the other in attempts to verbalize responses.

Teaching small group cooperative learning includes helping children prepare to work in groups. Just as we address activities for ''reading readiness,'' we should consider ''group readiness'' classroom programs. Many group experiences teach young children what happens in groups and how to be constructive members. By participating in some of these simple exercises, students can learn how to communicate with one another and get a taste of what it is like to be part of a group.

Using progressive stories, ''fun'' exercises that move toward group participation, is one method by which to involve children in group efforts. One student starts a story, and when the teacher claps her hands that child stops wherever he or she is in the tale. Then another student picks up the story where the first left off. This process continues until many children have had a chance to add their part to the story, often with hilarious results. This group story method is so much fun, and it teaches children ways to be group members, to listen, to wait their turn, and to make a contribution to a group effort. If a videotape is made of the story and the children can watch and listen to it later, they can also learn about their impact on the finished product. One second grade girl, for instance, was quite giggly during the story. When she watched the video she became quiet and subdued. Without the teacher saying a word, her disruptive behavior became much more controlled. Other group projects that allow these young creative beings their full individuality include group plays, pictures, and stories about themselves.

One important thing to remember when conducting ''group readiness'' activities in a class with primary school age children is that the process is as important as the outcome. Frequently, the results are discussed, but the manner in which they were achieved is not discussed. Even young children are old enough to learn that how they function in a group affects the outcome, even though it may not be as important to them now as it will be in later years. They are able to take a step back from the end result to see what happened along the way. This process can also be used as a problem-solving technique.

One third grade teacher put problem solving to good use when a dilemma arose at recess: one of the children had punched another who had come crying to the teacher. After the recess period was over, the teacher asked everyone in the class to draw a picture of what had happened at recess. Most of the children drew a picture of two children, one hitting the other. The teacher then asked them to put themselves into the picture, to draw in where they were and what they were doing. This activity led to a discussion of what some of the other children might have done to help avert the crisis. Some discovered they could have done nothing, and others saw that they might have helped. The process of working this through was the beginning of group awareness for most of the children in the class.

Helping children in the primary grades develop responsible, constructive ways of relating to each other is essential. While most primary grade students frequently do not develop strong group alliances, often group contagion occurs: one child begins a behavior that spreads like honey through the whole group. Helping the children learn how to become aware when this is happening may assist them in using this phenomenon constructively or in controlling it.

Beginning Management Skills

By the time children are in the second or third grade, they are ready to assume responsibility for classroom management. Beginning with some fun activity, such as planning a party, children can be taught to make decisions, to help make some rules, and to analyze and understand the consequences of their behavior. By the third grade, many children are members of natural friendship groups, so they must learn some of the things that happen in groups and take responsibility for making constructive contributions. How many teachers give their students a chance to understand what is making them happy or unhappy in their particular groups? How often do teachers give pupils an opportunity to discuss some of the things they can do to effect change? A teacher can use groups in a variety of ways to help "group learning." One is to give part of the classroom management over to the children, with the teacher acting primarily as consultant. Student-controlled decisions might be as simple as deciding how to line up for recess, how to assign seats, what stories or books to read, or how to distribute the various "jobs" that need to be done in the classroom. Whatever the question or situation, a committee of students can be formed to discuss the issue and make a report back to the class. Then the class can decide, by vote or consensus, what they want to do about the situation. This is democracy at work in a classroom; students are learning the democratic process.

At first, when third grade students are given a task, it may not work out very well because they have not had experience in the democratic form of management, and they will make mistakes. For example, they may come up with some irresponsible ideas about how to handle a reading assignment or job assignment. It is difficult, yet very important, that the teacher let the children really make the decision. The teacher may point out options and possible repercussions, but if at all possible, the final decision should belong to the students. This is also a time when children can be taught to use "step five" of the problem-solving process. They must ask themselves: What do we do if it does not work? How long should the trial period be? To allow students to make the decisions and learn from the results is of great value indeed.

Sometimes some of the craziest ideas that children suggest turn out to work beautifully; other times their ideas are disastrous, but teachers have an opportunity to help children pick themselves up, dust themselves off, and try again. How rewarding it is to see a group of children who have created a plan that did not work move beyond blaming each other to accepting some responsibility for the decision and to developing another plan. These are the years when children are most creative and most flexible. If teachers allow children to flex their creative muscles, they will continue to develop. Encouragement and faith that children can complete a task are of prime importance to these budding young group participants. The process of developing mutual goals, in a dyad or group, and individual accountability at an early age will augment the democratic principles of working together and academic achievement in areas such as reading.

Fourth through Sixth Grades

Children in the fourth through sixth grades begin to have close, natural affinities to one another in groups. Many sociologists call this stage of life the "pack age." During these years, young people have a powerful sense of identity with one another as well as a strong skill orientation as a way of being acceptable in their peer group. For this reason, every teacher in a classroom with this age group works with a group every day, whether he or she likes it or not. In addition, because groups are forceful at this age, teachers have the possibility of harnessing that group strength to encourage learning. Below are some significant characteristics of children in this age group:

- For most children in this age group, these years are a period of rapid mastery of a variety of skills that often improve self-concept.
- Athletic prowess, relationship skills, and academic achievement are all very important ways that fourth, fifth, and sixth grade children increase their feelings of self-worth.
- How children in this age group are treated by and communicate with their peers is directly linked not only to their relationship ability but also to their skill achievement.
- Whatever the kinds of groups, a collection of individuals or individuals with similarities that are easy or difficult to work with, there is no doubt that the group is a very powerful influence in grades four, five, and six.

Whether educators prefer it or not, fourth, fifth, and sixth grade students are working on their social skills, and consider the group a high priority. Also, each individual in this age group is struggling to find some area of competence that will make him or her feel more worthy, both individually and in the group.

Cooperative Learning

This is a good age to introduce small cooperative group projects as a way to enhance learning. For example, in a fourth or fifth grade language arts class using children's books, the small cooperative groups might read "The Gibble" from Prelutsky's *The Snopp on the Sidewalk*. Each group could make up an imaginary animal and describe it, then report where the animal lives and what it eats in poetry form. Each group might then interpret the poem and share it with the class (Laughlin and Watt, 1986).

When students work together as a group with mutual goals and individual accountability, students learn more. It is also advantageous for students who are fast learners, who can conceptualize very easily, and who work precisely, to have to slow down and participate in the group process. Part of the learning for these students is to develop the ability to listen to people who do not grasp concepts as quickly, and to become increasingly able to assist the group process without putting people down.

Small cooperative learning groups can enhance both cognitive learning and the students' abilities to cooperate in a group. The goal in group teaching should be to work on both of these issues simultaneously. Thus, evaluation of small groups should cover not only the final cognitive product but also how the members of the groups work together.

Group Management

If students have been allowed to set some of their own rules for participation in decision making, they can also be involved in the problem-solving process when something goes wrong. For example, problems might include those that occur outside at recess time or in the lunchroom, as well as something that is happening within the classroom. For classes to participate in effective problem solving, the following three conditions must be met:

(1) The focus must be on *what happened* and not on assessing guilt or blame. This is crucial, because otherwise youngsters in this age group will simply blame each other, and that is not very helpful. However, if the focus is on what happened, there is a good chance of educating these children on how to solve problems in constructive ways.

(2) The second condition that must be met is that there must always be some *plan of action* agreed upon to improve the problem situation. Particularly in sixth grade, students might be pulled into a gripe session involving comments such as "This isn't fair," or "That isn't fair." Problem solving requires some plan of action which the children develop and which they have a part in implementing.

(3) The third condition is that children as a group *should not set punishments* for one another. If some form of punishment is necessary, the choice of action belongs to the teacher and not the students. If students are asked to mete out punishment against a classmate, two things usually happen. One, children will be harder on that child than the teacher would be, which may or may not be appropriate. Two, the class as a whole may get thrown "up for grabs" because the children are worried. They may begin to wonder, "If they punish one child, then who is going to be next? What will the group do to *me* if *I* misbehave?" At this grade level, any disciplining should come from the teacher or principal and not from the children themselves.

Even while using the problem-solving process, fourth, fifth, and sixth grade students may face another student whom they cannot handle. In such a situation, they need help from the teacher to deal with that student. The teacher should not single out any one child for special attention, negative or otherwise, until he or she has a clear assessment from the class about what the problem was and how it occurred.

At this age level, a variety of different kinds of symptoms are exhibited by unhappy children. This is a prime time for lying, stealing, and being mean to one another. Most of this behavior has two parts to it. One involves the child himself or herself, who feels uncomfortable, unlovable, unable to achieve in the way he or she would like, or who lives in a community where learning antisocial behavior aids in survival. The other involves the group as a system—how group members feel about themselves and how the group treats others. In either event, helping the class as a whole will also help each individual feel better about himself or herself. Teachers must learn how to help children keep from being scapegoated or picked on in class.

Building on Commonalities

At times, teachers cannot work individually with a child who is being scapegoated. A child may be picked on because he or she is slightly retarded, slower than others in the class, or physically inept and cannot run as fast or play ball as well as the other children. In such cases, teachers should take some time in class to talk with the children about what it is like to be different. Children at this age tend to scapegoat most often those who remind them of a part of themselves. If somebody is unable to run fast, the children pick on that person not only because they might lose the game but also because that person represents the piece of them that is slow or left out.

Guidelines in dealing with scapegoating are threefold. First, the teacher can share an experience that he or she had. Teachers must never say to a class "Tell me about some time when you felt left out" without being ready to share first; teachers should model the sharing.

Second, a teacher should try to avoid, if possible, protecting the student who is being scapegoated. For example, a teacher who felt sorry for a boy who stuttered should not say, "Oh, please don't pick on Jimmy. Please don't do this; please don't do that." If a teacher protects a scapegoat and tells the children not to pick on a certain child, two things are communicated: the teacher cares about the scapegoat, which is fine, and the scapegoat is very different and needs the teacher's protection. This tends to perpetuate the scapegoating because the teacher's protectiveness makes the other children turn on that student even more. It may send the hostility underground, but it does not help the child's tormentors understand what he or she is going through.

Third, the teacher's approach must not shame the child. Saying, "Tell me about when you felt left out yourself" and saying, "How would you feel if somebody did this to you?" are very different. The subtle difference between helping children share with the teacher and putting them down for being cruel becomes a dramatic one.

Teachers can use groups in a variety of situations to foster learning and to help children take increasing responsibility for the classroom milieu. Understanding what is happening in groups and having the freedom to try something new can be good learning experiences for teachers and children.

PEER OR SAME-AGE TUTORING

Peer or same-age tutoring, dating to prehistoric times but used sparingly in the last fifty years, is a natural occurrence in small cooperative learning groups. Thelen (1969) explains:

The idea of students learning through helping each other is a very promising alternative to the traditional system of learning through competing with each other. It also makes the acquisition of knowledge and skills valuable, not in the service of competition for grades, but in the means of personally significant interaction with others. (p. 236)

The effectiveness of peer tutoring is supported by some of the research studies cited by Gibbs (1982) and other research findings from the ERIC system displayed in Figure 5.2. To illustrate, a peer tutorial program in reading was considered responsible for the reading growth at the Soto Street School in Los Angeles. When the program was initiated, fewer than 5 percent of the first grade students scored at the fourth stanine or higher on standardized reading tests. As fifth graders, 81 percent of those students scored at the fourth stanine or higher.

The findings of an experimental study of peer tutoring to measure vocabulary development among learning disabled students reveal that said students were able to tutor their resource-room classmates so effectively that the latter group's reading scores on criterion-referenced tests exceeded those of the teacher-instructed control group.

With the help and understanding of school administrators and teachers, almost all students can be tutors and learners while working in small cooperative learning groups. Hedin (1987, p. 47) concludes from her extensive research on tutoring that ''students at all levels of achievement, from those in special education to the gifted and talented, can be effective tutors.''

Peer or Same-Age Tutoring

1. Permits a teacher to add ''auxiliary teachers'' to teach more students
2. Creates linkages between and among learning content
3. Fosters a spirit of community in the classroom: cooperative rather than competitive
4. Enables peer tutors to fulfill both affective and cognitive needs
5. Improves the self-concept of learners and tutors
6. Increases time-on-learning
7. Improves the academic achievement of learners and tutors
8. Improves self-discipline and self-esteem
9. Enables teachers to be educational analysts and facilitators of learning
10. Is the most cost-effective

Figure 5.2. Peer tutoring effects. Sources: *Current Index to Journals in Education,* 1983 – 1988; and *Psychological Abstracts,* 1983 – 1989.

There is no substitute for a teaching format that provides personal-practical emphasis on basic academic skills. Learning, after all, is a personal, humanistic, and affective process. Peer or same-age tutoring that takes place in small cooperative learning groups can significantly enhance the ability to promote students' interpersonal growth as well as to promote higher academic achievement.

STRUCTURING SMALL COOPERATIVE GROUPS

Arranging small cooperative learning groups within a classroom of students requires a restructuring of the traditional teaching and learning processes. In reality, it requires the construction of knowledge through the interaction between pairs of students or among students in small cooperative learning groups numbering from three to six.

The guidelines to follow for establishing small cooperative groups in classrooms are relatively straightforward. However, these steps, according to Boschee (1989), are essential if students are to have a meaningful journey to knowledge.

Step One

Teachers should exhibit a positive attitude for this type of learning, which will show students that small group cooperative work can multiply the opportunities for interaction, responsibility, and learning.

Step Two

Teachers should know the composition of the students in the classroom. Using sociometric techniques illustrated in this chapter will enable teachers to group students according to their needs, attitudes, and concerns. *The Small Grouper*, a computer program, will make this a relatively easy task (approximately fifteen minutes).

Step Three

Teachers should plan the tasks by considering the reading curriculum goals and objectives that are to be achieved by students and should ask the following questions:

- What part of this reading lesson needs information about the content, objectives to be learned, and direction for covering the content from the teacher (direct teaching)?
- What can students learn from each other (small cooperative learning groups)?
- What should they learn by themselves (independent study)?

Teachers who are analysts and facilitators will know how much information must be given before small cooperative groups are able to function. The decisions about what instructional methods to use are as important as the content to be learned. Method connects students with content.

Step Four

The task to be completed should determine the length of meeting time for small cooperative groups. Teachers need to be flexible, however, and allow additional time to a group or groups if such is necessary.

Step Five

Teachers should determine the size of the small cooperative group(s) according to the content and objectives of the task and according to individual needs of the groups. For example, all students may be assigned to small cooperative groups to work on a reading assignment, or some students may be grouped to work on special assignments. Again, students, whether a dyad or a group of three, four, five, or six students, should be grouped with someone or others they have selected.

Step Six

Student leaders for the small cooperative learning groups should be considered. Using the information from a sociomatrix, the students chosen most often are natural candidates for group leaders. As the school year progresses, however, all students should assume the responsibility of being group leaders. Assigning group leaders should be correlated with the task to be completed. The need for group recorders and presenters should be determined by the content covered, the grade level, and the task to be completed. If the assignment is to have the groups make reports, then there is a need for a recorder and a presenter.

Instead of using the terms ''group leader'' and ''recorder,'' children at the eiementary school age may relate better to identifiers such as encourager, noise pollution controller, summarizer, secretary, runner, traffic controller, or committee member. All students in the small cooperative learning groups should have definite assignments, each assignee having a responsibility. This, coupled with mutual goals for the group(s), will result in active learning and higher achievement. Again, mutual goals and accountability are the ''key'' components for the success of small cooperative learning groups.

Step Seven

Each small cooperative group should be physically separated from others as much as possible to develop cohesiveness and to reduce the noise level. Also, members of a small group, unless paired, should be in a circular arrangement; however, in this arrangement students will communicate more with the individuals opposite them than with those to their immediate right or left.

Step Eight

Teachers should intervene only to keep group interaction going, to provide feedback, and when asked to join the group. The purpose of small cooperative group learning is to let the students learn by ''saying and doing.'' Figure 5.3 presents data on learning and remembering, which is applicable to all ages.

During group learning time, a teacher's actions are very significant. A teacher must actively observe students during group work. Imagine

---

Alcorn, Kinder, and Schunert (1970, p. 216) allege that people remember
- 10 percent of what they *READ*
- 20 percent of what they *HEAR*
- 30 percent of what they *SEE*
- 50 percent of what they *HEAR AND SEE*
- 70 percent of what they *SAY*
- 90 percent of what they *SAY* as they *DO* a thing

Figure 5.3. Learning to remember.

the message sent to groups when teachers correct papers or enter grades during prime-time learning moments for children.

By emulating the eight steps described, teachers already define the tasks for students, elucidate individual assignments and each student's role in the group, provide necessary resources or information about where to obtain resources, examine the progress of each group as each is held to a realistic schedule, and provide feedback to individual groups and to the larger group during the time small cooperative groups are working and after the groups have completed their tasks.

SOCIOMETRY

Sociometry, a method of discovering and analyzing patterns of friendship within a group setting, is a technique that teachers can use for determining student friendship preferences, for planning teaching strategies to overcome observed social weaknesses, and for assessing intervention induced changes in socialization (Roberts, 1986).

Historical Perspective

The earliest literature on sociometry is provided by Moreno (1934) in his book entitled *Who Shall Survive?* Since then, interest in the relationship between the affective and academic areas of growth has been reviewed in a myriad of research reports. The findings indicate that achievement in academic areas, as well as attitude toward learning, are improved when students are placed in an arrangement in which they can help one another work toward a common goal.

Several studies show that sociograms do reveal specific aspects of the classroom social structure that are beyond the teacher's level of awareness. Taba et al. (1951) concluded that sociograms can reveal important problems in student interrelationships that teachers did not see.

Do teachers perceive all students to be alike? Do teachers treat students as equals? They do not, according to Gronlund's (1950) findings. Sixth grade teachers, he found, have a tendency to overrate the sociometric status of students they most preferred and to underrate the status of students they least preferred. Furthermore, there was no relationship between teacher accuracy and the number of years of teaching experience or the gender of a teacher. A subsequent study by Bonney (1974, p. 135) suggested that "teachers . . . could not identify the poorly accepted students as well as they could the well accepted ones."

A study by Semple (1982) further refutes the assumption that teachers can predict, with a great degree of accuracy, the sociometric status of their students:

- Teachers and student teachers exhibit a wide range of accuracy (or, more precisely, inaccuracy) in predicting the sociometric status of individual students.
- Teachers who placed decreasing emphasis on intelligence as a correlation to student popularity could moderately predict social status.
- No teacher maintained any consistent level of accuracy.
- Teachers cannot predict which students will have favorable or impartial feelings toward the rejectee.
- Teachers cannot effectively discover the rejected student through observation. (pp. 1−2)

In a study conducted by Boschee (1991), elementary school teachers were asked to group students in their classrooms. Each of the forty-five teachers was to make sure that all students would have at least one of the five students that they thought students preferred to work with in a group. A comparison of "teacher choice vs. student choice" showed a 66 percent accuracy by the teachers. How well do teachers know the composition of their classrooms? Is it satisfactory to misplace one-third of the students in a class?

The research assuredly demonstrates that teachers can, at best, only moderately predict the social status of individual students in their class-rooms. School administrators and teachers should reflect on the research on sociometry and use this technique to appraise the classroom climate for organizing small cooperative learning groups.

Historically, affective learning, as well as cognitive learning, has been recognized in American education as an imperative educational aim by commissions and groups that drafted the Seven Cardinal Principles of Education in 1918, the Four Groups of Objectives in 1938, the Ten Imperative Needs in 1952, the Four Dimensions of the Task of the School in 1960, and Imperatives in Education in 1966 (Knezevich, 1969). Although public schools have been called upon to act on broad social issues, they have not shed the traditional conservatism to develop a school culture that is truly student-centered to meet students' needs. As Glasser (1986) indicates, about 50 percent of students fail in school because their basic needs are not being met.

Objective Student Data

Sociometry is a technique that, if used, will provide objective data about social relationships that exist among students in their classrooms. Figure 5.4 illustrates what information the sociogram can provide.

Below are the findings by Semple (1982) regarding the stability of student choices, attraction, and learning styles:

- The interaction between friends is more harmonious as well as more mutually directed than is the interaction between nonfriends.
- Changes in social structure occur more frequently if students are given the opportunity to interact in the classroom.
- Different sociometric questions yield different responses. For example, ''Who would you like to study with?'' and ''Who would you like to play with?'' will produce different answers.
- Asking students to identify disliked peers might well serve as a stimulus for group members to increase their negative interaction with unpopular students.
- If a classroom is organized so that students feel liked and respected, they will more likely behave in a manner that makes them worthy of the liking and respect.
- If a classroom is filled with anxiety, hostility, and self-doubt, students will behave in unconstructive and unproductive ways, thus perpetuating the negative climate.

The objective student data that can be obtained from the sociogram will show

- which students are the most desired to study with (group leaders can be selected from this assemblage)
- mutual choices
- ranked status scores
- which students are isolates (no one selected them)
- cliques (groups of students who restrict their choices to members of the same group)
- which students are neglectees (selected a minimum number of times)

Note: Teachers should *not* ask students to identify those with whom they would prefer *not* to study. To have students do this identifies the rejectees, and it also reinforces negative attitudes.

Figure 5.4. Sociometric objective student data. Source: Cockriel, I. W. 1973. ''Framing Instructional Groups from Sociometric Data,'' *Education*, 93:393.

- Classroom groups with diffuse friendship patterns exhibit a more positive climate than do classrooms that are centrally structured.
- Peer choices for formulating small group instruction lead to a positive learning situation for students. (pp. 6–10)

With the utilization of sociometrically derived data, small cooperative groups can be systematically established to maximize the learning for all students. To aid teachers in developing a sociogram of students in a classroom, the sociometric procedures are presented in step-like order.

Collect the Data

Just as a carpenter needs materials to build a house, teachers will need student data to begin construction of a sociogram. Because this procedure may be something new for students, the following approach will be helpful in collecting the needed data. The teacher could inform the students about the grouping process by saying,

> Next week, for our reading assignment on *The Hunter and the Animals*, we will start working together in groups of four. I think you will learn more, work better, and enjoy examining the illustrations in the book more if you are a member of a small cooperative learning group with those students with whom you would like to study, like a committee.

> Today you will be given a sheet of paper with the names of all the students in this class. Please write your first and last name on the blank provided at the top of the sheet of paper. Look over carefully the names of all the students; choose five students that you would like to have in your group. Place the numbers that are assigned to the names (e.g., #1 for Ryan Block, etc.) that you have chosen in the choice spaces provided (see Figure 5.5). I will do my best to put you in a group with some of the students you have chosen. No one but I will know what choices you make.

Research also shows that (1) five choices produce more reliable and useful data than items that require students to make fewer choices; (2) the validity of sociometric data is improved when students are assured that their choices are kept confidential; (3) sociometric tests should be administered when students are acquainted with all the students in the class; and (4) discouraging discussion of choices by students gives credence to the sociometric technique.

The classroom climate must be made favorable prior to data collection in order to obtain sincere answers. Students must feel free to make their

---

Student Choice Worksheet

Student Name:_____

Choices: 1. _____ 2. _____ 3. _____ 4. _____ 5. _____

Class List

1.   Ryan Block
2.   Susan Brady
3.   Jennifer Bumstead
4.   Gary Christenson
5.   Jeremy Crawford
6.   Etc.

Other student choice forms might ask the students to write the names of five students in rank order on a piece of paper or a form. Younger children, especially, might tell the teacher with whom they would like to work or play.

Figure 5.5. Student choice form.

choices without any influence from outside factors, and they must know that their selections are confidential. If teachers follow the correct procedure, students will quickly learn the value of naming their choices and help teachers make small cooperative group instruction work.

Building a Matrix

The students' choices from the ''Student Choice Worksheet'' (illustrated in Figure 5.5) must be entered into the computer using *The Small Grouper* software program. The printed sociomatrix (see Figure 5.6.) presents the student class list, the choices each student made, and the number of times each student was chosen by his or her classmates. The matrix will help teachers identify the group status for each student in the class. For example, students not selected are *isolates;* students selected between one and three times are identified as *neglectees;* and students chosen most often are *stars*.

Each entry that students make has equal weight. Research shows that little is gained if different weights are assigned to choices of dissimilar rank (Alcorn et al., 1964).

If a teacher was to pair students for a project or task to be completed in reading, especially in kindergarten through third grade, the sociomatrix illustrated in Figure 5.6 could be used for "pairing" students. Assume that student #3, Jennifer Bumstead, should be paired with a classmate who is a good reader to model reading for her. Examining

Sociomatrix

Sociometric Report for

School . . . . Any Elementary School
Teacher . . . . Any Teacher
Grade Level 2
No. Students 24
Date 2/14/91

Student List	Choices					# Times Chosen
1. Ryan Block	8	13	16	2	12	7
2. Susan Brady	15	16	17	12	19	3
3. Jennifer Bumstead	24	15	7	10	12	2
4. Gary Christenson	9	10	23	14	5	8
5. Jeremy Crawford	9	10	4	11	21	7
6. Karla Erickson	10	8	1	3	12	0
7. Jane Gross	8	1	17	24	12	4
8. Marsha Handover	17	1	12	19	24	7
9. Joseph Jackson	4	18	10	11	5	9
10. Michael Kemp	9	4	11	5	18	9
11. John Langely	10	22	1	7	21	6
12. Kathy Meyer	19	13	8	17	24	13
13. Cindy Nelson	17	19	12	7	1	5
14. Jerry Nixon	23	22	4	8	12	2
15. Mindy North	2	5	8	17	13	3
16. Karen Sails	10	20	5	4	9	2
17. Lisa Smith	13	12	19	24	15	9
18. Ronald Snow	9	4	12	22	10	3
19. Kristin Stone	12	17	13	7	1	5
20. Charles Toft	5	9	11	21	12	2
21. Brian Trimble	10	9	11	17	4	4
22. Mitch Underwood	18	9	11	1	20	3
23. Timothy Vail	14	21	4	5	9	2
24. Amy Waters	8	12	2	17	3	5

Figure 5.6. Compilation of student choices.

the choices that Jennifer made reveals that one of her choices is student #24, Amy Waters. It so happens that Amy Waters is a good reader and she has chosen #3, Jennifer Bumstead, as one of the students with whom she would like to study. Such a situation makes a near perfect match for pairing and peer learning.

Now assume that student #6, Karla Erickson, an isolate, has a low reading ability and interest. One of her choices is #12, Kathy Meyer, a group star or leader. It would be advantageous for Karla if the two could be paired as ''buddy'' readers because such a situation could enhance the reading skills and interest of Karla, permit Kathy to be a miniteacher and relearn reading skills herself, and build self-esteem for both students. After all, Karla did choose Kathy as one of five classmates with whom she would like to work or study in the reading class.

Constructing the Sociogram

The distribution of student choices is plotted by *The Small Grouper* software program. Groups are developed systematically with the following guidelines:

- Teachers determine the size of the group (four, five, or six students).
- Isolates are *not* placed into the same group.
- Every student, in most cases, will have at least one person with whom he or she chose to work in a small cooperative learning group.
- Clique members are dispersed among the different groups.
- High-rating students are dispersed among the small cooperative learning groups.
- In plotting the sociogram, the first students placed are the sociometrically poor – isolates and neglectees.

The Small Grouper, a computer program designed with the recommended guidelines for developing a sociogram, is available and is recommended by the authors.[4] Past experience and visits with many elementary school classroom administrators and teachers affirm that converting sociometric choices into data for grouping is time consuming. However, with the low-cost computer program available, a minimum

---

[4]To order *The Small Grouper,* send $139.95 to Wilkinsin Computer Systems, P.O. Box 5398, Albuquerque, NM 87185. Please indicate whether you would prefer Apple or IBM, and 5¼ " or 3½ ".

```
Sociometric Report for

                    School    . . . . . . . Any Elementary School
                    Teacher . . . . . . . Any Teacher
                    Grade Level   . . . . 2
                    No. Students  . . . . 24
                    Date     . . . . . . . 2/14/91

Suggested Grouping for Group Size  = 4

Group One

                              Kathy Meyer (star)
                              Kristin Stone
                              Susan Brady (neglectee)
                              Mindy North (neglectee)
Group Two

                              Lisa Smith (star)
                              Cindy Nelson
                              Jennifer Bumstead (neglectee)
                              Amy Waters
Group Three

                              Michael Kemp (star)
                              John Langley
                              Ronald Snow (neglectee)
                              Mitch Underwood (neglectee)
Group Four

                              Joseph Jackson (star)
                              Jeremy Crawford
                              Karen Sails (neglectee)
                              Charles Toft (neglectee)
Group Five

                              Gary Christenson (star)
                              Timothy Vail (neglectee)
                              Jerry Nixon (neglectee)
                              Brian Trimble
Group Six

                              Marsha Handover (star)
                              Ryan Block
                              Karla Erickson (isolate)
                              Jane Gross
```

Figure 5.7. Student choice sociogram.

```
                    School  . . . . . . . . Any Elementary School
                    Teacher  . . . . . . . Any Teacher
                    Grade Level . . . . .2
                    No. Students  . . . .24
                    Date  . . . . . . . . .2/14/91


Suggested Grouping for Group Size = 4

Group One
                            Kathy Meyer (star)
                            Ronald Snow
                            Mindy North
                            Amy Waters
Group Two
                            Kristin Stone (star)
                            Mitch Underwood
                            Charles Toft
                            Marsha Handover
Group Three
                            Jeremy Crawford (star)
                            Lisa Smith
                            Cindy Nelson (neglectee)
                            Michael Kemp
Group Four
                            Joseph Jackson (star)
                            Jennifer Bumstead
                            Jane Gross (isolate)
                            John Langley
Group Five
                            Brian Trimble
                            Karla Erickson
                            Gary Christenson
                            Ryan Block
Group Six
                            Jerry Nixon
                            Timothy Vail
                            Karen Sails (neglectee)
                            Susan Brady
```

Bold: Students who did not get any of their choices.

Figure 5.8. Teacher choice sociogram.

amount of effort and time (generally less than fifteen minutes) is required to group students in a classroom.

Figure 5.7 (p. 129) illustrates *The Small Grouper*'s edition of grouping students. Isolates, neglectees, and stars are identified in each group, which permits teachers to easily do several sociograms to meet the needs of children for different projects and subjects throughout the school year.

The knowledge that teachers can gain from the sociometric process is immeasurable. Sociograms are reliable short-term instruments that help teachers to understand the composition of their classrooms. As a result of generating sociograms, teachers gain additional insights into the behavior of their students, which are helpful for pairing or grouping students and decreasing intragroup tensions.

Figure 5.8 (p. 130) displays an example of a "Teacher Choice Sociogram." A comparison of the two sociograms, Student Choice vs. Teacher Choice, reveals the following results:

- *The Small Grouper* placed all students into groups with at least one of their choices.
- The teacher placed sixteen of the twenty-four students into groups with at least one of their choices.
- The teacher identified two of the six group leaders (stars).
- The wrong student was selected as an isolate by the teacher.
- The teacher identified one neglectee from a total of eight identified by the students.

The concrete evidence about the dynamics in classrooms will be an asset for developing learning experiences for cohesive groups. Teachers exposed to the sociometric process for the first time made the following comments: "It helped me to understand the composition of my class"; "I was surprised with the choices that students made"; "It was interesting to find that high achievers were not selected more often"; "This process will certainly help me in 'pairing' students for reading"; "This approach for pairing and grouping students is long overdue, why didn't they teach this process in my teacher preparation program?" and "Interdependence is a higher value than independence."

The combination of small cooperative learning groups and sociometric techniques can provide the "fresh view" needed to enhance the teaching and learning processes. Failure to apply the axioms brought forth in this chapter reinforces the statement that "no improvement is possible with unimproved people." Administrators, as well as teachers, need to be exposed to modern classroom management techniques to facilitate the teaching and learning processes in reading.

REFERENCES

Alcorn, M. D., J. S. Kinder, and J. R. Schunert. 1970. *Better Teaching in Secondary Schools*. Chicago, IL: Holt, Rinehart and Winston, Inc.

Berghoff, B. and K. Egawa. 1991. "No Rore 'Rocks': Grouping to Give Students Control of Their Learning," *The Reading Teacher*, 44:537.

Bonney, M. 1974. "Sociometric Study of the Agreement between Teacher Judgements and Student Choices: In Regard to the Number of Friends Possessed by High School Students," *Sociometry*, p. 135.

Boschee, F. 1989. *Grouping = Growth*. Dubuque, IA: Kendall/Hunt Publishing Company.

———. 1991. *A Comparison of Teacher Choice vs. Student Choice for Grouping Small Cooperative Learning Groups, Typescript*. Vermillion, SD: Division of Educational Administration, School of Education, University of South Dakota.

Brunner, J. 1986. *Actual Minds, Possible Worlds*. Cambridge, MA: Harvard University Press.

Cockriel, I. W. 1973. "Framing Instructional Groups from Sociometric Data," *Education*, 93:393.

Emberley, B. and E. Emberley. 1967. *Drummer Hoff*. Englewood Cliffs, NJ: Prentice-Hall, Inc.

Gibbs, S. G. 1982. *A Comparison of the Effects of Cross-Age and Same-Age Tutoring on the Reading Achievement of Elementary School Students*. Potsdam, NY: Potsdam College of Arts and Science. ERIC Document Reproduction Services No. ED 225 116.

Gifford, B. R. 1991. "Willie Mays, Big Blue, and Me," *The Chronicle of Higher Education*, 38:A22.

Glasser, W. 1986. *Control Theory*. New York: Harper & Row Publishers.

Gronland, N. 1950. "The Accuracy of Teachers' Judgements Concerning the Sociometric Status of Sixth Grade Pupils," *Sociometry*, 13:197–225.

Hedin, D. 1987. "Students as Teachers: A Tool for Improving School Climate," *Social Policy*, 17:47.

Holmes, N. C. 1991. "The Road Less Traveled by Girls," *The School Administrator*, 10:11.

Hoyle, J. R., F. W. English, and B. E. Steffy. 1985. *Skills for Successful School Administrators*. Arlington, VA: The American Association of School Administrators.

Johnson, D. W., R. T. Johnson, E. J. Houlubec, and P. Roy. 1984. *Circles of Learning*. Reston, VA: Association for Supervision and Curriculum Development.

Knezevich, S. J. 1969. *Administration of Public Education, Second Edition.* New York, NY: Harper & Row Publishers.

Laughlin, M. K. and L. S. Watt. 1986. *Developing Learning Skills through Children's Literature: An Idea Book for K−5 Classroom Libraries.* Phoenix, AZ: The Oryx Press, p. 153.

Moreno, J. L. 1934. *Who Shall Survive?* New York: Nervous and Mental Disease Publications.

Roberts, G. J. 1986. "Classroom Social Structure Analysis," *Equity & Excellence*, (Summer):26.

Schaps, E. and D. Solomon. 1990. "Schools and Classrooms as Caring Communities," *Educational Leadership*, 48:40.

Semple, E. E. 1982. *A Review of the Literature of Sociometry.* Garretsville, OH, pp. 1−2, 6−10. ERIC Document Reproduction Service No. ED 224 838.

Slavin, R. E. 1988. "Cooperative Learning and Student Achievement," *Educational Leadership*, 46:32.

———. 1990. "Research on Cooperative Learning," *Educational Leadership*, 47:52−54.

Taba, H., E. Brady, J. Robinson, and W. Vickers. 1951. *Diagnosing Human Relations.* Washington, D.C.: American Council on Education.

Thelen, H. 1969. "Tutoring Students," *School Review*, 77:236.

1983−1988. *Current Index to Journals in Education.*

1983−1989. *Psychological Abstracts.*

Classmates

"The fountains mingle with the river,
And the rivers with the ocean;
The winds of heaven mix forever
With a sweet emotion;
Nothing in the world is single;
All things, by a law divine,
In one another's being mingle.
Why not I with thine?"

PERCY BYSSHE SHELLEY

As you read and study:

. . . Differentiate between heterogeneous and homogeneous grouping.

. . . Determine how an elementary school principal can shape the composition of classrooms.

. . . Identify the characteristics that should be considered when assigning students to classes.

. . . Prioritize the characteristics that should be considered when assigning students to classes.

. . . Summarize the value of heterogeneous grouping.

. . . Compose a successful homogeneous classroom setting.

. . . Appraise the merits of *The Classmate*.

Who are Susan's classmates? Who are Michael's classmates? Are they boys or girls? Are they similar or dissimilar in academic ability? Are they in special programs? Are they from a minority group? Are they leaders or followers? Are they gifted? Is their learning rate fast, average, or slow? Is the reteaching frequency for them classified as never, seldom, or usually? Are their birthdays in the same month or different months? Is the sibling order the same: first child, second child, third child, and so on? Does it matter? Do any of the characteristics matter? Should it matter?

135

Over the years many have explained and offered answers to these questions. From philosophy and technology, from administrators and teachers have come insights, solutions, proposals, and models as well as more questions and problems yet to be solved. Some educators have focused on the issues and forces that affect the kind of classmates students have. Many, however, consider none or only some of the characteristics for students' classmates.

Following are the most vital questions to ask when placing elementary school students in classes: How does a vast accumulation of knowledge about heterogeneous and homogeneous grouping affect student learning? What does all this knowledge mean to the total growth of children? Should the nature of the relationship between theory and practice be left to the discretion or whim of individual administrators or teachers?

How can school administrators assimilate the important, yet terribly scattered, information offered by research? Or, consider the controversy among educators over the issue of heterogeneous versus homogeneous grouping. Is it fact or fiction? Once there is an arrangement of the particular type of consequence called reinforcement, the technique of placing students with appropriate classmates will permit the shaping of an organism almost at will. Can administrators shape the composition of a classroom? What must school administrators do? What must they *not* do? Should they mold the configuration of elementary school classrooms? Always? Never? Sometimes? Somewhat? These and a multitude of other issues and questions besiege elementary school administrators who take courses in educational administration. These are important issues; the research findings on heterogeneous and homogeneous grouping make important contributions to the work of elementary school administrators. A serious difficulty, however, arises in the all-too-common failure to employ the research findings in making school administrators more aware of how to group students.

GENDER PLACEMENT

It is a well-established certainty that in mixed sex classrooms, male students receive more teacher attention than do females. In several studies cited by French and French (1984, p. 128), boys interact more with teachers than do girls because ''teachers have a general and overall preference for male pupils.'' Why? According to some researchers, boys are more likely than girls to ask questions, to volunteer information, and to make heavier demands on a teacher's time. These behaviors could be the basis for explaining gender-differentiated patterns of student participation at the elementary school level.

To qualify and clarify the views on gender imbalances, French and French conducted a study to show an interactional account on turns taken by ten and eleven year old students from a teacher-class discussion of the topic "What I do on Mondays and what I would like to do on Mondays." As illustrated in Figure 6.1, not all boys monopolize the

Male Speakers	Turns	Female Speakers	Turns
Tom	17	Marie	5
Matthew	10	Rachel	3
Andrew	10	Angela	2
Simon	5	Sharon	2
Peter	3	Anne	1
Wayne	3	Claire	1
Jason	1	Laura	1
Warren	1	Rowena	1
Thomas	0	Anna	0
Andrew C.	0	Debbie	0
Allan	0	Gina	0
Martin	0	Helen	0
Paul	0	Jenny	0
		Joanne	0
		Linda	0
		Lorraine	0
Total	50		16

Numerical Breakdown of Turns

Turns taken by teacher	81
Turns taken by boys (13 out of 29 pupils)	50
Turns taken by pupils as "chorus"	33
Turns taken by girls (16 out of 29 pupils)	16
Turns taken by unidentified pupils	8
Total	188

Figure 6.1. Distribution of interaction turns. Source: French, J. and P. French. 1984. "Gender Imbalances in the Primary Classroom: An Interactional Account," *Educational Research*, 26:127–128.

interactional span of the lesson. Some boys take no more than or even fewer turns than most of the girls. A further analysis of the data indicates that the fifty instances of turn-taking are explicitly attributable to boys opposing solely girls. Considering that girls are in a majority (16:13) in the class, the ratio of imbalance becomes altogether more evident.

Factors contributing to gender interactional imbalances in elementary school classrooms may include:

- the tendency for boys to demand more of the teacher and hence receive more than their share of attention
- teachers (being) socially and psychologically predisposed to favor boys
- insensitivity to the interactional methods used by pupils in securing attention and conversational engagement
- teachers' immersion in the immediate concerns of "getting through" lessons, (leaving) them unaware of the activities performed by boys in monopolizing the interaction (French and French, 1984, p. 131)

Even though teachers consciously try to distribute their attention evenly between boys and girls, more time is spent with boys than girls. Spender (1982, p. 56), for example, consciously tried to distribute her attention evenly between the two sexes when teaching a class. She taped ten lessons and found herself interacting with girls 42 percent of the time. The minimum time spent with boys was 58 percent. As she said, "It is nothing short of substantial shock to appreciate the discrepancy between what I thought I was doing and what I actually was doing."

Gender Desegregation

School classrooms are "minisocieties" that replicate many structures of our larger society. Patterns of gender segregation account for substantial sex differences in adult earnings and occupational attainment (Lockheed, 1986). Understandably, sensible managers want the most productive employees for the lowest possible cost. Such rationale has merit, but the sex of the employee is, or should be, irrelevant. However, in adult workplaces, male or female managers and executives may prefer to work with same sex employees and, in some instances, are willing to pay for the privilege of working in a single-sex environment.

Where does the taste for sex segregation develop? How can it be changed? Although administrators have no control over sex-segregated activities for children prior to their attending school, Lockheed (1986, p. 619) believes that elementary schools are responsible for reinforcing sex-segregated attitudes. In this environment, "students have little cross-sex contact and rarely engage in equal-status cross-sex interaction. Instead, segregated patterns of study and play tend to permit stereotypes to be maintained unchallenged."

School administrators can reduce sex-segregated attitudes through school-based interventions by

- using gender variables as criteria for placing students in appropriate elementary school classrooms
- encouraging the use of small cooperative learning groups in the elementary school classrooms to counter gender imbalance
- providing appropriate inservice activities for staff on gender imbalance and interactional accountability in elementary school classrooms
- using *The Classmate*, a computer program designed to group students utilizing the gender variable[5]

The school-based interventions, utilizing the technology suggested, will assist with placing students into heterogeneous classrooms, encourage teachers to reexamine their attitudes about the appropriateness of student cross-sex friendships, and alter educators' methods of teaching and classroom organization. Teachers will also be able to provide direct instruction to students regarding the distinction between coworkers and friends.

ACADEMIC ACHIEVEMENT PLACEMENT

Should elementary school students be placed into classes on the basis of achievement or ability? Classes are homogeneous when the performances of students tend to cluster closely to the measure of central tendency, or they may be heterogeneous when performances are quite different and widely dispersed from the measure of central tendency. Both types of variability are important considerations in developing educational programs for elementary schools.

[5]Thanks are owed to Brenda Rae Dronen, a first grade teacher in the Eden Prairie, Minnesota school district, for originating the thought about *The Classmate*, and to the principal, Robert Bowker, and staff at Jolley Elementary School, Vermillion, South Dakota, for their cooperation.

The two most common forms of ability grouping are (1) where children are assigned to self-contained classrooms based on homogeneity of ability or achievement, and (2) within class ability grouping where children are assigned to smaller groups within classrooms. Dawson (1987, p. 348) notes "Other grouping practices include regrouping within a grade level for selected subjects, usually math and reading, and the Joplin Plan, in which regrouping takes place across grade lines."

Ability Grouping

The practice of ability grouping began at the turn of the century. Critics of the age-graded elementary schools, which were established in 1848, questioned the adequacy of such a model. They objected mostly to the classification of students exclusively by age in the new schools. "At each age level, the range in student mental age was likely to be as great as the number of their grade—a two-year range in mental age in the second grade, a three-year range in the third, and so on" (Kulik and Kulik, 1982, p. 619). The revisionists modified the age-graded elementary schools by accommodating individual differences with ability grouping, which is still prominent in an estimated 77 percent of all American schools today (Raze, 1985).

The reliance on ability grouping arrangements by educators is based on several assumptions:

- Students learn better when grouped with students considered academically similar.
- Low-ability students will develop more positive self-concepts when not forced to compete with students of far greater capability.
- Grouping decisions can be made fairly and accurately on the basis of native ability or past achievement.
- Teachers are better able to manage students and accommodate individual differences in homogeneous groups (Oakes, 1985).

Because grouping children of similar ability for reading instruction is as much a part of the classroom as the chalkboard, other assumptions arise:

- Teachers and administrators assume that ability groups offer the best way to manage the reading instruction of twenty-four or twenty-five young children.

- Teachers have used three reading groups simply to be able to manage the classroom. (Worthing, 1991, p. 4)
- If teachers can create groups of children that are alike in learning needs, instruction will proceed more efficiently and effectively. (Harp, 1989, p. 430)
- Teachers have fewer individual differences to contend with in ability-grouped classes, and students learn more when instruction can be aimed at the right level. (Kulik and Kulik, 1982, p. 619)

Negative Effects of Ability Grouping

The negative impact that grouping practices have on pupils' cognitive and affective behaviors has been thoroughly researched. A broad summary of the research by Unsworth (1984, p. 229) on homogeneous reading groups indicates the following.

- Ability grouping has not been effective in raising pupils' reading achievement.
- Ability grouping tends to harden the categories, especially for low-achieving pupils.
- Performances of children in the low-ability group declined significantly relative to the performances of the high-ability group members, even though they had only been in the group for a few months.

Other negative characteristics of ability grouping in reading are provided by Hiebert's (1983, pp. 231–255) summary of the research.

- Low-ability groups spent much more time on decoding tasks whereas high-ability group members spent more time on meaning-related activities.
- Low-ability groups spent more time on oral reading; high-ability groups spent more time on silent reading.
- Teachers spent more time on behavior management with low-ability groups. Because time spent on behavior management is negatively correlated with learning, lower-ability groups have diminished opportunity to share.
- Teachers were more prone to interrupt poor readers who made oral reading errors than good readers who made the same kind of errors, regardless of the semantic appropriateness of the error. Teachers also gave poor readers graphophonic cues to

target words, while they gave good readers syntactic and
semantic cues.

- In high reading groups, teachers discourage pupils from
  interrupting another pupil's oral reading with "call outs," but
  they do not do so in low reading groups.
- Some teachers clearly communicate messages to students about
  the status of reading groups, despite clever names or reverse
  numbering of groups.

An episode involving a fifth grade student who felt the effects of
homogeneous grouping is exemplified by Manning and Lucking (1990).
It is one example that could illustrate the situation of thousands of
students in American schools.

Early in the fall semester, the fifth grade teachers busily placed students
into homogeneous ability groups. Upon learning he was in the lower-
ability group, Carl spoke calmly and matter-of-factly: "Well, Mr. M.,
you put me in the dumb group."

"No, No, Carl," the teacher carefully explained, "you are not in a dumb
group . . . let me tell you what we did." He carefully explained to Carl
the process used to group students according to ability and that his being
in a lower-ability group meant he would receive more individual attention, help, and time. He felt good about his skills in explaining the grouping system to lower-ability children. Carl will feel better, he thought.

Carl's response [clearly expressed] the [negative] effects of homogeneous grouping as he again stated calmly and matter-of-factly: "Like I
said, you put me in the dumb group." (p. 254)

Such a practice of placing students is a near violation of human rights
and defies what research purports. For example, a study by Beckman
and Good, reported by Welbourn (1986), on the classroom ratio of high-
and low-aptitude students and its effects on achievement reveals some
significant results. Classrooms that included more than a third of the
students as high-aptitude learners and less than a third of the students as
low-aptitude learners were classified as "more favorable." The "less
favorable" classrooms contained the opposite ratio. Less than a third of
the students were high-aptitude learners and more than a third of the
students were low-aptitude learners. Beckman and Good "concluded
that both high- and low-aptitude students in more favorable classrooms
had greater achievement than comparable students in less favorable
classrooms" (Welbourn, 1986, p. 12).

Positive Homogeneous Grouping Technique

A place for homogeneous grouping in schools exists "if" students are grouped according to effective methods. One method of ability grouping that is successful for reading instruction at the elementary school level is the Joplin Plan. Students are regrouped across grade levels and age rather than within grade levels in order to create reading groups (Villa and Thousand, 1988). The plan creates reading groups that are homogeneous from the various ungraded classrooms.

The advantage of the Joplin Plan over traditional within-class grouping is the increased amount of direct instruction each student receives. "For example, in a traditional class with three reading groups and forty-five minutes of daily reading instruction, each group receives only fifteen minutes of instruction from the teacher. With the Joplin Plan, all students have teacher contact for the full forty-five-minute period" (Villa and Thousand, 1988, p. 149).

School administrators should use caution and permit homogeneous grouping only when

- The grouping plan measurably reduces student heterogeneity in the specific skill being taught.
- The plan is flexible enough to allow teachers to respond to misassignments and changes in student performance level after initial placement.
- Teachers actually vary their pace and level of instruction to correspond to students' levels of readiness and learning rates. (Slavin, 1987, p. 322)

In addition, elementary school students should be regrouped for no more than two subject areas. This allows pupils to spend the majority of each school day in a heterogeneous environment in which low-achieving students or students with handicaps have a heterogeneous student group as their primary reference. It also evades the detrimental psychological effects when students are associated with a low-ability track or special classes.

To achieve effective reading programs, the first step in creating effective elementary schools, school administrators must consider the implications of heterogenous grouping and the consequences of homogeneous grouping. As Brookover et al. (1982, p. 72) indicate, "Achievement of the goals of an organization is highly related to the structure of the organization." Given that our schools are organizations and that their goal is, or should be, to educate *all* students, their organizational structure must promote, or at the very least allow for, heterogeneity (Villa and Thousand, 1988). In doing less, school administrators indicate that either they don't know, they don't care, or they are under too much pressure from some people to care.

SPECIAL PROGRAM PLACEMENTS

- Section 504 of Public Law 93-112 (Rehabilitation Act of 1973)
- Public Law 94-142 (Education for All Handicapped Children Act of 1975)
- Public Law 99-457 (1986 Amendments to the Education for All Handicapped Children Act)
- handicapped children with communication disorders; learning disabilities; behavioral disabilities; cognitive disabilities; and physical, health, and sensory disabilities
- mainstreaming
- least restrictive environment
- individualized educational program (IEP)

The declarations above serve to illustrate that public school education today is geared to the unique needs and abilities of each individual child. The nearly 4.5 million students who receive special education services in the United States every year comprise the following categories (school-aged population percentages are in parenthesis):

- Blind or visually impaired: Students with special learning needs in areas requiring functional use of vision (less than 1 percent).
- Deaf or hard of hearing: Students with special learning needs in areas requiring functional use of hearing (less than 1 percent).
- Deaf and blind: Students with special learning needs in areas requiring functional use of hearing and vision (less than 1 percent).
- Orthopedically or other health impaired: Students with special learning needs in areas requiring functional use of hands, arms, legs, feet, and other body parts (less than 1 percent).
- Mentally retarded: Students with special learning needs in areas requiring functional use of intelligence and adaptive behavior (1.4 percent).
- Learning disabled: Students with learning needs in areas

requiring functional use of listening, speaking, reading, writing, reasoning, and math skills (5 percent).
- Emotionally disturbed: Students with special learning needs in areas requiring functional use of social and emotional skills (1 percent).
- Language impaired: Students with special learning needs in areas requiring functional use of language and communication (2.5 percent).
- Multihandicapped or severely impaired: Students with special learning needs in more than one area requiring functional use of skills (less than 1 percent). (Ysseldyke and Algozzine, 1990, pp. 13, 16)

Should handicapped children be taught reading in isolation, or can they benefit from a cooperative approach with nonhandicapped pupils? According to the research findings by Slavin, Stevens, and Madden (1988, p. 60), a heterogeneous cooperative approach increases reading achievement of *all* students, ''including mainstreamed and special education and remedial reading students.''

Cooperative Integrated Reading and Composition (CIRC)

An overview of the Cooperative Integrated Reading and Composition (CIRC) program suggests how students can work in heterogeneous learning teams. The planned activities should follow a cycle that consists of teacher presentation, team practice, peer preassessment, additional practice, and testing. The CIRC structure and activities illustrated by Slavin, Stevens, and Madden (1988), are presented below.

Reading Groups

Students are assigned to two or three reading groups consisting of eight to fifteen students per group. The group assignments should be made according to reading level determined by the students' teachers.

Teams within Reading Groups

Students should be assigned to pairs or triads within their reading groups. Following the reading assignment, pairs should be joined to form teams composed of partnerships from two different reading groups. For example, a team might be composed of two students from the top reading group and two from the low group. This process distributes the mainstreamed academically handicapped and remedial reading students among the teams.

Numerous activities within the teams should occur in pairs, whereas others involve the whole team. When one pair is engaging in some activity, the other pair should be accessible for help and encouragement. Most of the time, the teams should work independently of the teacher, which frees the teacher to work with reading groups selected from the different teams or to work with individuals.

This program requires students to follow a weekly schedule of activities. For accountability, partners should initial the assignment record forms as students complete each of the tasks assigned for the week. Teachers may use students' scores on quizzes, compositions, and book reports to form a team score. Teams that have an average weekly criterion of 90 percent on all activities can be designated as ''super teams'' and receive certificates. The 80 to 89th percentile performance can merit a ''great team'' certificate.

Basal-Related Activities

Using the regular basal readers, teachers should introduce basal stories and discuss them with students in teacher-led reading groups, meeting about twenty minutes each day. During the sessions, teachers should set a purpose for reading, introduce new vocabulary words, review old vocabulary words, discuss the stories after students have read them, and so on. For example, teachers should be taught to use vocabulary presentation procedures that require demonstration of word comprehension by each individual, review of methods of word attack, repetitive oral reading of vocabulary to achieve automaticity, and use of meanings of vocabulary words to help introduce the content of the stories. The story discussions should be structured to emphasize the skills needed in making and supporting predictions about the stories and understanding the major structural components of the story.

When students are not working with teachers, students should be given a series of activities to do in their teams. The recommended sequence is as follows:

(1) Partner reading: Students should read the stories silently first and then take turns reading aloud with their partners, alternating after each paragraph. The process of repeated reading contributes to

decoding and to comprehension of narratives. Further, the partner reading technique will give students an abundance of oral reading practice and enable teachers to assess student performance by circulating and listening without having to take the time of all students in the reading groups to allow individual students to read aloud.

(2) Story structure and story-related writing: Students should be given questions emphasizing the story grammar that relate to each narrative story. About halfway through the story, students should be instructed to stop reading and to identify the characters, the setting, and the problem in the story. They should also predict how the problem will be solved. At the end of the story, students should respond to the story as a whole and write a few paragraphs on the topic related to the story. Research on reading comprehension supports the importance of students' understanding the structure of stories and making predictions based on partial information about stories.

(3) Reading words out loud: Students should be given a list of new or difficult words used in the story, which they must be able to read correctly in any order without stumbling. The words should be presented by teachers in the reading groups and followed by students practicing their lists with partners or other teammates until they can read them smoothly. This activity will help students gain automaticity in decoding critical words, an essential prerequisite for comprehension.

(4) Word meaning: Students should be given a list of story words that are new in their speaking vocabularies, and asked to look them up in dictionaries, paraphrase the definitions, and write a sentence for each that shows the meaning of the words.

(5) Story retell: After the story has been read and discussed in the reading groups, students should summarize the main points of the story to their partners. The partners should have a list of the essential story elements that they use to check the completeness of the story summaries. Research shows that summarizing recently read material for a peer is an effective means of enhancing comprehension and retention of the material.

(6) Spelling: Students should pretest one another on a list of spelling words each week. They should also help each other master the list during the course of the week. Students should also use a ''disappearing list'' strategy whereby new lists of missed words are made until the list disappears and they can go back to the full list, repeating the process as many times as necessary.

Partner Checking

After students have completed each of the activities just listed, their partners should initial a student assignment form indicating completion of the task. Students should be given daily expectations regarding the number of activities to be completed. They should be encouraged to go at their own rate and complete the activities earlier, creating additional time for independent reading.

Tests

Students should be given a comprehensive test on the story at the end of three class periods. The test should ask them to write meaningful sentences for each vocabulary word and to read the word list aloud to the teacher. Students should *not* be permitted to help one another on the tests. Also, the test scores and evaluations of the story-related writing should be major components of students' weekly team scores.

Direct Instruction in Reading Comprehension

Once weekly, students should receive direct instruction from teachers in reading comprehension skills such as identifying main ideas, drawing conclusions, and comparing and contrasting ideas. Research does indicate that reading comprehension should be effectively taught as a skill separately from basal instruments.

Integrated Language Arts and Writing

Students should work on language arts on the same teams as in reading. For example,

(1) During three one-hour sessions each week, students should participate in a writer's workshop, working at their own pace on topics of their choice.
(2) Teachers should present ten-minute minilessons at the beginning of each hour on the writing process, style, or mechanics.
(3) Following the minilesson, students should spend the major portion of the hour planning, drafting, revising, editing, and publishing their writing. Informal and formal peer and teacher conferences can be held during this time.

(4) Ten minutes at the end of the hour should be reserved for sharing and celebration of student writing.

(5) Teacher-directed lessons on specific aspects of writing, such as organizing a narrative or a descriptive paragraph, using specific sensory words in a description, and insuring noun-verb agreement, should be conducted during two one-hour sessions each week.

A key in the design of a CIRC program is to integrate the activities of special education resource teachers and remedial reading teachers with regular classroom teachers. Resource and remedial pull outs for children should be at times other than reading or language arts/writing periods.

The CIRC program was presented for school administrators because it increased the reading achievement of *all* students, special and remedial as well as nonhandicapped. The three major studies using the CIRC program, involving third and fourth grade students, had the greatest impact on reading comprehension. This finding is crucial because reading researchers in the past found that standardized tests of reading comprehension are extremely difficult to influence.

The research results of the CIRC program also show that academically handicapped students can be effectively integrated into regular reading and language arts/writing classes if the regular classroom programs are designed to accommodate student differences.

Chapter 1

Should Chapter 1 money be expended for schoolwide reductions in class size? What is the ideal class size for Chapter 1 pull-out programs?

Class Size

Recent legislation by Congress is allowing Chapter 1 schools with 75 percent of their students classified "high poverty" to activate school-wide projects to reduce class size. Because high-poverty schools are normally located in school districts that are underfunded and, subsequently, have large class sizes, there will be pressure to use Chapter 1 funds to reduce class size (Slavin, 1989).

The intentions by school administrators to improve achievement scores in reading by reducing class size are noble. The research on class size by Slavin (1989, p. 107), however, "suggests that using Chapter 1 funds to reduce class size will not in itself make a substantial difference in student achievement." Although the findings on class size are disappointing, the justification for smaller class size is, at this point, teacher and student morale.

Based on evidence by the various research studies on what works, schools with Chapter 1 programs should consider one-on-one tutoring in reading as opposed to small-group pull outs or reduction in class size. Studies also show that in remedial reading programs where there are three to six students in a group, "teachers tend to revert to use of large numbers of worksheets and whole-group instruction" (Slavin, 1989, p. 107). With these facts, school administrators should seriously consider adding a second teacher with Chapter 1 funds for tutoring one-on-one only for at-risk students. Tutoring interventions in the first grade, especially, can prevent the development of reading deficits in at-risk students (Slavin, 1989).

Mainstreaming: Inclusion or Exclusion

Since mandatory special education laws were enacted and the successful mainstreaming research reports, e.g., CIRC, were published, it appears that there is still more exclusion than inclusion (see Figure 6.2) of students with special needs. Why? Because "historically, educators have created separate programs and systems to address unique student needs" (Cloud, 1992, p. 24).

The debate in educational communities about the value of inclusion could continue for some time unless administrators, professional staff, and community people begin to believe in equal opportunity in education for *all* students. As Schattman and Benay (1992, p. 12) so adequately state, "Inclusive education offers the school the opportunity to be truly effective," and "Education in a democratic society requires no less."

MINORITY PLACEMENT

Interracial schooling is a fact of life for millions of American children. What is known about the extent and nature of intergroup contact in desegregated schools? What should be known?

Data obtained through a computer-based auditing procedure (allowing students to audit the performance of classmates) from second, third, and fourth grade children indicates that they begin to show interest in the performance of their classmates early in the formal schooling process (Meisel and Blumberg, 1990). The research also shows that by fourth

Top Five States	Regular Class	Resource Room	Separate Class
Vermont	79.4%	8.1%	8.9%
North Dakota	74.0	10.4	12.3
Nebraska	60.0	22.7	14.2
Massachusetts	59.4	15.8	18.0
Oregon	59.0	26.8	11.1
Bottom Five States			
Alabama	0.0%	71.6%	26.3%
Georgia	1.1	69.7	26.7
Texas	3.9	78.7	10.0
New York	7.1	36.3	43.8
Arizona	9.9	62.9	22.9

Note: Remaining students, ages six to twenty-one, in each state were served in separate facilities or homebound.

Figure 6.2. Placement of students with disabilities in regular classrooms. Source: Conn, M. 1992. "1991 Annual Report to Congress on the Implementation of the Individuals with Disabilities Education Act" (February). "Aligning Our Beliefs with Action," *The School Administrator*, 49(2):23.

grade, or sooner, children constantly use "comparison information" to evaluate their own performance capabilities.

Everyone knows that children constantly compare their performance with that of classmates. However, the study by Meisel and Blumberg of a second and a third grade class consisting of eleven white males, six black males, ten white females, and five black females revealed the following results.

- Second and third grade students from all the subgroups tended to audit classmates that were of both a different gender and (a different) race far less than would be expected if only chance were operating.
- White males tended to over-audit other white males to a much greater extent than would be expected.
- Black students . . . tended (to audit) classmates of the same race but opposite gender, with black males over-auditing black females and black females over-auditing black males. (Meisel and Blumberg, 1990, p. 175)

The fourth grade class, comprised of nine white males, five black males, ten white females, and three black females, "audited classmates that were of both a different race and a different gender much less than would be expected" (Meisel and Blumberg, 1990, pp. 175–176). Additionally, there was a distinct trend for all subgroups to over-audit within their own subgroup; "This was most pronounced for white females and least evident among black males who actually over-audited white males to a greater extent than they did other black males."

Overall, this study indicates that children in this age group tend to avoid comparing their own performance with that of classmates who are both a different race and a different gender. Similar findings are reported by Sager, Schofeld, and Snyder (1983) from a study with sixth grade students in an urban desegregated school. It was found that

- Students interacted primarily with others of their own race and sex.
- Boys interacted more across racial lines than girls.
- Blacks were almost twice as likely as whites to be the source of cross-race interactions.
- No race effects were apparent in the children's own task orientation, but peer behaviors were more likely to be task-related when directed toward white rather than black interactants.
- A parallel study of sociometric choice . . . reinforced virtually all of the above conclusions. (p. 1032)

From these studies, it becomes quite clear that racial in-grouping is the mode in interracial schools. When assigning students to classes, teachers should consider minority placement because racial aggregation remains high throughout students' school years.

PULL-OUT PLACEMENT

Placement of elementary school students who have commitments to various special activities such as orchestra practice and so on during school hours should be considered. For example, an elementary school classroom that has a third or half the class absent at the same time may have some problems with normal classroom activities. As one elementary school principal said: "I would suggest 'pull out' as a program feature for *The Classmate* to ensure continuity in classrooms."

LEADERSHIP PLACEMENT

Leadership in school settings can be a perplexing concept. What is it? Who has it? How do students get it? A leader can be defined as an individual who has group support and who influences the group toward his or her preferences without exerting external authority (Shaw, 1971). Students who have those qualities should be identified as leaders by teachers for "leadership placement."

Elementary schools provide multiple opportunities for students to demonstrate leadership. During the course of a day or week, student roles and behaviors shift between formal and informal settings, across activities, and within teacher- and student-dominated settings. The melange of formal and informal school activities provides students with a basis to draw on to become astute in identifying student leaders in their classes and school. If teachers use sociometric techniques and small group cooperative learning, student leaders can be easily identified.

TALENTED AND GIFTED (TAG) PLACEMENT

Talented and gifted (TAG) students have special learning needs that require functional use of intelligence and artistic ability. This select group of students makes up about 3 percent of the school-age population.

Cluster Grouping

The majority of gifted elementary school-age children are placed in classes with peers of varying abilities, which can be frustrating to many. Heterogeneity is not the problem. The problem rests with the structural system in assigning students to classes and to the classroom teacher.

Assume that an elementary school has 120 third grade students comprising six different classes, i.e., twenty students per class. If 3 percent of the students qualify for the TAG program, the total number of gifted students would normally be three or possibly four students. Should these students be in the same class or different classes? Is it important to meet the special needs of these children?

If no provisions are made for a pull-out program for TAG students, unlikely in a setting with three or four students from one grade level in a small school district, a "cluster grouping" approach seems logical to meet the needs of TAG students. Both teachers and students benefit from a cluster grouping approach. Bryant (1987) indicates that

- It is more efficient for one teacher to plan for five students than for five teachers to make plans for single students.
- If the teacher knows gifted students will be placed in his or her class, planning, organizing, and developing appropriate materials can be accomplished in advance, thus making it easier to offer enriching experiences during the year.
- The cluster allows nongifted students to learn from their gifted peers (a disadvantage is that students in the other five classes will *not* have regular exposure to the TAG students).
- A cluster offers (students) the opportunity to work with others who have similar abilities, and they benefit from these interactions. (pp. 214–215)

The cluster grouping approach for TAG students is especially appropriate for economic efficiency. Many school districts are not large enough to employ a full-time teacher for TAG children. School districts should, however, make sure that regular classroom teachers receive appropriate inservice for TAG enrichment activities. Many programs are implemented without this consideration, and the enrichment activities are merely haphazard collections of unrelated games and puzzles.

What are the effects of "appropriate" enrichment activities for elementary school-aged children? A study by Kolloff and Feldhusen (1984, p. 57) of 392 third, fourth, fifth, and sixth grade students participating in a pull-out program, two hours per week, supports the effectiveness of an enrichment program. They concluded "that the creative thinking abilities of gifted elementary students can be developed through a systematic program of enrichment experiences," and "students maintained their self-concepts."

The size of schools and school districts should be the determining factors in the placement of TAG students in elementary school classes. Both approaches, cluster grouping and pull-out programs, can be effective if school administrators place students to fit the situation.

LEARNING RATE PLACEMENT

All elementary school students are assigned into classrooms for purposes of instruction and learning. In typical classrooms, students come from diverse cultural and educational backgrounds and, subsequently, learn specific subject matter at different rates (Brown and Saks, 1986). These factors play a dominant role in placement of students into classes, becoming important components for the composition of a classroom.

RETEACHING FREQUENCY PLACEMENT

Reteaching is a function that can be met several ways: by the teacher, by the student working with other students, by the student working alone, or by computer-assisted instruction (CAI). CAI in reading is effective in teaching a wide variety of reading skills and in concept areas (Darter and Phelps, 1990).

Intervention in the educational processes must occur in order to guarantee a high quality of learning for all students. Distributing students who need frequent reteaching among classes will permit more intervention by teachers as well as peers and CAI. In a heterogeneous group, teachers will have more time to spend with some students in need, rather than the whole class; high-achieving students can be helpful to slow learners; and because the number of computers is limited in most elementary school classrooms, heterogeneity will permit CAI for students in the acquisition and development of reading skills.

BIRTHDATE PLACEMENT

The concept of school readiness has propagated controversy among educators and psychologists for a long time. "Two aspects of this controversy focus on children's age at the time of school entry and on sex of the child" (May and Welch, 1986, p. 100). Most states specify cutoff dates for entry into kindergarten or first grade with a variance of six months. Yet, no systematic research supports any of the age variances. The problem in evaluating school entrance age is the lack of a definition for "readiness." At what age is a child ready for school?

Readiness Defined

The Concise Oxford Dictionary (1987, p. 862) defines readiness as a "ready or prepared state." A compilation of the research findings on "school readiness" by May and Welch shows that

- Children who are under six years of age, both mentally and chronologically, when entering first grade have little chance for school success.
- The older the child when entering school, the greater are his or her chances of success academically.
- Boys born late in the year were more likely to be referred for problems than were boys born early in the year.
- Boys are more negatively affected by early school entry than are girls. (p. 101)

Results of the research on birthdate and age group suggest "that the use of chronological age as the only eligibility criterion for school entry may result in some children being admitted to school who are not cognitively or emotionally ready" (Kinard and Reinherz, 1986, p. 366).

Considerable attention should be given to children's appropriate developmental placement, which can reduce school learning problems (Gesell Institute, 1980). Some school districts recommend that children born in September, October, or November (especially boys) wait a year before entering school. Others use the Gesell School Readiness Test, or the screening portion of it, to make placement recommendations based on developmental age rather than chronological age.

Noticeable birthdate effects are limited to school entry for children, and tend to disappear in the later grades. Since lower achievement dissipates in programs that accommodate individual differences, *The Classmate* can be a helpful tool to place students into appropriate classes.

SIBLING ORDER PLACEMENT

Much of the literature on sibling order in the past suggested that first-born children excelled over others in academic achievement and leadership. The inaccuracy of past research reports, according to Steelman and Powell (1985), is attributed to the collection of data from small, select samples that were confined to narrow age groups. Other contaminating factors that were not taken into account were family marital stability, family size, and family socioeconomic status.

Sibling Order Impact

The impact of sibling order and how it affects social skills and academic performance of children and adolescents provides some applicable clues to differential development and aids in placing students into classrooms. From two nationally representative studies with a sample population of 3,568 children, ages six to eleven, and youth, ages twelve to seventeen, Steelman and Powell (1985) found the following:

- Males profit from a later birth position with respect to being chosen when children pick sides and when children pick leaders.
- Birth order is not a significant predictor for females (when children pick sides and when children pick leaders).
- Neither male nor female children are influenced by their ordinal positions in terms of academic performance.
- Females profit from later birth order only with respect to outgoingness and getting along with other children.
- Males profit consistently from later birth order on all four aspects of social success (getting along, being outgoing, being chosen, and being perceived as leaders). (p. 121)

The implications for placing students into classes using birth order are abundant. To illustrate, if a whole class was made up of later birth order children, all the boys could be leaders, outgoing, well liked, and easy to get along with. The girls would be outgoing and easy to get along with. What would another class be like if most of the first born children were assigned to it? Perhaps there is a reason why teachers at times say, ''This is the best or worst group of students I have ever had.'' The problem could be how students are assigned to classes. Birth order should be placed high on the ''criteria for placement'' list.

THE CLASSMATE

An IBM-compatible computer program, *The Classmate*[6] assists elementary school principals in systematically making heterogeneous student placements in classes, which maximizes the learning for *all* students. It also lets the school principal ''work smarter, rather than harder.'' For example, an administrator should ask the following questions: How much time will it take to place third grade students into the fourth grade? What is the cost? Are the students grouped with a true heterogeneous procedure?

[6]To order *The Classmate,* send $400.00 plus 25¢ per student enrolled district-wide in grades K−5, to Excelltech, Inc., 300 West Third St., Yankton, SD 57078. Please indicate 3½ " or 5¼ ".

Several elementary school principals estimate that it takes approximately thirty hours per grade level. Whatever the number of hours, multiply them times the principal's hourly wage (e.g., $50 × 30 hours = $1,500). The total cost is even more when one includes teachers' time spent beyond completing the student data forms. Placing students into appropriate classes can be expensive and possibly ineffectual. *The Classmate* has a twofold purpose: letting elementary school principals use student data to make placement costs more efficient, and to make placement heterogeneously effective.

Elementary school principals and reading supervisors should now be knowledgeable about the values of and the need for appropriate student placement in classrooms. The process for truer heterogeneous assignments using *The Classmate* is presented in step-by-step order.

Step 1: Collect the Data

A bricklayer building a foundation will need some material to commence construction, just as an elementary school principal will require data to develop heterogeneous classes. A Student Data Worksheet form (see Figure 6.3) contains twelve identifying criteria for each student. Teachers are asked to identify and/or to evaluate each student's personal data comprised of gender, reading achievement, math achievement, special programs, minority, pull out, leadership, gifted, learning rate, reteaching frequency, birthdate, and sibling order. Teachers should be able to complete the Student Data Worksheet form, with the possible exception of the sibling order category.

Step 2: Prioritizing Criteria

After collecting the Student Data Worksheet forms, the elementary school principal may want to meet with grade level teachers to prioritize the established criteria (see Figure 6.4).

The student data is entered into the computer program. *The Classmate* computes the data entered and heterogeneously assigns students to classrooms. Figure 6.5 illustrates *The Classmate's* edition of placing students into a class. The following should be noted:

(1) Six sections of third grade students were assigned to classes in the fourth grade with *The Classmate*.

Student Data Worksheet

Student Last Name: _____ First Name: _____ Initial: _____

Grade Level: _____

Teacher: _____

School: _____

Date: __ / __ / __

Gender:
[ ] Male
[ ] Female

Reading:
[ ] High
[ ] High Average
[ ] Average
[ ] Low Average
[ ] Low

Math:
[ ] High
[ ] High Average
[ ] Average
[ ] Low Average
[ ] Low

Special Program:
[ ] None
[ ] Chapter 1
[ ] Communication Disorder
[ ] Learning Disabilities
[ ] Behavioral Disabilities
[ ] Cognitive Disabilities (MR)
[ ] Physical/Health/Sensory

Minority:
[ ] No
[ ] Yes

Pull Out:
[ ] No
[ ] Yes

Leader:
[ ] No
[ ] Yes

Gifted:
[ ] No
[ ] Yes

Learning Rate:
[ ] Fast
[ ] Average
[ ] Slow

Reteaching Frequency:
[ ] Never
[ ] Seldom
[ ] Usually

Birthdate:
[ ] Sept
[ ] Oct
[ ] Nov
[ ] Dec
[ ] Jan
[ ] Feb
[ ] Mar
[ ] Apr
[ ] May
[ ] Jun
[ ] Jly
[ ] Aug

Sibling Order:
[ ] First
[ ] Second
[ ] Third
[ ] Fourth
[ ] Fifth
[ ] Sixth

Figure 6.3. Student data characteristics.

159

Current Priority		New Priority	
[1]	Gender	[8]	Gender
[2]	Reading Performance	[1]	Reading Performance
[3]	Math Performance	[2]	Math Performance
[4]	Special Programs	[5]	Special Programs
[5]	Minority	[7]	Minority
[6]	Pull Out	[10]	Pull Out
[7]	Leader	[6]	Leader
[8]	Gifted	[12]	Gifted
[9]	Learning Rate	[3]	Learning Rate
[10]	Reteaching Frequency	[4]	Reteaching Frequency
[11]	Birthdate	[9]	Birthdate
[12]	Sibling Order	[11]	Sibling Order

Note: The "New Priority" column configuration was used to assign third grade students into fourth grade class sections.

Figure 6.4. Student class priority criteria.

Class Grouping for _____ School Third Grade Date _____
Group One

Nme	Gndr	Rdng	Mth	Spcl	Min	Plot	Ldr	Gft	Lrn	Rtch	Bd	Sib
A	F	L	LA	C1	N	Y	N	N	S	A	AG	3
B	M	L	LA	C1	N	Y	N	N	S	A	AP	2
C	M	L	L	C1	N	Y	N	N	S	A	AG	1
D	M	HA	A	CD	Y	Y	N	N	A	S	JN	1
E	M	A	HA	CD	N	Y	Y	Y	F	N	OC	1
F	F	H	H	N	N	Y	Y	Y	F	N	SP	1
G	M	LA	LA	C1	N	Y	N	N	S	A	AG	2
H	M	A	A	N	N	N	N	N	A	S	MR	2
I	F	L	L	C1	N	Y	N	N	S	A	JN	4
J	F	H	H	N	N	N	Y	N	F	S	FB	3
K	M	A	A	N	N	N	N	N	N	S	DC	2
L	F	A	LA	N	N	N	N	N	S	A	AG	1
M	F	HA	HA	N	N	N	Y	N	A	A	AG	5
N	M	LA	LA	N	N	N	N	N	A	S	MY	1
O	M	H	H	N	N	N	Y	N	F	N	AG	3
P	M	H	H	CD	N	Y	Y	Y	F	N	FB	3
Q	M	HA	HA	N	N	N	N	N	A	S	JY	2
R	M	HA	A	N	N	N	N	N	A	S	NV	1
S	M	H	H	N	Y	N	N	N	F	N	JY	1
T	M	A	A	N	N	N	N	N	A	S	SP	1
U	F	L	L	CD	Y	Y	N	N	S	A	NV	3
V	M	HA	HA	N	N	N	Y	N	F	S	JA	1
W	M	A	A	N	Y	N	N	N	A	A	OC	1
X	F	LA	A	N	N	N	N	N	A	S	JY	4
Y	M	HA	A	CD	N	Y	N	N	A	S	JA	3
Z	M	H	HA	N	Y	N	Y	N	F	S	MY	2

Note: The names of students have been omitted for usual reasons. *The Classmate* printout provides a key for the abbreviated terms (e.g., Bd = Birthdate, CD = Communication Disorder, etc.).

Figure 6.5. Class grouping computed by *The Classmate*.

(2) Each class had about the same mix of students among the twelve categories.

(3) *The Classmate* creates heterogeneous class groups based on students' abilities and attributes.

Grouping of students is a delicate and complicated process, which can have a significant impact on student performance and student attitude toward the learning process. Done incorrectly, grouping can stigmatize and demoralize students. But if done with care and intelligence, grouping can stimulate students and provide them with a positive attitude toward reading and learning that will last a lifetime.

REFERENCES

Brookover, W., L. Beamer, H. Efthim, D. Hathaway, L. Lezzotte, S. Miller, J. Passalacqua, and L. Tornatzky. 1982. *Creating Effective Schools: An Inservice Program for Enhancing School Learning Climate and Achievement.* Holmes Beach, FL: Learning Publications.

Brown, B. W. and D. H. Saks. 1986. "Measuring the Effects of Instructional Time on Student Learning: Evidence from the Beginning Teacher," *American Journal of Education*, p. 94.

Bryant, M. A. 1987. "Meeting the Needs of Gifted First Grade Children in a Heterogeneous Classroom," *Roeper Review*, 9:214–215.

Cloud, J. D. 1992. "Ending Our Practice of Compartmentalization," *The School Administrator*, 49(2):24.

Conn, M. 1992. "Aligning Our Beliefs with Action," *The School Administrator*, 49(2):23.

Darter, C. L., Jr. and L. N. Phelps. 1990. *The Impact of the Computer on the Teaching of Reading: A Review of the Literature*, ERIC Document Reproduction Service No. ED 326 836.

Dawson, M. M. 1987. "Beyond Ability Grouping: A Review of the Effectiveness of Ability Grouping and Its Alternatives," *School Psychology Review*, 16:348.

French, J. and P. French. 1984. "Gender Imbalances in the Primary Classroom: An Interactional Account," *Educational Research*, 26:127–128, 131.

Gesell Institute of Human Development. 1980. *A Gift of Time . . . A Developmental Point of View.* New Haven, CT: Gesell Institute of Human Development.

Harp, B. 1989. "What Do We Know Now about Ability Grouping?" *The Reading Teacher*, 42:430.

Hiebert, E. H. 1983. "An Examination of Ability Grouping for Reading Instruction," *Reading Research Quarterly*, 18:231–235.

Kinard, E. M. and H. Reinherz. 1986. "Birthdate Effects on School Performance and Adjustment: A Longitudinal Study," *The Journal of Educational Research*, 79:371.

Kolloff, P. B. and J. F. Feldhusen. 1984. "The Effects of Enrichment on Self-Concept and Creative Thinking," *Gifted Child Quarterly*, 28:57.

Kulik, C. C. and J. A. Kulik. 1982. "Research Synthesis on Ability Grouping," *Educational Leadership*, 39:619.

Lockheed, M. E. 1986. "Reshaping the Social Order: The Case of Gender Segregation," *Sex Roles*, 14:617, 619.

Manning, M. L. and R. Lucking. 1990. "Ability Grouping: Reality and Alternatives," *Childhood Education*, 66:254.

May, D. C. and E. Welch. 1986. "Screening for School Readiness: The Influence of Birthdate and Sex," *Psychology in Schools*, 23:100, 101.

Meisel, C. J. and C. J. Blumberg. 1990. "The Social Comparison Choices of Elementary and Secondary School Students: The Influence of Gender, Race, and Friendship," *Contemporary Educational Psychology*, pp. 15, 175–176.

Oakes, J. 1985. *Keeping Track: How Schools Structure Inequality*. New Haven, CT: Yale University Press.

Raze, N. 1985. *Overview of Research on Ability Grouping*. San Mateo County Office of Education. ERIC Document Reproduction Service No. ED 252 927.

Sager, H. A., J. W. Schofeld, and H.N. Snyder. 1983. "Race and Gender Barriers: Preadolescent Peer Behavior in Academic Classrooms," *Child Development*, 54:1032.

Schattman, R. and J. Benay. 1992. "Inclusive Practices Transform," *The School Administrator*, 49(2):12.

Shaw, M. E. 1971. *Group Dynamics: The Psychology of Small-Group Behavior*. New York, NY: McGraw-Hill.

Slavin, R. E. 1987. "Ability Grouping and Student Achievement in Elementary School: A Best-Evidence Synthesis," *Review of Educational Research*, 57:293–336.

———. 1989. "Class-Size and Student Achievement: Small Effects of Small Classes," *Educational Psychologist*, 24:107.

Slavin, R. E., R. J. Stevens, and N.A. Madden. 1988. "Accommodating Student Diversity in Reading and Writing Instruction: A Cooperative Learning Approach," *Remedial and Special Education (RASE)*, p. 9.

Spender, D. 1982. *Invisible Women: The Schooling Scandal*. London: Writers and Readers Publishing Co-Operative Society with Chameleon Editorial Group.

Steelman, L. C. and B. Powell. 1985. "The Social and Academic Consequences of Birth Order: Real, Artifactual, or Both?" *Journal of Marriage and Family*, 47:121.

Unsworth, L. 1984. "Meeting Individual Needs through Flexible Within-Class Grouping of Pupils," *The Reading Teacher*, 38:298–299.

Villa, R. A. and J. S. Thousand. 1988. "Enhancing Success in Heterogeneous Classrooms and Schools," *Teacher Education and Special Education*, 11:148–149.

Welbourn, V. 1986. *The Effect of Class Composition on Achievement*. Information analysis, p. 12. ERIC Document Reproduction Service No. 277 461.

Worthing, J. 1991. "Reading Groups: Problems, Solutions," paper presented at the *Annual Meeting of the International Reading Association, Las Vegas, NV, May 6–10, 1991*, p. 4. ERIC Document Reproduction Service No. 327 833.

Ysseldyke, J. E. and B. Algozzine. 1990. *Introduction to Special Education, Second Edition*. Geneva, IL: Houghton Mifflin Company.

1987. *The Concise Oxford Dictionary, Seventh Edition*. New York, NY: Oxford University Press, p. 862.

Outcome-Based Education

*"Change is inevitable. In a progressive
country change is constant."*

EDINBURGH
29 OCT. 1867

As you read and study:

. . . Analyze the National Assessment of Educational Progress reading
assessment report.

. . . Define a paradigm.

. . . Analyze "paradigm paralysis."

. . . Compare traditional education and outcome-based education.

. . . Summarize the dramatic success of outcome-based programs.

. . . Analyze the procedure for an outcome-based language arts
program.

. . . Determine the value of identifying learning experiences, learner
outcome assessments, and resources used for learning.

American students today are reading less both in and out of the classroom than students who were assessed in 1988. The National Assessment of Educational Progress (NAEP) reading assessment, released in
May 1992, "shows 45 percent of fourth graders, 63 percent of eighth
graders, and 59 percent of twelfth graders reported reading ten or fewer
pages each day" (Lucas, 1992, p. 1). Alarmingly, nearly one-third of
the students in all three grades reported they never read for pleasure.

Although there is a considerable amount of research on effective
reading instruction that emphasizes combining reading and writing

activities, the NAEP reading assessment report confirms that "teachers still rely heavily on workbooks to teach reading skills" (Lucas, 1992, p. 1). For example, "44 percent of fourth graders and 25 percent of eighth and twelfth graders reported using workbooks daily" (Lucas, 1992, p. 1). From the representative sample of 25,000 public and private school students, only "50 percent of the fourth graders reported writing in a journal at least weekly about their reading, compared with 28 and 29 percent of eighth and twelfth graders" (Lucas, 1992, pp. 1–2).

Are we enhancing continuous learning with our reading programs today? According to the NAEP reading assessment report, the resounding answer is "no" because the frequency of student library use declines as students progress through school. To illustrate, "Two-thirds of fourth graders . . . use the library at least weekly, compared with 25 percent of eighth graders and 10 percent of twelfth graders" (Lucas, 1992, p. 2). The report also indicated that more than 33 percent of twelfth graders and nearly 25 percent of eighth graders visit the library only once a year.

The ability to work smarter, not harder, is the measure of achievement for future generations. As Thomas Jefferson so eloquently said: "Any nation that expects to be both ignorant and free . . . expects what never was and never will be." Those words are as true today as they were nearly two centuries ago. The responsibility for developing and implementing effective reading programs is awesome, but the opportunity to restructure them is promising.

Reading has been, and continues to be, regarded as the essential cornerstone to prepare children for adult lives. In essence, through reading programs our schools equip children with the knowledge and skills to learn, to think, to live, and to work more effectively.

Past reading program practices, many of which still exist today, placed a strong reliance on basals and workbooks. The programs served as a good resource for an agrarian and industrial nation. However, reading programs of yesteryear lack the capacity to respond to the rapid shifts and new demands of a changing society.

The tried-and-true reading programs of the past are not wrong, but they must be updated to ensure that *all* students have the skills to learn what is germane today and in the future. Along with the knowledge explosion, urban centers are in decay with a pervasive drug culture woven into their social fabric. Countless children, as well as adults, live in poverty, and the gap even widens between the haves and have-nots. America has become a much different society than it was shortly after World War II and through the 1960s (Hodgkinson, 1991). In reality,

America is once again turning to public education for solutions and the Model-T Ford reading program cannot be used to deliver the load required of a supersonic jet transport program.

"Broad brush" reading programs with detailed lists of concepts to be "covered" in some mysterious style with an unidentified audience run the risk of producing unessential and perhaps even harmful experiences for students. The information-oriented society is demanding a new model of organizational excellence for reading programs, a model that has the characteristics and operational components that will lead to more consistency, have higher productivity, and demonstrate incomparable outcomes.

AN EMERGING PARADIGM

Outcome-based education represents a paradigm shift for all of education, and especially for language arts programs, the cornerstone of all learning.[7] What is a paradigm? Joel A. Barker (1992), in *Future Edge,* defines a paradigm as

> a set of rules and regulations (written or unwritten) that does two things: (1) it establishes or defines boundaries; and (2) it tells you how to behave inside the boundaries in order to be successful. (p. 32)

To develop and implement effective language arts programs, school administrators must be able to manage within a paradigm and lead between paradigms. The current rules, guiding principles, standards, and protocols of school systems permit administrators to manage a language arts program. However, to lead in the development and implementation of an outcome-based education language arts program, school administrators must be able to "instill the courage in others to follow them" (Barker, 1992, p. 164).

Paradigm Paralysis

Educators need to be aware of paradigm paralysis and learn from the following example. In 1968, Switzerland dominated the watchmaking

---

[7]Thanks are owed to Dr. Mark A. Baron, Assistant Professor, Division of Education, School of Education, University of South Dakota, for his contributions on outcome-based education.

industry because the Swiss made the best watches in the world. The invention of the minute hand and the second hand attributed to a dominant market along with the research in discovering better techniques to manufacture the gears, the bearings, and the mainsprings of contemporary watches. They also produced the best waterproof and self-winding watches. The Swiss were leaders and innovators in the watch industry.

The successful Swiss watch industry captured more than 65 percent of the sales in the world watch market and more than 80 percent of the profits. Without a doubt, the Swiss were the world leaders in watchmaking.

In 1980, twelve years later, the Swiss watch market experienced a catastrophe. The overwhelming market share was less than 10 percent and the profit portion dropped to less than 20 percent of the world market. What caused the dilemma?

Electronics!

The electronic quartz watch, invented and rejected by the Swiss themselves in 1967, was displayed at the World Watch Congress that year. Seiko, a Japanese watch manufacturer, immediately saw it as the "watch of the future." Paradigm paralysis dethroned the Swiss as the largest and best watchmakers in the world, and 50,000 of the 62,000 watchmakers lost their jobs (Barker, 1992).

Many school administrators are hesitant about accepting innovative ideas because they assume that the future is an extension of the past. The NAEP reading assessment report should be cause enough for school administrators to advocate reform in language arts programs. It could well be the paradigm that will determine the success or failure of the nation's future, our children.

OUTCOME-BASED EDUCATION: WHAT IS IT?

Outcome-based education is "a comprehensive approach to teaching and learning and to instructional management that has its origin in mastery learning and competency-based education" (Bonaiuto, Davidson, Harmon, and Monteith, 1991, p. 3). It is a strategy for realizing the mission of a school district whose curriculum and programs emphasize the intellectual, social, physical, emotional, aesthetic, and moral growth of each student. The basic beliefs guiding a school district's approach to outcome-based education should be articulated in direct statements such as:

- Every child can learn.
- Success creates success.
- Schools control conditions of success (Johnson, Snyder, and Berry, 1989).

Outcome-based education is a dynamic system (see Figure 7.1) where learning goals, teaching techniques, instructional resources, and school

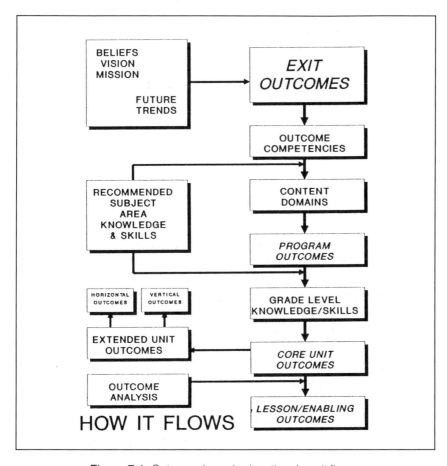

Figure 7.1. Outcome-based education: how it flows.

organizations interact to ensure successful learning for each student. It is a practical, results-centered approach to make sure that each student develops the knowledge, skills, and character traits necessary for life today and in the future. More specifically, students at every level are able to use reading, writing, speaking, listening, problem-solving, decision-making, and critical-thinking skills to continue to learn and to make personally appropriate decisions in daily life. The three guiding principles for outcome-based education, an individual-centered learning system, are:

(1) Outcome focus: Instructional organization and activity are designed in terms of precise, personally significant outcomes the student can demonstrate.

(2) Extended opportunity: Time and interaction with teacher and materials are flexibly designed to meet the specific learning requirements of each student.

(3) Success expectations: Each learner is expected to reach rigorous and developmentally appropriate performance standards (Johnson, Snyder, and Berry, 1989).

When school districts are guided by outcome-based principles, they are "success based" rather than "selection oriented."

Traditional vs. Outcome-Based Education

Traditional and outcome-based education paradigms differ in their applications and implications for education, and specifically language arts programs. Figure 7.2 presents a comparison of the basic principles between traditional and outcome-based education paradigms. The transition from the traditional educational paradigm to an outcome-based model requires attitudinal changes and strategic planning. We must avoid the mistake the Swiss made: paradigm paralysis.

Outcome-based education: the big picture, illustrated in Figure 7.3, presents a transparent approach for strategic planning. By identifying alternative futures, selecting the future of choice, and creating the future of choice, strategic planning for student exit outcomes will generate:

- a commitment to prepare students for future opportunities and challenges
- a commitment to change education

Traditional Model	Outcome-Based Model
• System is time driven	• System is performance driven
• Units measured in time	• Units measured by performance
• Calendar dictates curriculum structure	• Outcomes dictate curriculum structure
• Calendar drives advancement	• Performance drives advancement
• Emphasis is on *when* and *how* students learn	• Emphasis is on *what* and *why* students learn
• Outcomes are uncertain and undocumented	• Outcomes are determined and documented
• Comparative standards and results	• Criterion standards and results
• Cover the curriculum	• Teach for competency
• Focus on activities	• Focus on ultimate outcomes
• Grading and averaging of grades	• Evaluating outcome of significance

Figure 7.2. Comparison of traditional and outcome-based education. Source: Baron, M. A. 1992. *Strategic Planning for Outcome-Based Education*. Vermillion, SD: University of South Dakota, p. 55.

- a commitment to base all decisions on student exit outcomes that are life-role based and futuristic
- a process for determining the future of individual choice
- a process for involving all ''stakeholders'' in the creation of a school district focus
- a process that will create beliefs, a school district vision, a school district mission, and student exit outcomes

A strategic planning process for an outcome-based education curriculum will eradicate the ''quick fix'' or ''textbook'' approach to curriculum development. To have a balanced and comprehensive language arts instruction program, broad-based support and involvement are required from the internal and external publics. Strategic planning for curriculum development to include exit outcomes for students involves a paradigm shift. It is a change to a new game with a new set of rules. In a sense, the new paradigm, ''tells you that there is a game, what the game is, and how to play it successfully'' (Barker, 1992, p. 37).

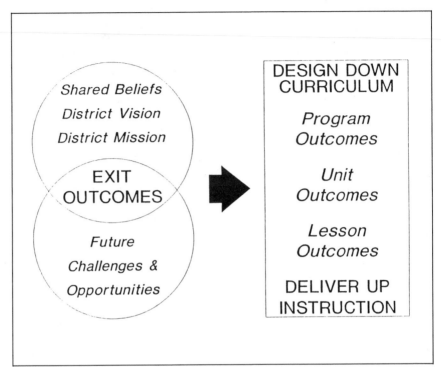

Figure 7.3. Outcome-based education: the big picture.

Exemplary Outcome-Based Education Models

The Johnson City Central School District, Johnson City, New York, was honored nationally twice in a five-year period for its exemplary outcome-based instructional program and commitment to success for all students and staff. The American Association of School Administrators presented the ''Leadership for Learning Award'' to the superintendent in 1982 and the U.S. Department of Education's National Diffusion Network designated the district's entire K−8 program exemplary in all subject areas in 1985. The awards were based on the following results:

(1) At least 50 percent of the sixth graders finished at least the first half of Algebra I, and some students completed quadratic equations—their designated ending to Algebra I content.
(2) About 60 percent of the sixth graders hit the top of the Metropolitan Achievement Test for pre-algebra mathematics.

(3) At least 30 percent of the fifth graders hit the top of the same test.

(4) No more than two students in the entire school of about 420 failed to reach grade level on the Metropolitan, and this included all of the school's mildly handicapped students.

(5) (During) a typical year, the lowest scoring sixth grader scored 6.3 and the lowest scoring fifth grader scored 5.9 on the Metropolitan. (Spady, 1986, p. 53)

Outstanding success was also experienced in the North Sanpete School District in Utah where both the primary and middle school children averaged a gain of over seventeen months on the California Achievement Test in the very first year of implementation. Districts using the outcome-based education model report similar, dramatic gains for their students (Spady, 1986).

OUTCOME-BASED EDUCATION CURRICULUM DEVELOPMENT

The guidelines to follow for developing and implementing an outcome-based curriculum require strategic planning, changes in attitudes, changes in structure, and changes in expectations for school board members, school administrators, teachers, students, staff, parents, and members of the community. Outcome-based education encompasses interacting structural elements that are presented in this chapter.

Mission Statement and Philosophy

Outcome-based education is the overall strategy for realizing the mission of a school district. A mission statement should be driven by a school district's philosophy, which includes statements about the learner, the school staff, the parent, and the community.

An example of a mission statement is "Lifelong Learning for All." Philosophy statements regarding the learner might be:

- We believe that each student must have successful experiences in order to develop positive attitudes and approaches to learning.
- We believe that each student needs to become an increasingly effective citizen of the home, the school, the community, the nation, and the world.

For each category, six or eight philosophy statements should be developed. Regarding the school staff, these philosophy statements could include:

- We believe that each school staff member affects the individual learner's motivation, growth, and success.
- We believe that the probability of learning increases when each school staff member uses varied learning plans that provide for the unique learning styles of individual learners, the individual learner's rate of learning, and active individual participation in learning.

Philosophy statements centering on the parent might be:

- We believe that the parent has fundamental responsibilities for education of the child. This requires that the parent be fully informed about the child's learning.
- We believe that the parent is responsible for a home environment in which the importance of learning is emphasized.

A few sample philosophy statements centering on the community are:

- We believe that the community has the responsibility to provide for the learning needs of all.
- We believe that the community should work with the schools and all other public and private, formal and informal community agencies to provide for the growth needs of citizens of all ages.

Student Exit Outcomes

Student exit outcomes[8] consist of knowledge, skills, and attitudes that a school district expects *all* students to demonstrate upon graduation. The student exit outcomes should be driven by trends and shifts in society, future conditions, and the school district's mission. The criteria to consider in developing student exit outcomes are as follows:

(1) General statements (about five to ten in total)
(2) High-powered action verbs (see Figure 7.4)

[8]The mission statement, belief statements, and exit statements were excerpted from curriculum materials supplied by the Rochester Public Schools, Independent School District No. 535, Rochester, Minnesota. Thanks are extended to Dr. R. Berry, Director of Instructional Programs, for his cooperation.

CATEGORIES	CUE WORDS			
KNOWLEDGE *Recall* Remembering previously learned information	acquire abbreviate alphabetize circle copy define	describe find identify label list locate	mark match note omit place print	recite search sort spell state
COMPREHENSION *Translate* Grasping the meaning	add arrange balance calculate chart classify	compare convert diagram divide estimate explain	express indicate interpret manipulate measure operate	recognize separate subtract suggest trace
APPLICATION *Generalize* Using learning in new and concrete situations	apply change collect compute construct demonstrate	differentiate discuss dramatize draw graph induce	infer make predict present produce question	react respond solve structure translate

Figure 7.4. Taxonomy of thinking.

(continued)

CATEGORIES	CUE WORDS			
ANALYSIS *Break Down/Discover* Breaking down an idea into component parts so that it may be more easily understood	analyze categorize conduct convert determine	dissect itemize outline rearrange reconstruct	rename rephrase retell review revise	select simplify specify tabulate transfer
SYNTHESIS *Compose* Putting together to form a new whole	alter combine and organize compile compose design	develop discover extrapolate formulate generate imagine	integrate organize paraphrase propose prove reproduce	role-play systematize verify

EVALUATION
Judge
Judging value for a given purpose
	agree or disagree
	appraise
	compare and
	  contrast
	conclude
	criticize
		critique
		decide
		defend
		discriminate
		document
		editorialize
			evaluate
			expose beliefs
			express an
			  opinion
			make a
			  decision
				make a
				  judgment
				recommend
				summarize
				supply evidence
				take a stand

Figure 7.4 (continued). Taxonomy of thinking.

(3) Product orientation (relate to ends, not means)
(4) Capacity to impact all students, staff, and instruction
(5) Create common purpose
(6) Future orientation
(7) Life-role focus

Sample Student Exit Outcomes

Student exit outcomes, such as the following, set the direction for identifying learning outcomes and selecting learning experiences.

- Demonstrate the skills and processes required for effective communication, problem solving, decision making, and computation.
- Develop objectives, methods, and creative alternatives for achieving personal and group learning goals.

Note: The two exit outcomes listed are examples of the five to ten needed for "student exit outcomes."

Language Arts Philosophy, Program Outcomes, and Objectives

To develop an outcome-based language arts curriculum, the language arts philosophy statement must do the following.

- Include a well-written philosophy statement.
- Incorporate student exit outcome competencies into the curriculum for each subject area.
- Indicate the profile of a student having completed the K − 12 subject area curriculum.
- Address subject area content for identifying more specific unit and lesson outcomes for grades K − 12.

Sample Language Arts Philosophy Statement

The following is an example of a language arts curriculum philosophy statement:

Learning is a complex process of discovery, cooperation, and inquiry; language facilitates this process. Language processes of reading, listening, speaking, writing, viewing, and representing are interrelated and interdependent. Language is not only systematic and rule governed, but also dynamic and evolving, facilitating communication with others and flexibility of meaning. Through interaction with the social, cultural, intellectual, emotional, and physical aspects of the environment, the learner acquires language developmentally along a continuum.

Language learning thrives when the learner engages in meaningful use of the language. The learner's attitudes influence the process of constructing meaning, previous knowledge, experiences, and abilities. All forms of communication, both oral and written, expressive and receptive, are equally valuable. The language arts curriculum utilizes an integrated approach which treats skills as part of processes, processes as part of communication, and communication as part of all subject areas. Through the study of language, literature, and media, the student broadens experiences, weighs personal values against those of others, becomes appreciative of the past, sensitive to the present, and inquisitive about the future.

The language arts curriculum accommodates the learner's interests, abilities, and background by allowing for a range of learning styles, teaching styles, instructional strategies, and resources. The curriculum supports a classroom environment that encourages mutual respect, risk-taking, and experimentation. Effective evaluation is an integral part of the learning process. Continual evaluation that encompasses both process and product and both cognitive and affective domains allows the learner to take ownership of and responsibility for learning. The learner is already processing information and constructing meaning when formal schooling begins and continues to refine the processes of communication throughout the years of formal education and beyond.

A well-written philosophy will give explicit direction for developing program outcomes. It should precede the development of program outcomes.[9]

Sample Language Arts Program Outcomes (Primary Grades)

Program outcomes should consist of five to ten goals identifying how each subject area contributes to realizing "exit outcomes." A sampling of the primary grades' program goals, objectives, and learning objec-

[9]The language arts philosophy, program goals, and objectives were excerpted from the *Language Arts English Primary—Graduation Curriculum Guide,* Ministry of Education, Province of British Columbia, Victoria, BC, Canada.

tives (outcomes) needed for the language arts curriculum and common to primary grades through high school are presented. The objectives, which constitute the program goals, are given specific implementation direction at the proposed groupings of primary, intermediate, middle school, and high school (see Figure 7.5).

P I MS HS	Indicates the proposed program groupings: primary, intermediate, middle school, and high school.
O	Indicates orientation stage: preparatory activities are undertaken prior to the explicit teaching and learning activities suggested in the learning outcomes related to the objective. Refer to learning outcomes at the next appropriate stage.
E	Indicates an emphasis stage: learning outcomes are suggested at each emphasis stage. Learning outcomes are provided in this curriculum guide as examples of appropriate activities and observable behaviors. Explicit teaching and learning activities are expected.
M	Indicates maintenance stage: provisions are made to reinforce learning outcomes related to the objective.
Program Goal #1:	To develop knowledge, skills, and processes needed to communicate effectively by reading, listening, speaking, viewing, and representing

Note: Approximately five to ten program goals should be stated for the language arts curriculum.

Sample Objectives		P	I	MS	HS
1.1	To develop the student's ability to set and identify purposes for communicating	E	E	E	E
1.2	To develop the student's ability to understand that the communication skills and processes are interrelated avenues for constructing meaning	E	E	M	M

Note: Approximately three to six objectives should be stated for the language arts curriculum.

Figure 7.5. Matrix for the objectives.

Sample Learning Objectives (Outcomes)

At least eight learning objectives should be stated to address each objective in the language arts curriculum. For example, the student may demonstrate increasing ability by:

(1) Choosing to read for a variety of purposes (for example: for enjoyment, to find new information, to confirm ideas)
(2) Applying knowledge acquired by reading, listening, or viewing (for example: taking the role of a story character in a drama presentation after listening to a story)

Sample activities to implement the first objective might include:

- Use the interest inventory to select books of each student's choice (students will learn how to read by reading).
- Have students become familiar with and use the library.
- Have students find references to help clarify what they are learning.

Sample activities to implement the second objective might include: "Students will act out the story of *The Three Bears*."

It is important to develop assessments for learner outcomes to ensure that the objectives are achieved.

A sample assessment for the first objective above could be: "Students will illustrate or retell their favorite story." While for the second objective a good assessment would be child watching (i.e., observation).

Proper resources are critical, especially if the aim is to develop a lifelong love of reading.

Sample resources for the first objective include big books, little books, paperbacks, fairy stories, cowboy stories, mysteries, poems, poetry books, nursery rhymes, encyclopedias, trade books, basal readers, and the library.

Sample resources for the second objective include materials and supplies necessary for students to use for drama.

Sooner or later, a decision must be made on how important it is for *all* students to learn what it is we want them to learn. Many educational systems today operate much as they did when the purpose was not to educate all children but merely some of them. The transformation in education must shift from covering the textbook materials to teaching children.

The shifts in perspective and practice outlined in this chapter for educational change can be evolutionary. It will take time and actual results will be determined by the people involved—school administrators, school board members, teachers, students, staff, parents, and citizens in each community. The hope is that new understandings about education will develop and emerging needs will be identified. "Our greatest contribution is to be sure there is a teacher in every classroom who cares that every student, every day, learns and grows and feels like a real human being" (Selection Research, Inc.).

REFERENCES

Barker, J. A. 1992. *Future Edge*. New York, NY: William Morrow and Company, Inc.

Baron, M. A. 1992. *Strategic Planning for Outcome-Based Education*. Vermillion, SD: University of South Dakota, p. 55.

Bonaiuto, W., L. Davidson, J. Harmon, and B. Monteith. 1991. *Outcome-Based Education*. Mitchell, SD: South Dakota Association for Supervision and Curriculum Development.

Hodgkinson, H. 1991. *Beyond Schools: How Schools and Communities Must Collaborate to Solve the Problems Facing America's Youth*. Arlington, VA: The American Association for School Administrators and the National School Boards Association.

Johnson, V., G. Snyder, and R. Beery. 1989. *Learning through Outcome-Based Education in the Rochester Public Schools*, a district document. Rochester, MN: The Rochester Public Schools, Independent School District No. 535.

Lucas, J. 1992. "Turn Off TV; Do More Reading, Alexander Urges," *Leadership News*, 102:1−2.

Selection Research, Inc. "Our Greatest Contribution," a greeting card. Lincoln, NE: SRI Gallup.

Spady, W. G. 1986. "The Emerging Paradigm of Organizational Excellence: Success through Planned Adaptability," *Peabody Journal of Education*, 63(3):53.

CHAPTER EIGHT

Developing Successful Public Relations Strategies

"The true wealth of a country lies in its men and women.
If they're mean, unhappy, and ill, the country is poor."

RICHARD ADDINGTON

As you read and study:

. . . Consider the impact public relations can have on a school reading program.

. . . Determine the role of an elementary school principal in developing a public relations program for reading.

. . . Compose a public relations plan to strengthen a reading program.

. . . Summarize the importance of internal and external groups for a sound public relations program in reading.

. . . Establish criteria that should be used to assess a public relations program for reading.

This chapter highlights the importance of public relations (PR) skills, which are a necessary component in promoting successful reading programs. Interestingly enough, administrators are usually aware of how important public relations skills are, but rarely use them. Many building administrators are not knowledgeable about the "how to's" of public relations in education. They need to know how to sell their successful reading program to teachers, parents, board members, and the general public. They also need to know how to keep the public informed about new developments in reading such as grouping through technology, alternative assessment techniques, and literature-based in-

183

struction. In addition, administrators need to know how to deal with negative issues. They need to be able to take negative situations and turn them into positive ones. In a nutshell, administrators need to know how to make sure that everyone understands and supports the reading and language arts program (Conners, 1988).

Making sure everyone understands and supports the reading program means that administrators are going to have to become more effective communicators. Effective communication and good school-community relations should be based on farsighted goals and well-planned strategies. As a result, you might develop some strategies in determining how well your school is doing in public relations. For example, let's say that you, as the building administrator, begin asking questions about your reading program from a school-community standpoint. During your investigation, you

- determine that you have an excellent reading program, but no one knows about it
- notice that some teachers are hesitant in having parent-aide volunteers in their classrooms
- find that only 60 percent or less of the community's parents are attending parent-teacher conferences
- want to pass a mill levy or building reserve, but suspect that the voters will vote it down
- discover that an opportunity for a media event was missed because the local newspaper or television reporter became lost while trying to locate your school

Many administrators miss out on great opportunities to promote their staffs and successful reading programs because they are too busy with other problems such as student discipline, staff conflicts, parent concerns, budget, and evaluations to think about PR opportunities. Even though administrators are rightfully concerned with these problems, it is critical that administrators also develop a public relations program to share information with the community. Formulating a public relations program is a key to becoming an effective administrator in reading.

The initial step to develop a public relations program in reading is to ask the following questions.

- What is the role of the building administrator in public relations, and how does that role apply to reading?
- Why do we need to promote public relations in the field of reading?

- What key components make up the public relations process?
- What are some specific communication strategies administrators can use?
- Where should we go from here?

ADMINISTRATIVE ROLE IN PUBLIC RELATIONS

A review of the literature reveals a consensus that the role of the principal has a major impact on a school's reading program and student achievement. Being leaders, administrators hold a major role in public relations. Effective administrators are dynamic and creative in their communications with others. According to Calabrese (1991), effective principals and supervisors are committed to excellence. They have demonstrated a high level of involvement in community work, staff development, instructional supervision, and climate improvement. They are personally committed to reading and to communicating with the public.

The effectiveness of administrators in reading comes as no surprise. Coleman et al. (1966), and later Edmonds and Fredrickson (1983), found that successful schools with high reading rates have strong administrative leadership. According to both studies, effective principals and supervisors

- provide clear goals and objectives
- develop high expectations for children
- exercise control and effective decision making
- provide adequate materials and resources
- monitor assessment of student progress

Most recently, the role of administrators in reading is best exemplified by a study conducted by Crane (1989, p. 38), who writes, "A review of the literature reflects a consensus that the role of the principal has a major impact on a school reading program and student achievement." Principals and supervisors are realizing that their roles are broadening. Specifically, they are finding that their expertise should include a wide range of public relations skills.

As a result, the instructional leader of the 1990s is becoming the image maker of the twenty-first century. Roles of administrators in public relations are only limited by the creativity of the administrators; as such, the many roles are too numerous to cover in this chapter. We have, however, provided examples below of some of the more common PR roles found among effective principals and supervisors today.

- developing a sense of what the public needs to hear, being able to write journalistically, and knowing how to deal with the press
- developing a public relations advisory board to address reading curriculum issues
- responding to local and state legislation as it relates to reading
- improving administrative and staff relations as well as increasing staff morale
- preparing communications vehicles, e.g., newsletters and brochures, to inform the public about changes in reading curriculum
- developing school and business partnerships as they relate to reading

The list of administrative roles in public relations is endless. In fact, the demand on any administrator's time is endless. The days of the principal sitting endlessly in the teachers' lounge drinking coffee are over. As noted in Figure 8.1, the average work week of an elementary school principal is 47.5 hours.

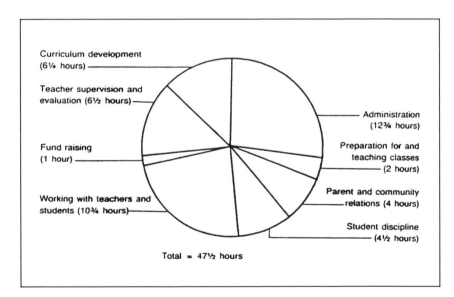

Figure 8.1. Average work week of elementary school principals, by major activity area: 1987–88. Source: Snyder, T. D. 1990. "Trends in Education," *Principal*, 70(1):7. Reproduced by permission.

Time spent on parent and community relations, according to Snyder (1990), is only four hours. Administrators are therefore limited in what they can and cannot achieve. The key is to enlist the help of everyone in the PR process. Everyone benefits when community and staff are fully informed about successful reading programs and activities.

[Macauley], in his book, *America and Its Discontents,* addresses the importance of public relations by stating that "it's folly to look at education reform and look only at the school. You have to look at the whole educational ecology" (Decker and Schoeny, 1992, p. 17). In this day and age, with schools encountering numerous problems, administrators have found that a little PR goes a long way, especially when everyone is included.

PROMOTING PUBLIC RELATIONS AND READING

Schools are in trouble. After eighteen months of hearings, debates, and study, the National Commission on Excellence in Education found little excellence in our nation's schools (Hill, 1990). The Commission's report indicates that societal changes are influencing our schools. Many factors have had an impact on reading achievement in schools. For example, alterations in our school populations affect overall achievement records. By the year 2000, minority students and non-English speaking students will make up 39 percent of our school-age population (Lincoln and Higgins, 1991). In addition, children from broken homes are becoming more prevalent, and poverty is on the rise. In our sluggish economy, many schools are underfunded and understaffed. Because changes in reading programs have not been implemented to meet the needs of a changing school population, reading achievement levels have suffered.

One reason for the unsuccessful implementation is a lack of community support. According to Seeley (1990a), reading reform movements of the past were often based on educational ideas that did not necessarily have widespread support. This has created a "pressure cooker" for principals and supervisors alike.

Administrators should respond to pressure cooker-type problems in education by

- reassessing what principals and supervisors can do to help promote their reading programs

- creating and implementing strategic public relations plans for our schools
- establishing professional relationships with businesses
- learning to handle conflict and criticism
- building trust
- establishing clear and open communications with parents and community members
- responding to reform by creating, adopting, and implementing sound board policies on public relations and expanding how they relate to reading

School reform, however, has been slow and not everyone has been pleased with its progress. The Commission on Excellence report found our nation ''at risk'' but said little or nothing about the thousands of successful schools in the United States.

As a result, many administrators are developing public relations programs as a method of self-protection. The idea is not to avoid bad news, but to do just the opposite—address the problems and talk about the success stories in education. Recognition must be given to schools with successful reading programs. Good PR programs will highlight schools with high success rates in student achievement, develop new approaches to reading and instruction, and begin the process of change.

THE PUBLIC RELATIONS PROCESS

School and community communication problems and a lack of PR planning have been well documented. For example, Figure 8.2 shows the results of a National Gallop Poll taken in 1970 that addressed the question: ''During the past year, have you received any newsletter, pamphlet, or any other material telling what the schools are doing?''

According to Walker (1983), the poll indicates that a significant problem in community-school communication existed in the 1970s. Very little communication in the way of newsletters or pamphlets was coming from the school, as noted by the 61 percent negative response nationally. School and community communication problems continued through the 1980s (Criscuolo, 1985) and are evident today (Dietz, 1990).

Researchers are working to rectify the problem. Armistead (1989) believes that public relations programs should emphasize planning,

Question: During the past year have you received any newsletter, pamphlet, or any other material telling what the schools are doing?
Gallup Poll—1969   ( ) Yes   ( ) No   ( ) Can't Recall

National Gallup Poll (1970)

	National Totals	Public School Parents	No Children in Schools
	%	%	%
Yes	35	57	16
No	61	39	81
Can't Recall	4	4	3

Figure 8.2. Communication by school to residents. Source: Adapted from Walker, J. E. 1983. "Polls of Public Attitudes Toward Education—How Much Help to Principals?" *NASSP Bulletin*, 67(459):30.

research, communication, and evaluation. These components are not necessary in every project, but do reflect a step-by-step process. Let's take a closer look at each of these steps and at how they relate to an effective public relations program that has been successful in many schools across the United States.

PUBLIC RELATIONS PLAN

Successful administrators include key ingredients in their PR planning document. Psencik (1991) states that a PR plan should include a mission statement, research, internal and external analysis, objectives and strategies, and action plans as shown in Figure 8.3.

Psencik's model helps provide a guideline for administrators wishing to review and update their current PR program. Following is a sample sketch of this planning process.

Mission Statement

A PR advisory board, consisting of administrators, teachers, parents, and community members, brainstorms to clarify its goals in order to

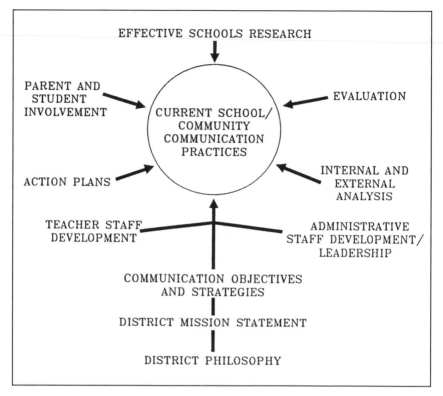

Figure 8.3. Communications model. Source: Developed from concept noted in article by Psencik, K. 1991. "Site Planning in Strategic Context in Temple, Texas," *Educational Leadership*, 48:29–31. Reproduced by permission.

develop a philosophy and a mission statement. The philosophy should reveal a general understanding of the beliefs, concepts, and attitudes of the group for a PR reading program. A mission statement must clearly address the need to increase school-community relations. For instance, a declaration stating ''The entire community will be informed about all aspects of the reading program'' adequately addresses this need.

Internal and External Analysis

Internal and external analysis involves viewing variables from both a school (internal) or community (external) based position. The PR advisory board discusses both school and community strengths and weaknesses. For example, the PR advisory board should address the basic delineations of educational responsibilities as they relate to reading and language arts on the part of students, parents, educators, and the public. Responsibilities can be categorized as seen in Figure 8.4. In addition, the PR advisory board can address demographic, political, socioeconomical, and educational trends as well.

Objectives and Strategies

After its analysis, the PR advisory board develops objectives and strategies, which should relate back to the philosophy and mission

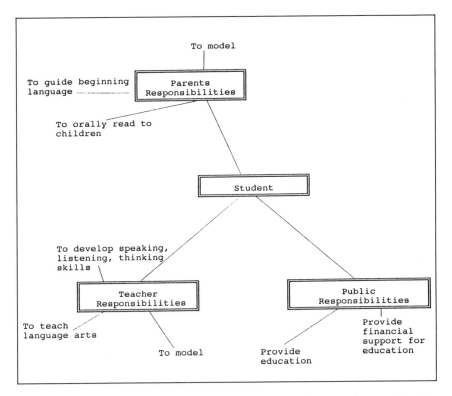

Figure 8.4. Educational responsibilities of parents, teachers, and general public as they apply to student development in the area of language arts.

statement, to improve school-community relations. A possible objective might stress the need to develop a newsletter about the reading and language arts program.

Action Plans

Following the development of philosophy, mission statement, and objectives, an action team composed of both members of the original PR advisory board and of new participants is selected to address each strategy. This team later reports back to the original board regarding the completion and success of specific objectives.

An action committee assigned to develop a strategy for creating a newsletter begins by drawing a set of guidelines for the letter. Topics are then researched, and data is collected. Next, calendar deadlines are set, assignments are made, and materials and resources are acquired. After a galley proof with a layout is made, revisions and adjustments are addressed, and the newsletter goes to print. Following printing, the newsletter is distributed to target groups.

PR plans, such as the one outlined above, allow administrators to anticipate problems. As a result, both principals and supervisors begin to research and to think through problems in strategic ways. PR planning works.

Research

Research is one key to the public relations process; however, this component is rarely used. To be effective, top administrators need to target messages for specific audiences (Armistead, 1989). This means having access to research data without requiring professional researchers. Many effective administrators can find accessible research data right in their own schools. Data simply needs to be collected, organized, and clearly presented (Tankard, 1974). A partial list of local data sources might include

- former publications of the school district
- test scores
- high school and college dropout statistics
- superintendent and principal reports
- special education and Chapter 1 reports
- official student records

- former single purpose surveys and opinions
- interviews with staff members
- interviews with parents and students

A partial list of nonschool data resources might include

- state departments of education and other state agencies
- U.S. Department of Education and other federal agencies
- community and business leaders
- area resource councils
- universities
- professional organizations, such as the International Reading Association

Data sources such as those listed above provide administrators with quality information. For example, let's assume that an administrator reviews a single purpose survey on student reading achievement and finds

- an analysis of reading achievement test scores revealing students who are making two-year gains in nine months
- teachers on staff who have been using new strategies such as Cooperative Learning, Writing Across the Curriculum, Telecommunications, and/or Teaching and Learning with Computers (TLC)
- a new computer lab using Writing to Read software is helping children achieve big gains in the first grade
- a specific staff member who has been recognized by the International Reading Association for his or her work in reading
- several teachers on staff who have discovered a new vocabulary game and wish to share it with the staff
- students who have indicated a desire to participate in the local Young Authors' Conference

Special projects, such as the Young Authors' Conference, can provide a wealth of data about students, curriculum, and schools. Materials displayed reveal writing abilities, understanding, special skills, as well as creative and artistic talents of teachers and children. Administrators who want to develop projects such as the Young Authors' Conference need to work collaboratively with reading and language arts teachers to formulate a management plan for program implementation. Administrators can be especially helpful because of their knowledge of

End Result:	Children from district schools submit student novels, stories, and poetry to be displayed on tables during a day long Young Authors' Conference.
Facilities:	Gymnasium, auditorium, or lunchroom is scheduled.
Activities:	Book and literature displays, speakers, and writing sectionals are established.

Figure 8.5. Young Authors' Conference plan.

programming techniques. Administrators and teachers have worked cooperatively to develop Young Authors' Conferences that draw thousands of student entries each year.

A Young Authors' Conference plan and planning schedule are illustrated in Figures 8.5 and 8.6. Innovative public relations projects such as the Young Authors' Conference not only provide administrators with information about their schools, but also provide a plethora of ideas for newspaper articles, television stories, and newsletters. Yet, administrators and PR advisory groups have to set priorities as to what should be highlighted in public relations projects. As a result, administrators planning a public relations project should address the following questions:

- Is the project exemplary?
- Is the project unique to school and community?

December:	Leadership, site selection, and specific calendar date(s) are established.
January:	Administrative approval is acquired and contact persons are selected. Speaker and sectional presenters are scheduled. Layout and specific details are approved by the committee.
February:	Information packet is given to teachers and prepublicity is given to parents. Students begin making books and displays.
March:	Final preparations are made. Radio, television, and newspapers are notified.
April:	Young Authors' Conference is implemented. Committee meets to evaluate and replan for next year.

Figure 8.6. Young Authors' Conference planning schedule.

- What aspects of the project can be easily identified?
- Is the project timely?
- Are financial resources available for the project?
- Is there enough time to complete the project?
- Does commitment exist on the part of staff and community to complete the project?
- Is the project administratively manageable?

Administrators can use information gained from the above questions to determine the scope of the PR plan and to formulate effective communication strategies.

Communication Strategies

The strength of any PR program lies with effective communication strategies, sometimes referred to as PR survival skills. They are crucial in improving school climate as well as in promoting success in reading. Effective administrators must relate their communication skills and techniques to the basic tenets of public relations (Conners, 1988): proximity, timeliness, prominent people, dramatic events, and ease of reporting.

Proximity

Proximity often determines how PR messages are received by parents and community members. Articles involving national schools are usually not as popular as stories involving the local school or community. For example, parents and community members are more interested in finding out about a local telecommunications program at the school than reading about one in a national magazine.

Timeliness

Timeliness can make the difference in successful PR programs. Newspapers, radio, and television do not want yesterday's news. When promoting an event, administrators must always remember a fundamental rule: ''Publicize an event before it happens and not after.'' Information about the new Reading Recovery program coming out of New Zealand is much more interesting than information about a phonics program.

Prominent People

Prominent people usually attract reporters. If administrators really want to get their stories in the newspaper or on TV, they should invite someone ''important'' to their school. Sports figures, politicians, and authors are good choices. For example, one school invited children's writer Betsy Byars, author of *The Summer of the Swans,* to share her experiences in writing with students. The event was a media success, with television and newspaper coverage. When special people are not available due to distances, satellite downlink operations can also prove useful in providing students access to special personalities. In all cases of providing special presenters, administrators should contact the media early because editorial decisions on story selection must be made as soon as possible.

Dramatic Events

Dramatic events often generate '' media play.'' The more controversial the stories, the greater the chance of having reporters arrive at schools. For example, if a school large-purchased a great number of computers, reporters might be more inclined to visit. This is especially true if several community members have been vocal about the amount of money spent on technology. For example, Seven Oaks School in Lacey, Washington has developed a model Teaching and Learning with Computers program (TLC). The TLC approach emphasizes the use of computers in the classroom in an integrated unit approach rather than in a traditional lab setting. Early in the development of the TLC program at Seven Oaks School, there was some skepticism as to the success of the program. With effective planning and a positive communication program on the part of administration and staff, the Seven Oaks School is now a nationally recognized TLC demonstration site and a leader in computerized education.

If the situation is extremely controversial, which is often the case, administrators should try to put a positive edge on the situation. This is particularly important when dealing with the press. The best policy is to say as little as possible, to be honest, and to hope that community members and news reporters hear ''what you thought you said.'' If in doubt, administrators should write out a statement and give it to media representatives.

Ease of Reporting

Ease of reporting can be a factor in the success of public relations. When media people are under the gun, they become increasingly selective about stories. For example, becoming aware of "the time of day" in which reporters like to cover a story is important. Newspaper reporters sometimes meet with editors in the morning and thus prefer to cover stories in the afternoon or evening if possible. Television reporters have a real "crunch time" just before the evening and late news. They often prefer stories earlier in the day, which allows more set-up time in the afternoon or evening. If administrators are out of sync with reporters and their time frames, they are not likely to get their story in the media. In addition, administrators can make reporters' lives a whole lot easier, and increase the chance of coverage, if they submit written information to the media about the event. Typing and double spacing information is very helpful. This allows reporters a chance to check details they might have missed.

When dealing with newspapers, administrators should ask editors to send a photographer because pictures are better remembered by the general public. In addition, the editor is more likely to print the story due to the expense of the film shot on the project.

An important step in effective communication is to identify target groups—either internal or external. Internal target groups include individuals directly associated with the school such as administrators, teachers, staff, board members, and students. External groups consist of individuals outside school such as parents, business and community leaders, and the general public.

COMMUNICATION STRATEGIES FOR INTERNAL GROUPS

Classroom Teachers

According to Conners (1988), high school teachers have the ability to reach 160 (or more) sets of parents and children per day. Primary teachers see fewer students and parents per day, but usually have closer communication ties with both (Dietz, 1990). Classroom teachers' relationships with students and with parents is a key to school-community relations.

An old saying applies: "If classroom teachers are happy, students are happy. And if students are happy, parents are happy. And if parents are happy, school board members are happy. And if school board members are happy, superintendents and principals are happy." The "bottom line" is that if teachers are happy, everyone is happy. This may sound too simple, but it works.

Some educators believe that raising salaries will increase teacher morale. This may be a possibility, but few principals and supervisors are able to address this issue. Other educators believe that fostering pride in schools and providing teacher recognition will help increase staff morale (Wherry, 1986). If the latter is true, then administrators are going to have to focus on motivational approaches.

The following motivational strategies are utilized by administrators wanting to become more effective instructional leaders as they learn how to increase staff morale. All of the strategies listed below have been successfully used by the authors as administrators in actual school settings—they do work.

Improving Communication through Instructional Leadership

As instructional leaders, administrators can improve communication with classroom teachers by doing the following.

- Become knowledgeable about reading programs in your schools. (Administrators need to observe reading classes and to stay current by reviewing professional journals such as *Reading Improvement, Reading Today,* and *The Journal of Reading.*)
- Utilize clinical supervision approaches for teacher improvement in reading. (Administrators need to know the difference between clinical supervision and formal evaluation. Many teachers need supervision via guidance, knowledge, and understanding, rather than just a formal evaluation.)
- Work to keep schools small, enabling administrators to know all of the children by name and many of the parents as well. An ideal size for elementary and middle schools is 450 or less; high schools should be capped at 1,500. (As shown in Figure 8.7, many elementary schools in large urban communities have 500 children or more.)
- Offer to teach reading classes or to read stories or poems to children. (Most students, including high school students, enjoy

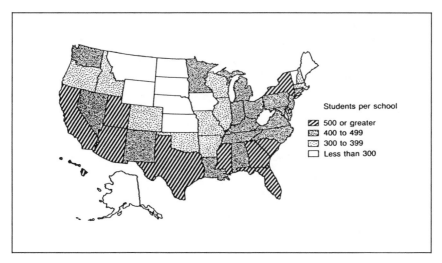

Students per school

- 500 or greater
- 400 to 499
- 300 to 399
- Less than 300

Figure 8.7. Average number of students in public elementary schools: 1988–89. Source: Snyder, T. D. 1990. "Trends in Education," *Principal*, 70(1):8. Reproduced by permission.

working with an administrator. A little time taken by an administrator in reading to a few students pays big dividends.)

- Work to maintain class size at twenty or less at the primary level, regardless of economics. (The state of Montana is one of the few states to set a limit on class size at twenty in the primary grades.)
- Minimize duties as much as possible, allowing teachers more planning time in reading. (Teachers are afforded very little planning time during the day and many times duties intervene in what little planning time is available. Administrators are going to have an easier time doing their jobs when teachers are well organized.)
- Involve teachers in school planning. (Teachers usually do have good suggestions if someone is listening. More ideas presented often means more options for administrators, if they are willing to take the risk and listen.)
- Act as a resource for materials and equipment used in reading. (Who better knows how to get their hands on money, equipment, or supplies when needed during "crunch time" than an administrator? When a problem with reading materials or resources surfaces, most administrators can get on the phone to other administrators and find out what is available—fast.)

- Set priorities in building-level budgets to assist classroom teachers with special reading projects. (Setting priorities simply means setting goals. Administrators are known to have a knack for finding money for those items that they feel are most important.)
- Provide early dismissals and/or specific days for teacher inservice in reading. (The best way to provide staff development is to provide opportunities for teachers and staff to view new ideas in reading and/or to provide the time for staff to develop and implement new ideas. Some schools have established an early student dismissal the second Tuesday of each month for staff development and inservice. This has allowed staff in reading and language arts to implement innovative practices such as cooperative teaching, talents unlimited, learning styles, literature-based instruction, writing across the curriculum, language experience, and writing to read.)
- Assist staff with organizing special reading programs. (Newspapers in Education, No Textbook Days, Young Author Week, and Reading Fairs are just a few of the many programs developed in schools with the assistance and coordination efforts of local administrators.)

Improving Staff Morale

Administrators can improve communication and increase staff morale in the following ways.

- Visit with teachers individually and informally about reading programs and/or about student needs. (Many administrators are now providing teacher goal sheets that are not part of the evaluation process. As a result, teachers feel more inclined to take risks and set higher professional goals in reading and language arts.)
- Acknowledge teachers' roles in developing successful reading programs, either verbally or publicly. (Much research exists revealing the importance of recognizing specific teachers for their contributions to their schools. A well-written note of thanks to a staff member for his or her work in reading generates a lot of positive feelings.)

- Create special packets to be given to substitutes, informing them about the school's unique reading program (see Figure 8.8). (Many administrators have developed simple handbooks for substitutes which can be updated each year. Substitutes can be a school's greatest public relations resource. Substitute teachers visit many other schools and talk with numerous individuals about their experiences—both positive and negative.)
- Recognize successful teachers of reading in daily memos or in monthly newsletters as shown in Figure 8.9. (Good administrators take advantage of every opportunity to highlight the achievements of their school and staff. When it comes to public relations, administrators should ''buy ink by the barrel.'')

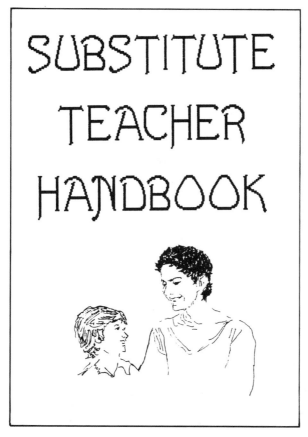

Figure 8.8. Cover of substitute teacher handbook.

SCHOOL DAYS

October 24, 1990

SPOOK AND GOBLIN TIME is nearly upon us once again. Please help keep our children safe by allowing them to "Trick or Treat" only in familiar neighborhoods, have an adult accompany them, have them wear reflective costumes or tape, be sure their vision is not obscured by masks (make-up is a great alternative and does not affect vision), they should carry plainly visible lights (no candles) after dark, and do not allow them to eat any treats until you have inspected them. We wish everyone a spooktacularly great evening that is just the cat's meee-ooow!!!

SETTING TRENDS

Teacher Noted in Publication

Mrs. Dunie Solander recently received news that her teaching activity "Wheel of Fortune" will be noted in an upcoming publication of the Mail Box. The Mail Box is a well known magazine for teachers published by the Education Center, Inc. of Greensboro, North Carolina. Mrs. Solander is a 2nd grade teacher at Hellgate Elementary. Congratulations Dunie!

Teachers Sing at Carnegie Hall

Candy Johnson and Judy Harvey had the honor of singing with their nationally recognized "Sweet Adelines" group at Carnegie Hall this past summer. Mrs. Johnson is widely recognized as a top director for "Sweet Adelines". Mrs. Johnson, our music and P.E. teacher, and Mrs. Harvey, a second grade teacher at Hellgate Elementary, have been singing with the "Sweet Adelines" for a number of years.

Fourth Grade Teacher President of Reading Council

Sue Rowe is currently President of the Five Valley's Reading Council. This is one of the largest and most prestigous reading councils in the state. Over 500 individuals from Western Montana attend the Five Valley's Reading Conference held each year at the University of Montana. This year's conference featured nationally recognized children's author, Betsy Byars. Mrs. Rowe will begin working toward her doctorate at the University of Montana this winter.

Figure 8.9. School newsletter highlighting teachers in reading.

- Promote leaves of absences, conferences, summer workshops, and professional libraries as illustrated in Figure 8.10. (The essence of good schools is innovation and a determination by the administration and staff to find the best way to teach students. Teachers, administrators, and board members who have an opportunity to attend special programs get exposed to new

material and new ideas that can add a new dimension to the
school to enrich the lives of children.)

Scheduling Total Staff Social Events

Administrators wanting to improve communication and increase staff
morale via staff meetings and social events can

- Have an "Open House and Back to School Night" to introduce
  new staff, to discuss new variations of the reading program, and
  to review new equipment. (Figure 8.11 illustrates an invitation
  to parents.)
- Provide optional continental breakfasts hosted by the school or
  social committee at which teachers can share titles of favorite
  books or discuss reading ideas. (A special Pancake Breakfast
  can be held to honor the contributions of the staff. The principal
  can be the cook.)
- Organize staff picnics based on reading themes. Administrators
  should try to hold picnics in appropriate settings that are
  convenient for spouses and fun for children. (Staff picnics can

Teachers and Principals Attend Major Reading Conference

Reading and Language Arts has also been in the spotlight. The k-5 elementary had the honor of having Beth Ray, Elaine Messmer, Pam Davy, Patty Peck, Gloria Melnikoff, Gretchen Jones, Mark Walton, and Bruce Whitehead attend the International Regional Reading Conference in Billings on October 8 and 9. This conference was the largest reading conference ever held in the State of Montana. Beth Ray, a fifth grade instructor, was one of the major organizers of this conference. Beth Ray and Bruce Whitehead, Principal of grades 1-5, were asked to present sectionals at this outstanding reading conference.

Figure 8.10. Newsletter article about reading teachers and the principal attending a reading conference.

Just A Reminder...

OPEN HOUSE
&
BACK TO SCHOOL NIGHT

WILL BE HELD ON
THURSDAY, SEPTEMBER 19, 1991
FROM 6:00 TO 8:00 P.M.

EVERYONE IS WELCOME!

Figure 8.11. Open house public notice.

be held in the evening, adjacent to a baseball park and basketball
courts. The picnic is a combination potluck with the
administration providing barbecued hamburgers and hotdogs.)

- Have short meetings after school, allowing staff to share new
  information about reading programs. (Inter- and intra-grade
  level meetings are organized to increase communication.)
- Organize cabinet meetings, before school or after school, to
  discuss any concerns that are not negotiable. All grade levels
  should be represented. Cabinet meetings provide good
  opportunities to discuss problems. (One staff member from each
  grade level provides representation, but any individual should be
  able to attend.)
- Develop optional Secret Pal programs. Teachers randomly
  choose secret pals and acknowledge them during special times
  such as birthdays. (Secret pals exchange novels, or works of
  literature, as well as other little gifts throughout the year. Most
  of the staff enjoy getting the boss as a secret pal.)
- Assist the PTA in providing special luncheons honoring reading
  teachers. (Luncheons are usually in conjunction with parent-
  teacher conferences.)
- Organize a potluck for Reading Awareness Week. The first ten
  minutes are used for a ''News Report,'' during which staff
  members report on positive or interesting ideas in reading. (It

can be used as a "Bring a Boss to Breakfast" format or used as a unique way of involving administrators in reading.)
- Develop an in-school task force committee whose purpose is to generate ideas regarding how the entire staff can help to promote reading. (Provides a way for parents to work with staff on reading issues.)

NONCERTIFIED STAFF MEMBERS

Successful administrators quickly learn the importance of noncertified staff. Day-to-day operations in the classroom would not run smoothly without the help of secretaries, clerks, custodians, and other support staff. A positive and enthusiastic secretary often sets the tone for the entire school. A cheerful custodian makes children feel secure and comfortable. There is no doubt that these individuals are a tremendous resource for our schools.

Utilizing Noncertified Staff

Administrators can best utilize noncertified staff in the following ways.
- Ensure that noncertified staff efforts do not go unnoticed. For instance, children can use reading and writing skills to make cards acknowledging positive contributions of these individuals. (A special day can be set aside to honor custodians. Students can make special cards acknowledging the contributions of the custodians to the school.)
- Encourage noncertified staff to share their special skills with students. For example, secretaries can share computer word processing skills with children in the classroom. (A school secretary discusses how one uses a computer and word processing in a clerical position. Students then write a paper on the importance of word processing in the office setting.)
- Have noncertified staff who have hobbies share their special interests with students in a reading classroom. (A custodian who also makes model airplanes can attend classrooms and discuss how to make and fly model airplanes. Children then read stories about airplanes and flight.)

- Organize a career day. Students could read about various careers of their choice. As part of career awareness, certain students can visit and work with specific school noncertified staff for a period of time. Journals or reports could be written about their experience. (Selected students visit the food service department, special education classrooms, and maintenance department and write about their experiences.)
- Acknowledge school staff in newsletters or at public gatherings. Students can write articles about the contributions of noncertified staff and submit them to the school paper. Student leaders can also provide staff with special awards during assemblies. (Students write an article about the many duties and responsibilities of the school clerk in the school newspaper.)

BOARD MEMBERS

Successful schools have positive and progressive school board members. Board members often reflect the political, economical, and social commitment of the community. Without their support, administrators will have a difficult time developing an effective public relations program. Board support is vital.

Board Member Communication

Communication with board members can be improved in a number of ways.

- Board members should be encouraged to attend the International Reading Association Conference. This conference, held around the country each year, provides board members with a positive experience about reading. (Board members receive no remuneration for their services, and thus feel more appreciated and knowledgeable when able to attend state and national meetings.)
- Board members should be encouraged to attend the National School Boards' Association Conference. (Board members are able to interact with other trustees who are supportive of reading. They are also able to compare notes on their school district with others around the country and usually come away impressed with the folks at home.)

- Administrators should continually make sure that board members are aware of successful activities in the reading program. Teachers and staff can give presentations to the school board. (School board members are invited into classrooms to work directly with students on computers. The kids love to "show off" and board members enjoy interacting with the youngsters.)
- Board members should be provided copies of all public relations communications. (Copies of all notices, newsletters, and other forms of communication can be given to board members each month as part of an informational packet.)

STUDENTS

How students feel and act sets the tone for a school. Students often communicate their feelings about teachers, administrators, and staff to their parents. Parents, in turn, communicate children's feelings directly to the teacher, the principal, and, if needed, to the superintendent or members of the school board. Principals and supervisors should be aware that problems can develop because of poor communication with students.

Student Communication

Successful administrators have learned to improve communication with students by doing the following.

- Keep an open door and allow students to discuss problems. (Utilizing a student council format allows students to develop a sense of ownership in the school.)
- Monitor reading groups to make sure that students are being challenged with appropriate reading material. (By having children read stories to the principal, students can receive a special certificate entitled *Principal Reading Award*. Figure 8.12 illustrates an award that can be given to students after reading with the principal.)

This program gives the principal a chance to do some checking on reading levels and student progress as well as provide some recognition to students.

Figure 8.12. Reading with the principal certificate.

- Stay current on new reading research that might improve student learning. (Subscribing to various reading journals, e.g., IRA publications, keeps administrators up to date on the latest in reading instructional techniques.)
- Reward students who excel in reading and language arts by giving honor passes to children making significant gains in reading. The passes provide freedom of movement within the building. (Students love them!)
- Reward students who excel or simply show extra effort in reading by allowing them to join the "Lunch with the Principal" program. (Figure 8.13 depicts a *Lunch with the Principal* certificate that can be given to students participating and usually wind up on the refrigerator door at home.)
- Support student council activities that are related to reading. For example, a class play can be supported financially by the student council. (Student councils can also support special speakers such as authors and illustrators when the regular budget is already "tapped out.")
- Support special minicourses or electives. (Minicourses allow

It's Time
for
LUNCH
with the
PRINCIPAL

Figure 8.13. Lunch with the principal certificate.

students to learn about specialty areas such as storytelling, drama, and writing. Special funds can be set aside for teachers incorporating minicourses within their curriculum.)

- Set up "Homework Clubs" as well as special "Homework Help Sessions for Parents" (see Figure 8.14). (Teachers can be encouraged to allow groups of students to stay in the classroom or library during recess, noontime, or after school for the purpose of studying. These groups can be labeled as clubs with the idea that all of the students in the group help each other with homework problems. Special sessions to help parents understand homework strategies can be scheduled through the PTA.)
- Encourage teachers to display stories and written work done by

---

"HOMEWORK HELP FOR PARENTS"
For Parents of Students Grades 5 through 8
* Monday, Oct. 15, at 7:15 P.M., Bldg. #1 Library
Presented by Mr. Terry Vanderpan, Principal
Parents need not register.

Figure 8.14. Homework help for parents program notice.

students. (Students' work can be displayed in hallways, display cases, or even in area businesses. Local banks take great pride in displaying student written work as well as art work in their lobbies.)

- Maintain open communications with parents. (Teachers need a time of the day when they can be easily accessible to parents via the phone or by personal visits. One-half hour before or after school should be set aside for this purpose. This time also gives teachers a time to talk to each other and share ideas about reading.)
- Encourage teachers to provide positive reinforcement. Students and parents enjoy having teachers call with positive news. (Some administrators use cordless phones to call parents ''on the spot'' when a child has finished a book or written a story. Kids love it!)

COMMUNICATION STRATEGIES FOR EXTERNAL GROUPS

Parents and the School

Parents are a critical component of the educational process. Children learn more and like school better if parents are part of the school process. According to Rasinski and Fredericks (1989), ''The research is clear: given proper guidance and support, parents can supplement, in powerful fashion, learning that takes place in the school.'' Durkin's (1966) studies also indicate that children who learned to read early had parents who played a role in the reading process. As a result of research, educators in reading are speaking out about the need to involve parents in education. With this in mind, administrators need to ask these questions: What are some ways that principals and supervisors can involve parents in reading; and how can administrators increase communication between home and school? The answers lie within the following communication strategies.

Involving Parents in School

Administrators can involve parents in school through many different methods.

- Develop a Parent-Aide Volunteer program (see Figure 8.15). The first step is selecting an enthusiastic parent and teacher willing to coordinate the program jointly. The parent coordinator organizes and administrates the program while the teacher acts as a liaison for the staff. (Some parent coordinators schedule a minimum of 100 parent-aide volunteers each year.)

- Encourage parents working in Parent-Aide Volunteer programs to be assigned to a grade level not occupied by their children. Some parents working with their children in classrooms can cause problems due to a lack of objectivity. Procedures for a successful program include encouraging parents to choose a level above their child's grade. This procedure enables parents to learn more about the reading process and curriculum and allows parents to become better able to assist their children for the coming year. This process also enables parents to develop a more positive attitude towards the school.

PARENT AID PROGRAM

Hellgate Elementary School is very fortunate to have a strong and visible Parent-Aide Program. It affords the teacher some much-appreciated help in the classroom and allows the parent a chance to see the educational process at work.

From the teacher's viewpoint, help in the classroom is always needed. It could be correcting papers, testing a new student, creating bulletin boards or working one-on-one with a student.

Sharon Thorson, Director of the program, and Mary Ruth Conley, School Coordinator, have seen the number of Parent-Aide volunteers increase to over 67 participants. According to Mrs. Thorson, the parents have enjoyed being a part of the school, and the children enjoy having their parents involved in the school process. She feels the program has been very rewarding to teachers, parents, and children.

If you are interested in participating in the program in the future, please contact the school principal, Mrs. Thorson, or Mrs. Conley. We are always pleased to have our parents participate in our school.

Figure 8.15. Newsletter article on parent-aide program.

- Set up an open house using the SWAP concept. Parents are able to swap places with students for a demonstration of a reading lesson. (Administrators should use caution in developing a SWAP program, because some parents feel insecure about being asked questions. Being aware of parent feelings can make the difference between a positive program or an ineffective one.)
- Advertise a Library Night or Book Fair, as illustrated in Figure 8.16. Many schools have had success with parents organizing these special events to help other parents and students check out books. (Administrators need to use care in making sure that book fairs do not turn into carnivals, with the sale of knick knacks and other accessories.)
- Develop an advisory board with which parents can discuss problems, and by which parents can provide input into the reading program. (Such meetings are becoming more pronounced with the advent of site-based management and shared decision-making concepts.)

Increasing Communication with Parents

Administrators can increase communication with parents in the following ways.

- Have special PTA or Parent Nights. New reading materials, computer software, videos, and textbooks can be displayed. A special program having success nationally is the PTA Reflections

Figure 8.16. Book fair notice.

The National PTA
Reflections Program

1991-92 Theme
Exploring New Beginnings

In this program students have an opportunity to use their creative talents by expressing themselves through their own original works.

Students may interpret the theme in any way they feel appropriate. World peace, space exploration, the first day of school and the new opportunities that were made available due to Columbus's explorations of the western Hemisphere are all examples of new beginnings. The theme must be reflected in the student's work, or used in the entry's title.

Projects do not have to be done at school, although some teachers may use the theme for class projects. Entries may be done at home, but all projects must be a student's own original work.

This is an optional contest. Know the rules-- they will be posted on January's bulletin board. The deadline for entries is <u>January 27th.</u> Start <u>exploring</u> your ideas and <u>begin</u> your project today!

Judging will be done in our school and winners in each age group and each category will receive ribbons. First and second place entries will be sent to the State PTA Convention.

Age Divisions
1. Primary -- Kindergarten through third grade
2. Intermediate -- Grades four through six
3. Junior High -- Grades seven through nine

Literature:
Poetry
Prose Drama

Music:
Scores of
original
composition
with or without
words

Photography:
Prints up to
11x14 inches in
color or black
and white

Visual Arts:
Drawing
Painting
Collage
Printmaking

Figure 8.17. PTA Reflections program notice.

program. This program allows students to share their art, music, and literature with others, as shown in Figure 8.17.

- Encourage teachers to report student progress on a regular basis. Some teachers make personal calls or write notes. (Many teachers are using sophisticated computer programs linked to phone systems that replicate message boards. Parents simply dial a phone number with a precoded extension and wait for a message describing the days' language arts homework assignment. Students are not happy about this innovation.)
- Develop a Clinical Summer Reading program. (Hellgate Elementary in Missoula, Montana is working jointly with the University of Montana to provide a unique eight-week summer

reading program for students. Clinicians, who are often teachers working on postgraduate-level degrees, provide instruction under the direction of a university professor. As illustrated in Figure 8.18, children are able to receive a diagnostic reading assessment and subsequent remediation. Research has shown children in the program have made substantial growth during the eight-week session.)

- Arrange to have at least one parent-teacher conference held at night to assist those parents who work during the day. Parent-teacher conferences should be used to discuss special reading activities. (Many working parents are grateful for the opportunity to meet with their child's teacher.)

- Set up coffee meetings in parents' homes. Many individuals enjoy having the principal or supervisor join a group of parents in their homes. Numerous positive communication ideas are nurtured at these sessions. (The coffee klatch is an old idea that is being rediscovered by administrators across the country.)

Figure 8.18. Summer reading and writing practicum brochure.

BUSINESS AND COMMUNITY LEADERS

We also need to involve business and community leaders in our PR projects. Business involvement in education is important (Seeley, 1990b); a major development in the 1980s and early 1990s has been the growth of school-business partnerships. Business leaders now recognize that they can play an important role in improving education. For instance, corporate executives are assisting school administrators with public relations and marketing ideas. Executives are opening businesses to students exploring career options and/or completing research.

Other community leaders can be helpful as well. Mayors, commissioners, police chiefs, and fire marshals enjoy working with children and are usually willing to come to schools. Many people in the community want to help schools, they just need to be asked.

Communicating with Business and Community Leaders

The following are examples of how businesses and public leaders can work collaboratively with schools.

- School administrators can invite community and business leaders as well as their employees to share ideas about reading. (A bank teller can discuss the feeling of handling millions of dollars, and why an ability to read helps him or her on the job.)
- Community and business leaders and their employees can read stories to children. (At one elementary school in Montana, employees of the Rocky Mountain Elk Foundation read stories about elk and their habitat to first grade children. The children have subsequently made a special wooden trunk that includes information about elk that travels to schools across Montana. The box contains pictures of elk, written materials, bones, teeth, hides, and other artifacts the children have collected.)
- Business leaders can provide special programs such as Pizza Hut's ''Book It'' program, shown in Figure 8.19. (Most elementary children will read extra books and stories if they think they can win a free pizza.)
- Individuals in the business world using word processing skills in their jobs can inservice teachers. In many instances, computer workshops are specifically arranged for teachers (see Figure 8.20) utilizing an employee from a local finance company. The

BOOK IT PROGRAM

The BOOK IT PIZZA HUT PROGRAM started October 1st. The purpose of the program is to motivate students to read more by offering free pizza on behalf of Pizza Hut. Teachers have set individual reading goals for their students. Any child who completes the minimum amount of required reading each month earns a free Personal Pan Pizza. If all the children in a class achieve their reading goals, the entire class can have a free Pizza Party.

As a parent or guardian, you can help your child reach his or her reading goals by giving your support and encouragement. We believe your involvement is very important to your child's success in reading.

Figure 8.19. Pizza Hut "Book It" program.

employee senses the satisfaction of working with teachers and devotes extra time to the school.

- Students can display their stories and illustrations in lobbies of various businesses or in the offices of public leaders. (Many shopping malls throughout the United States display children's stories and illustrations.)

- Community and business leaders and their employees can come to the school and explain what they do in their jobs. (In some schools, bank officers discuss with children how they use reading and math in their positions. Students use these visitations as a catalyst to read and write about banking careers.)

COMPUTER CLASS
FOR TEACHERS

Sentinel Elementary teachers will be participating in a computer education workshop. Instructor, Jerry Williams will work with groups of 14 teachers in four - 2 hour sessions. Mr. Williams will be instructing the teachers in the use of the computer, how to use the software and selection of good computer programs. The classes are being held after school hours, so as not to interfere with the regular school day.

Figure 8.20. Computer class for teachers.

- Business and community leaders can provide field trips for children in order to develop new experiences. (Some schools in the Rocky Mountain region have school-business partnerships with local ski resorts. Figure 8.21 illustrates a school-business partnership. One resort, Snowbowl Ski Inc., takes every child in the third grade downhill skiing. The children then read and write stories about their experiences. The resort also displays the children's work in their ski lodge.)

MISSOULA
ELEMENTARY SCHOOL
SKI PROGRAM

We are lucky to have a ski area the caliber of Snowbowl Inc. as our school/business partner at Hellgate Elementary. Snowbowl is offering our children a special opportunity to make a special skiing field trip as part of our physical education and recreation program. A two hour ski lesson by a certified instructor will be provided. This is a great chance for your child to experience a truly exciting life sport.

Third grade classes will go to Snowbowl on Thursday February 14th. A warm jacket, pants, hat and gloves are a must. Snowbowl will provide ski equipment for each child.

Figure 8.21. Big Sky elementary ski program.

These examples are just a few of the many school-business activities that can be undertaken. More and more schools are working with business and community leaders to expand students' horizons in new learning environments. The mobilization of community-wide relations has provided some dramatic improvements in school PR reform.

SCHOOL-COMMUNITY RELATIONS

Building trust is an important factor in school-community relations. Building trust means that administrators consistently make decisions in the best interests of children (Fuller and Martin, 1991). Maintaining that trust, however, implies two-way communications and involves parents and community members working with administrators to create successful schools. School-community relations are noted in this section as being either teacher directed or administratively directed. All activities or programs should be accompanied by a card or sign recognizing the school as the sponsor.

Teacher Directed Community Relations

Successful teachers of reading can improve school-community relations in the following ways.

- Provide special community programs that include plays, poetry, choral readings, and skits written and produced by children. (As shown in Figure 8.22, some school PTAs sponsor variety shows each year. Children are encouraged to share special readings, poetry, and musical acts.)
- Provide student publications for the public, which might include newspapers, newsletters, and yearbooks. (Lee Newspapers Inc. has been very supportive of displaying children's work in their newspapers across the United States.)
- Arranging public displays of student writing, often called "Reading Windows" in store fronts and in shopping malls. (Businesses are very supportive in volunteering windows for student displays as part of a project for the International Reading Association.)
- Formulate a "Bring Your Boss to Breakfast" program, encouraging businesses and schools to have their administrators

AMERICAN SCHOOL BANDSTAND

1990 VARIETY SHOW

UNDER THE DIRECTION OF CANDY JOHNSON AND CAROL GRINSTEINER

Sponsored by **Prescott** Elementary PTA

Figure 8.22. Prescott Elementary's PTA's American Bandstand brochure cover.

participate in an activity where children's stories are read and issues about reading are discussed. (This program has been developed by many reading councils and schools.)

- Help students to obtain books for homeless centers and nursing homes. (This program has been a success in a number of states.)
- Develop reading fairs in malls. Students read their own stories to young children. For example, a program entitled "Books, Beasts, and Balloons" has students reading fun books that have a dinosaur or dragon theme to other children. The children receive balloons at the end of the story. (This program occurs yearly in shopping malls.)
- Provide "Newspapers in Education" programs. (As noted in Figure 8.23, children must utilize newspapers in all aspects of the curriculum. This program is called No Books Day.)
- Have an Ice Cream Social based on a reading theme. (This program was developed at the National Reading Conference.)

- In the spring, T-shirts having a "Bloom with Books" logo can be given away. (This program was developed by schools in Spokane, Washington.)
- Develop a "Baskets of Books" program. Donated books are placed in baskets in offices of pediatricians and dentists where there are numerous children. (This program was developed by IRA state reading councils.)
- Provide a "Beans and Books" reading meeting by having a chili dinner at a reading meeting where new children's books are reviewed and reading issues are discussed. (This program was developed by IRA state reading councils.)
- Assist students in obtaining books to be given to new mothers in hospitals. Often called "Books for Babes," this program includes a tiny T-shirt that has a picture of a Teddy Bear and the inscription "Read to Me" on it. The school logo can also be added to the T-shirt. (This program was developed by IRA state reading councils.)
- Provide a "Reading Christmas Tree" in a mall or store front with miniature books as ornaments. Students enjoy making the books. (This program was developed by IRA state reading councils.)

Newspapers in Education

Mrs. Rowe's first grade class has become actively involved in a new program at school--Newspapers in Education (NIE). NIE provides the students with newspapers of their own once a week. The first graders have learned that the various functions of the newspaper are to inform, to spread news, to entertain and to advertise.

The children have written their own advertisements, shopped for Thanksgiving dinner and written their own captions for pictures. These are only a few of the activities in which these first graders participated.

NIE is a very exciting and educational program for children. They are learning that newspapers are for children as well as adults. They are now enthusiastic about the news and, of course, they love reading the comics!

Figure 8.23. "Newspapers in Education" program.

- Develop a ''Reading Christmas List of Books'' for parents. (This program was developed by IRA state reading councils.)
- Have a ''Sweet Pea Parade'' with children in a mall or park. The parade should start at a designated area, be centered around a reading theme, and end at a designated spot with balloons, book fair, and face painting. (This program was developed by IRA state reading councils.)

Administrator Directed

Administrators can improve school-community relations in many ways.

- Encourage staff to submit articles to media about their successful reading programs or activities. (Using local TV stations and newspapers to share student material is common in most states. *The Missoulian,* a western Montana newspaper, provides a special section for children's work entitled ''Bulletin Board.'')
- Be visible and available on a daily basis to work with parents or community members regarding reading programs or other activities. (Problems in schools usually need to be addressed with alacrity. Accessible administrators solve problems — inaccessible administrators do not.)
- Take part in a special program to catch the interest of children. (As illustrated in Figure 8.24, having a ''Turkey Walk Through'' around Thanksgiving time can spark the imaginations of elementary students into writing a creative story about turkeys, Thanksgiving, or principals.)
- Encourage staff to share unique reading projects with the board of education. (Having board members directly involved in working with primary children using a computer word processing program, e.g., Children's Publishing software.)
- Arrange for a distinguished visitor tour of the school by community, civic, business, media, and political leaders. The agenda should provide a broad picture of the reading program and be flexible, allowing consideration of visitors' needs. Some visitors may want to spend more time observing students working with reading on the computer, whereas others like to visit with students about their written stories. [This program

Principal Plans "Turkey Walk Through"

On November 24, Bruce Whitehead, principal of grades 1 - 5, will walk a full grown turkey through the various classrooms. The students should be very excited to see a "live" turkey in their own school just before the Thanksgiving Holiday.

The turkey is being provided by Sandy and Tom Knuchel who live in School Dist. 4. The Knuchels have two sons, Michael and Tony, who attend our school.

Thanks to the Knuchels, the students should get the opportunity to find out just who the real turkey is in building #2!!!

Figure 8.24. "Turkey Walk Through" notice.

(Ross, 1991) has been used extensively in the Aurora, Colorado School District, Aurora, Colorado.]

- Work with bookstores to provide or sponsor books to be used in a "Book a Month Club." One book can be given away each month to the student showing the most effort in reading. (B. Dalton Bookstores have supported these types of programs nationally.)
- Arrange with staff to cut an inch off the principal's tie if students read a specified number of books. (This is one of the authors' favorite ways to motivate children to read.)
- Provide a Literacy Award to an outstanding volunteer helping

with reading. (Literacy Awards are given each year by state reading councils under the direction of the International Reading Association.)

- Work with PTA or parent groups to develop a reader board or newspaper advertisement listing the names of community members supporting reading. (The PTA can sell lines that list the supporter's name for one dollar to help pay for the program. A newspaper advertisement could be from a half page to a full page in length. The advertisement might read: "Central Michigan Supports Reading." This idea has been developed successfully by IRA state reading councils.)
- Plan honors banquets for students excelling in reading and language arts. Parents are especially pleased to have their children honored. (Some vocational centers cater the whole event, considering it excellent "on line" training for vocational students.)
- Arrange "Senior Reading Volunteer" banquets. Many senior citizens work in the schools as volunteers in reading classes. They are extremely appreciative about being honored. The banquet or luncheon also offers students a chance to share their stories, plays, and poetry. (Local retirement associations are usually willing to assist school administrators.)
- Designate an "I Love to Read" day. (As noted in Figure 8.25, February has been selected by the International Reading Association as a special month for reading, with February 14 being "I Love to Read" day.)
- Develop weekly calendars and newsletters given to faculty, parents, and key community leaders. This is an old idea that should never be forgotten. Specific dates of reading events and stories about students and faculty make them popular with community members. (Placing newsletters in public places and grocery stores helps administrators reach community members who do not have children.)
- Develop special public relations brochures, as shown in Figure 8.26, which include a special section on reading. (Real estate agents are especially grateful to receive the brochures because they give a good synopsis of the quality of the school.)
- Be alert for possible articles for professional journals. Reading activities can be published in professional journals to help bring

recognition to school and community. (Examples of journals are *The Reading Teacher*, *Reading Today*, and *The Journal of Reading*.)

- Be willing to speak to local community organizations. Various groups need to hear and to understand what is happening in

Figure 8.25. A "Celebrate Reading" notice.

HELLGATE ELEMENTARY SCHOOL

Missoula, Montana

We thought you should know . . .

Hellgate Elementary School is currently receiving local, state and national attention as having outstanding educational programs.

Located just west of Missoula, near the confluence of the Clark Fork and Bitterroot Rivers, Hellgate Elementary is rich in history as one of the oldest school systems in the state of Montana. Named after the famous Hellgate Canyon, our school has grown and developed into one of the most innovative and technologically advanced elementary schools in our area. Visitors from schools throughout Montana regularly visit Hellgate Elementary to see first-hand new and exciting programs. The following items have been noted to reflect a partial list of how Hellgate Elementary has changed to become a leader in the educational field over these past years.

A STRONG, EFFECTIVE DISCIPLINE PROGRAM:

Hellgate Elementary was one of the first schools in the state and Western region to develop an In-School Suspension Program and an Assertive Discipline Program linked to a positive school climate.

RECOGNIZED STATE WIDE IN READING:

Hellgate Elementary and the University of Montana have established a Clinical Summer Reading Program which is recognized across the State of Montana.

This reading program provides post graduate level training in the teaching of reading as well as direct instruction for elementary students. Our reading program has been noted in the publication *Clearing House*.

Figure 8.26. Hellgate Elementary public relations brochure.

reading at individual schools, as well as across the nation. (Toast Masters, Kiwanis, Lions, and Rotary organizations are a few examples that welcome presentations on educational issues.)

- Volunteer to work on community projects. Involvement in civic organizations shows interest in the community. (For example, a principal can work with a local service club to provide eye glasses to needy children.)
- Develop a recorded message service. Parents can call a publicized number for information on special events, school activities, and student and faculty accomplishments. (Reading activities can be highlighted in the message.)
- Utilize information from professional organizations. (For example, the International Reading Association and Phi Delta Kappa have excellent materials on reading that can be disseminated to communities.)

In sum, it should be noted that all the ideas mentioned have been successfully used by the authors as well as other administrators around the United States. These ideas work. Many of the references used in this chapter are derived from school programs in the state of Montana because it has been cited by the U.S. Department of Education as being one of the top four states nationally in the field of education. Montana continues to be one of the leading states in the area of reading, math, and media technology. Administrators needing more information about any of the above communication strategies should consult the National Elementary or Secondary Principals Association, the International Reading Association, a public relations professional in a neighboring district, or a local media specialist.

EVALUATION OF THE PUBLIC RELATIONS PROGRAM

Every public relations project should be evaluated; evaluating PR programs helps develop the whole picture. In evaluations, the success of goals and objectives developed by an action planning team can be checked against the district PR mission statement. In addition, administrators and PR advisory councils can make adjustments in their plans, and communication strategies and ideas can be strengthened, adjusted, or discarded. Internal and external target groups can be reassessed regarding their importance to reading and to school-community relations. Outcomes, learned from current public relations project evaluations, can help enhance future projects.

Evaluations do not have to be complicated. The evaluation process can include a simple checklist, as shown in Figure 8.27 which helps to determine if key components are present in the public relations program.

WHERE SHOULD WE GO FROM HERE?

Where we go from here depends largely on where we have been. In this chapter, we discussed the importance of public relations in reading. We also discussed the role of administrators in the public relations process. In our search, we found that administrators play a key role in promoting reading and that administrators are becoming public relations specialists. As specialists, principals and supervisors should be working to get the word out about successful school reading programs. Parents and community members want to know what is happening in reading.

Research indicates that there are some exciting new developments in reading. New advances in media technology continue to make inroads

---

PROGRAM CHECKLIST

___ Provides evidence of administrative support

___ Has written philosophy incorporated into board policy

___ Establishes a reading task force or advisory council to establish goals and objectives

___ Facilitates community partnership in reading

___ Provides for a public relations plan relating to reading

___ Allows for the development of PR action teams

___ Provides for research development

___ Includes communication strategies for internal groups

___ Includes communication strategies for external groups

___ Allows for entire staff participation

___ Provides for evaluation procedures

Figure 8.27. Reading program evaluation checklist.

in reading instruction. Smaller, faster, and more compact computers are allowing teachers to develop individual education plans (IEPs) in reading for all students. Touch screen software is just now becoming available, and voice commands will become reality in the near future. Most libraries are becoming computerized. Students, teachers, and administrators are now able to obtain information from a vast network of city, county, and university libraries.

In the field of public relations, new technology will allow administrators to use interactive video over phone lines. Media editors and reporters will be able to actually visualize activities as they happen in the reading classroom. From their observations, editors and reporters will be able to make better editorial decisions on story selection. Life will be easier for reporters because they will have a daily collection of possible stories on video that can be used.

All of these changes will affect future administrators. Education and public relations are changing, and administrators need to keep pace with these changes. Our goal should be to stay abreast of new changes in technology and public relations. Sharing this information will require more knowledge about public relations programs and new communication techniques used to improve school-community relations.

As administrators responsible for shaping the future, we need to make collective decisions about our children's education. Educational priorities must be established to promote successful reading programs. As Wherry stated, ''The very heart of the public relations concept as we know it today, is action in the public interest'' (National School Public Relations Association, 1986). The result will be greater community support for the school and greater community support for reading.

REFERENCES

Armistead, L. 1989. ''A Four-Step Process for School Relations,'' *NASSP Bulletin*, 73(513):6,8,10−13.

Calabrese, R. L. 1991. ''Effective Assistant Principals: What Do They Do?'' *NASSP Bulletin*, 75(533):51−57.

Coleman, J., E. Campbell, C. Hobson, J. McPartland, A. Mood, F. Wenfield, and R. York. 1966. *Equality of Educational Opportunity*. Washington, D.C.: U.S. Printing Office, Superintendent of Documents.

Conners, A. J. 1988. ''Let's Hear about the Good Stuff!'' *The Clearing House*, 61(9):399−402.

Crane, G. M. 1989. ''Leadership Characteristics of Elementary School Principals Related to Reading Achievement,'' Ed.D. dissertation, University of Montana, pp. 15−38.

Criscuolo, N. P. 1985. ''A Little PR Goes a Long Way,'' *Principal*, 64(3): 33−34.

Decker, L. and D. Schoeny. 1992. ''National Educational Leaders Speak Out on Community Education,'' *The Community Education Journal*, 19(2):17.

Dietz, M. E. 1990. ''On the Road to Change,'' *Instructor*, 99(8):35−37, 52.

Durkin, D. 1966. ''The Achievement of Preschool Readers: Two Longitudinal Studies,'' *Reading Research Quarterly*, 1(4):5−36.

Edmonds, R. R. and J. R. Fredrickson. 1983. ''Search for Effective Schools: The Identification and Analysis of City Schools That Are Instructionally Effective for Poor Children,'' East Lansing, MI: Michigan State University. ERIC Document Reproduction Service No. ED 170 396.

Fuller, S. and G. Martin. 1991. ''Nine Ways to Build Better Relations with Your Board,'' *The Executive Educator*, 13(1):22−23, 28.

Hill, D. 1990. ''What Has the 1980's Reform Movement Accomplished?'' *The Education Digest*, 55(6):3−6.

Lincoln, C. A. and N. Higgins. 1991. "Making Schools Work for All Children," *Principal*, 70(3):6−8.

National School Public Relations Association. 1986. Preface to *School Public Relations: The Complete Book*. Arlington, VA: National School Public Relations Association.

Psencik, K. 1991. "Site Planning in a Strategic Context in Temple, Texas," *Educational Leadership*, 48(7):29−31.

Rasinski, T. and A. Fredericks. 1989. "Working with Parents: Can Parents Make a Difference?" *The Reading Teacher*, 43(1):84−85.

Ross, V. J. 1991. "VIP Tours for Local Leaders Turn School Critics into Fans," *The Executive Educator*, 13(6):27−28.

Seeley, D. S. 1990a. "A New Paradigm for Parent Involvement," *The Education Digest*, 55(6):37−40.

―――. 1990b. "Carrying School Reform into the 1990s," *The Education Digest*, 55(9):3−6.

Snyder, T. D. 1990. "Trends in Education," *Principal*, 70(1):6−10.

Tankard, G. G., Jr. 1974. *Curriculum Improvement: An Administrator's Guide*. New York, NY: Parker Publishing Company, Inc., pp. 95−120.

Walker, J. E. 1983. "Polls of Public Attitudes Toward Education−How Much Help to Principals?" *NASSP Bulletin*, 67(459):30.

Wherry, J. H. 1986. "A Public Relations Secret: Enlist Entire Staff for PR Effectiveness," *NASSP Bulletin*, 70(494):3−4, 6−8, 10−13.

AUTHOR INDEX

SUBJECT INDEX

THE AUTHORS

Floyd Boschee is an associate professor, Division of Educational Administration, School of Education, University of South Dakota, where he teaches and conducts research in educational leadership, supervision, and curriculum. For eighteen years he was a teacher, coach, athletic director, and assistant superintendent for curriculum and instruction. He has also served as chairman of departments of education, published extensively in national journals, and authored the book, *Grouping = Growth*.

Bruce M. Whitehead is a practicing elementary school principal at Hellgate Elementary School, Missoula, Montana, as well as a visiting assistant professor at the University of Montana. He has coauthored and illustrated four books and has published numerous articles in the field of education. As a result of his work in reading, administration, and media technology, he has received numerous awards and was recently recognized as a National Distinguished Principal by the National Association of Elementary School Principals. He is currently developing one of the few elementary schools to utilize IBM computer classroom networking programs and satellite downlink feed in the area of remedial reading.

Marlys Ann Boschee is an assistant professor, Division of Curriculum and Instruction, School of Education, University of South Dakota, where she is an academic advisor and teaches the language arts methods courses for undergraduate and graduate students. She has also taught the reading methods course for undergraduate elementary education majors. She began her career as a teacher in a one-room, rural school and was an elementary teacher, grades one through six, prior to completing her master's and doctorate degrees in school administration and curriculum and instruction.